Spring Microservices

Build scalable microservices with Spring, Docker, and Mesos

Rajesh RV

PUBLISHING

BIRMINGHAM - MUMBAI

Spring Microservices

First published: June 2016

Production reference: 1200616

Published by Packt Publishing Ltd.
Livery Place
35 Livery Street
Birmingham B3 2PB, UK.

ISBN 978-1-78646-668-6

www.packtpub.com

Credits

Author
Rajesh RV

Reviewer
Yogendra Sharma

Commissioning Editor
Edward Gordon

Acquisition Editor
Rahul Nair

Content Development Editor
Anish Sukumaran

Technical Editors
Taabish Khan
Kunal Chaudhari

Copy Editors
Shruti Iyer
Sonia Mathur

Project Coordinator
Izzat Contractor

Proofreader
Safis Editing

Indexer
Hemangini Bari

Graphics
Jason Monteiro

Production Coordinator
Melwyn D'sa

Cover Work
Melwyn D'sa

About the Author

Rajesh RV is a seasoned IT architect with extensive experience in diversified technologies and more than 16 years of airline IT experience.

Rajesh received a degree in computer engineering from University of Cochin, India. He joined the JEE community Spring during the early days of EJB. During the course, as an architect, he worked on many large-scale, mission-critical projects, including New Generation Airline Passenger Reservation System (iFlyRes) and Next Generation Airline Cargo Reservation systems (Skychain and CROAMIS) in the airlines domain.

At present, working as chief architect at Emirates (http://www.emirates.com/), Rajesh is handling the solution architecture portfolio, which is spread across various architecture capabilities, such as JEE, SOA, NoSQL, IoT, mobile, UI, integration, and more. At Emirates, Open Travel Platform (OTP) architected by Rajesh earned the group the prestigious 2011 RedHat Innovation Award in the Carved Out Costs category. In 2011, he introduced the innovative concept of the Honeycomb architecture based on the hexagonal architecture pattern used to transform the legacy mainframe system.

Rajesh has a deep passion for technology and architecture. He also holds several certifications, such as BEA Certified WebLogic Administrator, Sun Certified Java Enterprise Architect, Open Group Certified TOGAF Practitioner, Licensed ZapThink Architect in SOA, and IASA global CITA-A Certified Architecture Specialist.

Previously, Rajesh reviewed the book *Service Oriented Java Business Integration*, *Packt Publishing* by Binildas A. Christudas.

Rajesh's social profile is available at https://www.linkedin.com/in/rajeshrv.

Acknowledgments

I would like to thank everyone I worked with closely at Packt Publishing to make my dream come true. A special thanks to the reviewers; your in-depth reviews helped improve the quality of this book.

This book would have never been possible without the encouragement from my excellent colleagues at Emirates. A very special thanks goes to Neetan Chopra, Senior Vice President, and Thomas Benjamin, Vice President, for their constant support and help.

I would like to extend my thanks to Daniel Oor, who works as an independent enterprise architect, for his quality input and inspiration throughout the development of this book.

A heartfelt thanks goes to my wife, Saritha, for her tireless and unconditional support that helped me focus on this book. I would like to thank my kids, Nikhil and Aditya; I took away a lot of their playing hours to author this book. A huge thanks is due to my father, Ramachandran Nair, and mother, Vasanthakumari, for their selfless support that helped me reach where I am today.

About the Reviewer

Yogendra Sharma is a Java developer with Python background and with experience mainly in backend development. He has completed his bachelors of technology in computer science.

Yogendra is currently working in Pune at Siemens Industry Software Pvt. Ltd as a product development engineer. He is constantly exploring technical novelties and is open-minded and eager to learn about new technologies and frameworks.

Yogendra was also the technical reviewer of *Mastering Python Design Patterns, Sakis Kasampalis*, and *Test-Driven Development with Django, Kevin Harvey*, both by Packt Publishing.

His LinkedIn profile is available at `http://in.linkedin.com/in/yogendra0sharma`. He blogs at `http://TechiesEyes.com`.

I would like to thank my parents for allowing me to learn all that I did. I would also like to thank my friends for their support and encouragement.

www.PacktPub.com

eBooks, discount offers, and more

Did you know that Packt offers eBook versions of every book published, with PDF and ePub files available? You can upgrade to the eBook version at www.PacktPub.com and as a print book customer, you are entitled to a discount on the eBook copy. Get in touch with us at customercare@packtpub.com for more details.

At www.PacktPub.com, you can also read a collection of free technical articles, sign up for a range of free newsletters and receive exclusive discounts and offers on Packt books and eBooks.

https://www2.packtpub.com/books/subscription/packtlib

Do you need instant solutions to your IT questions? PacktLib is Packt's online digital book library. Here, you can search, access, and read Packt's entire library of books.

Why subscribe?

- Fully searchable across every book published by Packt
- Copy and paste, print, and bookmark content
- On demand and accessible via a web browser

Table of Contents

Preface

Microservice is an architecture style and pattern in which complex systems are decomposed into smaller services that work together to form larger business services. Microservices are services that are autonomous, self-contained, and independently deployable. In today's world, many enterprises use microservices as the default standard for building large, service-oriented enterprise applications.

The Spring framework is a popular programming framework with the developer community for many years. Spring Boot removed the need to have a heavyweight application container and provided a means to deploy lightweight, server-less applications. Spring Cloud combines many Netflix OSS components and provides an ecosystem to run and manage large-scale microservices. It provides capabilities such as load balancing, service registry, monitoring, service gateway, and so on.

However, microservices come with their own challenges, such as monitoring, managing, distributing, scaling, discovering, and so on, especially when deploying at scale. Adopting microservices without addressing the common microservices challenges would lead to catastrophic results. The most important part of this book is a technology-agnostic microservice capability model that helps address all the common microservice challenges.

The goal of this book is to enlighten readers with a pragmatic approach and guidelines for implementing responsive microservices at scale. This book will take readers on a deep dive into Spring Boot, Spring Cloud, Docker, Mesos, and Marathon. Readers of this book will understand how Spring Boot is used to deploy autonomous services server-less by removing the need to have a heavyweight application server. Readers will learn different Spring Cloud capabilities and also realize the use of Docker for containerization and of Mesos and Marathon for compute resource abstraction and cluster-wide control, respectively.

I am sure readers will enjoy each and every section of this book. Also, I honestly believe that this book adds tremendous value by successfully conceiving microservices in your business. Throughout this book, I have used practical aspects of microservices implementation by providing a number of examples, including a case study from the travel domain. In the end, you will have learned how to implement microservice architectures using the Spring framework, Spring Boot, and Spring Cloud. These are battle-tested, robust tools to develop and deploy scalable microservices. Written to the latest specifications of Spring, with the help of this book, you'll be able to build modern, Internet-scale Java applications in no time.

What this book covers

Chapter 1, Demystifying Microservices, gives you an introduction to microservices. This chapter covers the fundamental concepts of microservices, their evolution, and their relationship with service-oriented architecture, as well as the concepts of cloud native and Twelve-Factor applications.

Chapter 2, Building Microservices with Spring Boot, introduces building REST- and message-based microservices using the Spring framework and how to wrap them with Spring Boot. In addition, we will also explore some core capabilities of Spring Boot.

Chapter 3, Applying Microservices Concepts, explains the practical aspects of microservices implementation by detailing out the challenges that developers face with enterprise-grade microservices. This will also summarize the capabilities required to successfully manage a microservices ecosystem.

Chapter 4, Microservices Evolution – A Case Study, takes the readers into a real-world case study of microservices evolution by introducing BrownField Airline. Using the case study, this chapter explains how to apply the microservices concepts learned in previous chapters.

Chapter 5, Scaling Microservices with Spring Cloud, shows how to scale the previous example using Spring Cloud stack capabilities. It details out the architecture and different components of Spring Cloud and how they integrate together.

Chapter 6, Autoscaling Microservices, demonstrates the use of a simple life cycle manager to attain elasticity and the self-management of microservices by orchestrating services with service gateways. It explains how, in the real world, one can add intelligence to service gateways.

Chapter 7, Logging and Monitoring Microservices, covers the importance of logging and monitoring aspects when developing microservices. Here, we will go into the details of some of the best practices when using microservices such as centralized logging and monitoring capabilities using open source tools and how to integrate them with Spring projects.

Chapter 8, Containerizing Microservices with Docker, explains containerization concepts in the context of microservices. Using Mesos and Marathon, this chapter demonstrates a next-level implementation to replace a custom life cycle manager for large deployments.

Chapter 9, Managing Dockerized Microservices with Mesos and Marathon, explains the autoprovisioning and deployment of microservices. Here, you will also learn how to use Docker containers in the previous example for large-scale deployments.

Chapter 10, The Microservices Development Life Cycle, covers the process and practices of microservices development. The importance of DevOps and continuous delivery pipelines is also explained in this chapter.

What you need for this book

Chapter 2, Building Microservices with Spring Boot, introduces Spring Boot, which requires the following software components to test the code:

- JDK 1.8
- Spring Tool Suite 3.7.2 (STS)
- Maven 3.3.1
- Spring Framework 4.2.6.RELEASE
- Spring Boot 1.3.5.RELEASE
- `spring-boot-cli-1.3.5.RELEASE-bin.zip`
- RabbitMQ 3.5.6
- FakeSMTP

In *Chapter 5, Scaling Microservices with Spring Cloud*, you will learn about the Spring Cloud project. This requires the following software components in addition to the previously mentioned ones:

- Spring Cloud Brixton.RELEASE

In *Chapter 7, Logging and Monitoring Microservices*, we will take a look at how centralized logging can be implemented for microservices. This requires the following software stack:

- Elasticsearch 1.5.2
- `kibana-4.0.2-darwin-x64`
- Logstash 2.1.2

In *Chapter 8, Containerizing Microservices with Docker*, we will demonstrate how we can use Docker for microservices deployments. This requires the following software components:

- Docker version 1.10.1
- Docker Hub

Chapter 9, Managing Dockerized Microservices with Mesos and Marathon, uses Mesos and Marathon to deploy dockerized microservices into an autoscalable cloud. The following software components are required for this purpose:

- Mesos version 0.27.1
- Docker version 1.6.2
- Marathon version 0.15.3

Who this book is for

This book is primarily for Spring developers who are looking to build cloud-ready Internet-scale applications to meet modern business demands. The book will help developers to understand what exactly microservices are and why they are important in today's world by examining a number of real-world use cases and hands-on code samples. Developers will understand how to build simple RESTful services and organically grow them to truly enterprise-grade microservices ecosystem.

This book will be interesting to architects who are seeking help on designing robust Internet-scale microservices using the Spring framework, Spring Boot, and Spring Cloud and managing them using Docker, Mesos, and Marathon. The capability model will help architects devise solutions even beyond the tools and technologies discussed in this book.

Conventions

In this book, you will find a number of text styles that distinguish between different kinds of information. Here are some examples of these styles and an explanation of their meaning.

Code words in text, database table names, folder names, filenames, file extensions, pathnames, dummy URLs, user input, and Twitter handles are shown as follows: "The following properties can be set in `application.properties` to customize application-related information."

A block of code is set as follows:

```
<parent>
  <groupId>org.springframework.boot</groupId>
    <artifactId>spring-boot-starter-parent</artifactId>
    <version>1.3.4.RELEASE</version>
</parent>
```

When we wish to draw your attention to a particular part of a code block, the relevant lines or items are set in bold:

eureka-server2.properties
```
eureka.client.serviceUrl.defaultZone:http://localhost:8761/eureka/
eureka.client.registerWithEureka:false
eureka.client.fetchRegistry:false
```

Any command-line input or output is written as follows:

```
$ java -jar fakeSMTP-2.0.jar
```

New terms and **important words** are shown in bold. Words that you see on the screen, for example, in menus or dialog boxes, appear in the text like this: "Click on the **Make Request** button."

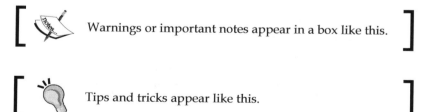

[Warnings or important notes appear in a box like this.]

[Tips and tricks appear like this.]

Reader feedback

Feedback from our readers is always welcome. Let us know what you think about this book—what you liked or disliked. Reader feedback is important for us as it helps us develop titles that you will really get the most out of.

To send us general feedback, simply e-mail `feedback@packtpub.com`, and mention the book's title in the subject of your message.

If there is a topic that you have expertise in and you are interested in either writing or contributing to a book, see our author guide at `www.packtpub.com/authors`.

Customer support

Now that you are the proud owner of a Packt book, we have a number of things to help you to get the most from your purchase.

Downloading the example code

You can download the example code files for this book from your account at `http://www.packtpub.com`. If you purchased this book elsewhere, you can visit `http://www.packtpub.com/support` and register to have the files e-mailed directly to you.

You can download the code files by following these steps:

1. Log in or register to our website using your e-mail address and password.
2. Hover the mouse pointer on the **SUPPORT** tab at the top.
3. Click on **Code Downloads & Errata**.
4. Enter the name of the book in the **Search** box.
5. Select the book for which you're looking to download the code files.
6. Choose from the drop-down menu where you purchased this book from.
7. Click on **Code Download**.

You can also download the code files by clicking on the **Code Files** button on the book's webpage at the Packt Publishing website. This page can be accessed by entering the book's name in the **Search** box. Please note that you need to be logged in to your Packt account.

Once the file is downloaded, please make sure that you unzip or extract the folder using the latest version of:

- WinRAR / 7-Zip for Windows
- Zipeg / iZip / UnRarX for Mac
- 7-Zip / PeaZip for Linux

The code bundle for the book is also hosted on GitHub at `https://github.com/PacktPublishing/Spring-Microservices`. We also have other code bundles from our rich catalog of books and videos available at `https://github.com/PacktPublishing/`. Check them out!

Errata

Although we have taken every care to ensure the accuracy of our content, mistakes do happen. If you find a mistake in one of our books—maybe a mistake in the text or the code—we would be grateful if you could report this to us. By doing so, you can save other readers from frustration and help us improve subsequent versions of this book. If you find any errata, please report them by visiting `http://www.packtpub.com/submit-errata`, selecting your book, clicking on the **Errata Submission Form** link, and entering the details of your errata. Once your errata are verified, your submission will be accepted and the errata will be uploaded to our website or added to any list of existing errata under the Errata section of that title.

To view the previously submitted errata, go to `https://www.packtpub.com/books/content/support` and enter the name of the book in the search field. The required information will appear under the **Errata** section.

Piracy

Piracy of copyrighted material on the Internet is an ongoing problem across all media. At Packt, we take the protection of our copyright and licenses very seriously. If you come across any illegal copies of our works in any form on the Internet, please provide us with the location address or website name immediately so that we can pursue a remedy.

Please contact us at `copyright@packtpub.com` with a link to the suspected pirated material.

We appreciate your help in protecting our authors and our ability to bring you valuable content.

Questions

If you have a problem with any aspect of this book, you can contact us at
questions@packtpub.com, and we will do our best to address the problem.

Demystifying Microservices

1

Microservices are an architecture style and an approach for software development to satisfy modern business demands. Microservices are not invented; they are more of an evolution from the previous architecture styles.

We will start the chapter by taking a closer look at the evolution of the microservices architecture from the traditional monolithic architectures. We will also examine the definition, concepts, and characteristics of microservices. Finally, we will analyze typical use cases of microservices and establish the similarities and relationships between microservices and other architecture approaches such as **Service Oriented Architecture (SOA)** and Twelve-Factor Apps. Twelve-Factor Apps defines a set of software engineering principles of developing applications targeting the cloud.

In this chapter you, will learn about:

- The evolution of microservices
- The definition of the microservices architecture with examples
- Concepts and characteristics of the microservices architecture
- Typical use cases of the microservices architecture
- The relationship of microservices with SOA and Twelve-Factor Apps

The evolution of microservices

Microservices are one of the increasingly popular architecture patterns next to SOA, complemented by DevOps and cloud. The microservices evolution is greatly influenced by the disruptive digital innovation trends in modern business and the evolution of technologies in the last few years. We will examine these two factors in this section.

Business demand as a catalyst for microservices evolution

In this era of digital transformation, enterprises increasingly adopt technologies as one of the key enablers for radically increasing their revenue and customer base. Enterprises primarily use social media, mobile, cloud, big data, and Internet of Things as vehicles to achieve the disruptive innovations. Using these technologies, enterprises find new ways to quickly penetrate the market, which severely pose challenges to the traditional IT delivery mechanisms.

The following graph shows the state of traditional development and microservices against the new enterprise challenges such as agility, speed of delivery, and scale.

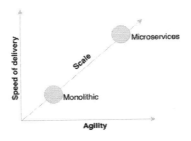

 Microservices promise more agility, speed of delivery, and scale compared to traditional monolithic applications.

Gone are the days when businesses invested in large application developments with the turnaround time of a few years. Enterprises are no longer interested in developing consolidated applications to manage their end-to-end business functions as they did a few years ago.

The following graph shows the state of traditional monolithic applications and microservices in comparison with the turnaround time and cost.

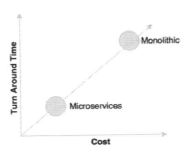

Microservices provide an approach for developing quick and agile applications, resulting in less overall cost.

Today, for instance, airlines or financial institutions do not invest in rebuilding their core mainframe systems as another monolithic monster. Retailers and other industries do not rebuild heavyweight supply chain management applications, such as their traditional ERPs. Focus has shifted to building quick-win point solutions that cater to specific needs of the business in the most agile way possible.

Let's take an example of an online retailer running with a legacy monolithic application. If the retailer wants to innovate his/her sales by offering their products personalized to a customer based on the customer's past shopping, preferences, and so on and also wants to enlighten customers by offering products based on their propensity to buy them, they will quickly develop a personalization engine or offers based on their immediate needs and plug them into their legacy application.

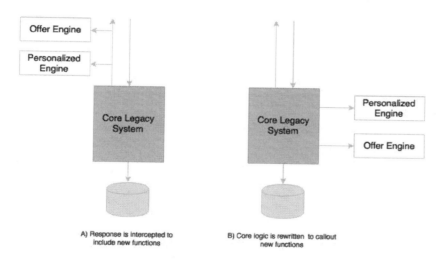

As shown in the preceding diagram, rather than investing in rebuilding the core legacy system, this will be either done by passing the responses through the new functions, as shown in the diagram marked **A**, or by modifying the core legacy system to call out these functions as part of the processing, as shown in the diagram marked **B**. These functions are typically written as microservices.

This approach gives organizations a plethora of opportunities to quickly try out new functions with lesser cost in an experimental mode. Businesses can later validate key performance indicators and alter or replace these implementations if required.

[Modern architectures are expected to maximize the ability to replace their parts and minimize the cost of replacing their parts. The microservices approach is a means to achieving this.]

Technology as a catalyst for the microservices evolution

Emerging technologies have also made us rethink the way we build software systems. For example, a few decades back, we couldn't even imagine a distributed application without a two-phase commit. Later, NoSQL databases made us think differently.

Similarly, these kinds of paradigm shifts in technology have reshaped all the layers of the software architecture.

The emergence of HTML 5 and CSS3 and the advancement of mobile applications repositioned user interfaces. Client-side JavaScript frameworks such as Angular, Ember, React, Backbone, and so on are immensely popular due to their client-side rendering and responsive designs.

With cloud adoptions steamed into the mainstream, **Platform as a Services** (**PaaS**) providers such as Pivotal CF, AWS, Salesforce.com, IBMs Bluemix, RedHat OpenShift, and so on made us rethink the way we build middleware components. The container revolution created by Docker radically influenced the infrastructure space. These days, an infrastructure is treated as a commodity service.

The integration landscape has also changed with **Integration Platform as a Service** (**iPaaS**), which is emerging. Platforms such as Dell Boomi, Informatica, MuleSoft, and so on are examples of iPaaS. These tools helped organizations stretch integration boundaries beyond the traditional enterprise.

NoSQLs have revolutionized the databases space. A few years ago, we had only a few popular databases, all based on relational data modeling principles. We have a long list of databases today: Hadoop, Cassandra, CouchDB, and Neo 4j to name a few. Each of these databases addresses certain specific architectural problems.

Imperative architecture evolution

Application architecture has always been evolving alongside demanding business requirements and the evolution of technologies. Architectures have gone through the evolution of age-old mainframe systems to fully abstract cloud services such as AWS Lambda.

Using AWS Lambda, developers can now drop their "functions" into a fully managed compute service.

Read more about Lambda at: `https://aws.amazon.com/documentation/lambda/`

Different architecture approaches and styles such as mainframes, client server, N-tier, and service-oriented were popular at different timeframes. Irrespective of the choice of architecture styles, we always used to build one or the other forms of monolithic architectures. The microservices architecture evolved as a result of modern business demands such as agility and speed of delivery, emerging technologies, and learning from previous generations of architectures.

Microservices help us break the boundaries of monolithic applications and build a logically independent smaller system of systems, as shown in the preceding diagram.

 If we consider monolithic applications as a set of logical subsystems encompassed with a physical boundary, microservices are a set of independent subsystems with no enclosing physical boundary.

What are microservices?

Microservices are an architecture style used by many organizations today as a game changer to achieve a high degree of agility, speed of delivery, and scale. Microservices give us a way to develop more physically separated modular applications.

Microservices are not invented. Many organizations such as Netflix, Amazon, and eBay successfully used the divide-and-conquer technique to functionally partition their monolithic applications into smaller atomic units, each performing a single function. These organizations solved a number of prevailing issues they were experiencing with their monolithic applications.

Following the success of these organizations, many other organizations started adopting this as a common pattern to refactor their monolithic applications. Later, evangelists termed this pattern as the microservices architecture.

Microservices originated from the idea of hexagonal architecture coined by Alistair Cockburn. Hexagonal architecture is also known as the Ports and Adapters pattern.

 Read more about hexagonal architecture at `http://alistair.cockburn.us/Hexagonal+architecture`.

Microservices are an architectural style or an approach to building IT systems as a set of business capabilities that are autonomous, self-contained, and loosely coupled:

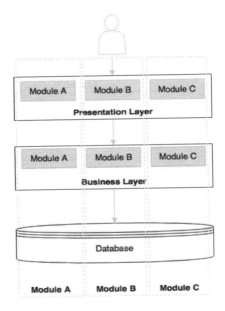

The preceding diagram depicts a traditional N-tier application architecture having a presentation layer, business layer, and database layer. The modules **A**, **B**, and **C** represent three different business capabilities. The layers in the diagram represent a separation of architecture concerns. Each layer holds all three business capabilities pertaining to this layer. The presentation layer has web components of all the three modules, the business layer has business components of all the three modules, and the database hosts tables of all the three modules. In most cases, layers are physically spreadable, whereas modules within a layer are hardwired.

Let's now examine a microservices-based architecture.

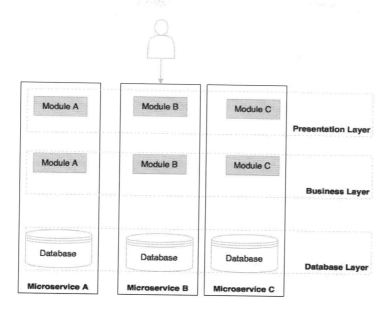

As we can note in the preceding diagram, the boundaries are inversed in the microservices architecture. Each vertical slice represents a microservice. Each microservice has its own presentation layer, business layer, and database layer. Microservices are aligned towards business capabilities. By doing so, changes to one microservice do not impact others.

There is no standard for communication or transport mechanisms for microservices. In general, microservices communicate with each other using widely adopted lightweight protocols, such as HTTP and REST, or messaging protocols, such as JMS or AMQP. In specific cases, one might choose more optimized communication protocols, such as Thrift, ZeroMQ, Protocol Buffers, or Avro.

As microservices are more aligned to business capabilities and have independently manageable life cycles, they are the ideal choice for enterprises embarking on DevOps and cloud. DevOps and cloud are two facets of microservices.

 DevOps is an IT realignment to narrow the gap between traditional IT development and operations for better efficiency.

Read more about DevOps:

`http://dev2ops.org/2010/02/what-is-devops/`

Microservices – the honeycomb analogy

The honeycomb is an ideal analogy for representing the evolutionary microservices architecture.

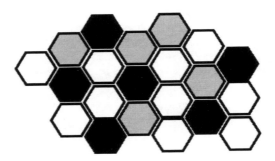

In the real world, bees build a honeycomb by aligning hexagonal wax cells. They start small, using different materials to build the cells. Construction is based on what is available at the time of building. Repetitive cells form a pattern and result in a strong fabric structure. Each cell in the honeycomb is independent but also integrated with other cells. By adding new cells, the honeycomb grows organically to a big, solid structure. The content inside each cell is abstracted and not visible outside. Damage to one cell does not damage other cells, and bees can reconstruct these cells without impacting the overall honeycomb.

Principles of microservices

In this section, we will examine some of the principles of the microservices architecture. These principles are a "must have" when designing and developing microservices.

Single responsibility per service

The single responsibility principle is one of the principles defined as part of the SOLID design pattern. It states that a unit should only have one responsibility.

Read more about the SOLID design pattern at:

`http://c2.com/cgi/wiki?PrinciplesOfObjectOrientedDesign`

This implies that a unit, either a class, a function, or a service, should have only one responsibility. At no point should two units share one responsibility or one unit have more than one responsibility. A unit with more than one responsibility indicates tight coupling.

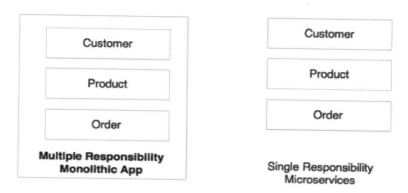

As shown in the preceding diagram, **Customer**, **Product**, and **Order** are different functions of an e-commerce application. Rather than building all of them into one application, it is better to have three different services, each responsible for exactly one business function, so that changes to one responsibility will not impair others. In the preceding scenario, **Customer**, **Product**, and **Order** will be treated as three independent microservices.

Microservices are autonomous

Microservices are self-contained, independently deployable, and autonomous services that take full responsibility of a business capability and its execution. They bundle all dependencies, including library dependencies, and execution environments such as web servers and containers or virtual machines that abstract physical resources.

One of the major differences between microservices and SOA is in their level of autonomy. While most SOA implementations provide service-level abstraction, microservices go further and abstract the realization and execution environment.

In traditional application developments, we build a WAR or an EAR, then deploy it into a JEE application server, such as with JBoss, WebLogic, WebSphere, and so on. We may deploy multiple applications into the same JEE container. In the microservices approach, each microservice will be built as a fat Jar, embedding all dependencies and run as a standalone Java process.

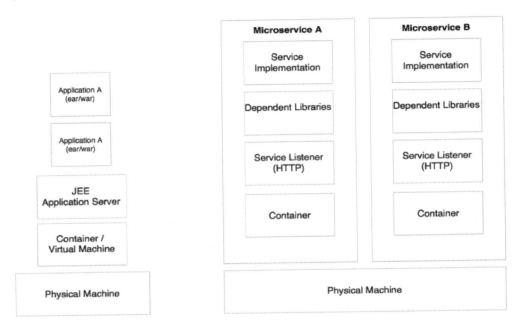

Microservices may also get their own containers for execution, as shown in the preceding diagram. Containers are portable, independently manageable, lightweight runtime environments. Container technologies, such as Docker, are an ideal choice for microservices deployment.

Characteristics of microservices

The microservices definition discussed earlier in this chapter is arbitrary. Evangelists and practitioners have strong but sometimes different opinions on microservices. There is no single, concrete, and universally accepted definition for microservices. However, all successful microservices implementations exhibit a number of common characteristics. Therefore, it is important to understand these characteristics rather than sticking to theoretical definitions. Some of the common characteristics are detailed in this section.

Services are first-class citizens

In the microservices world, services are first-class citizens. Microservices expose service endpoints as APIs and abstract all their realization details. The internal implementation logic, architecture, and technologies (including programming language, database, quality of services mechanisms, and so on) are completely hidden behind the service API.

Moreover, in the microservices architecture, there is no more application development; instead, organizations focus on service development. In most enterprises, this requires a major cultural shift in the way that applications are built.

In a **Customer Profile** microservice, internals such as the data structure, technologies, business logic, and so on are hidden. They aren't exposed or visible to any external entities. Access is restricted through the service endpoints or APIs. For instance, Customer Profile microservices may expose **Register Customer** and **Get Customer** as two APIs for others to interact with.

Characteristics of services in a microservice

As microservices are more or less like a flavor of SOA, many of the service characteristics defined in the SOA are applicable to microservices as well.

The following are some of the characteristics of services that are applicable to microservices as well:

- **Service contract**: Similar to SOA, microservices are described through well-defined service contracts. In the microservices world, JSON and REST are universally accepted for service communication. In the case of JSON/REST, there are many techniques used to define service contracts. JSON Schema, WADL, Swagger, and RAML are a few examples.

- **Loose coupling**: Microservices are independent and loosely coupled. In most cases, microservices accept an event as input and respond with another event. Messaging, HTTP, and REST are commonly used for interaction between microservices. Message-based endpoints provide higher levels of decoupling.

- **Service abstraction**: In microservices, service abstraction is not just an abstraction of service realization, but it also provides a complete abstraction of all libraries and environment details, as discussed earlier.

- **Service reuse**: Microservices are course-grained reusable business services. These are accessed by mobile devices and desktop channels, other microservices, or even other systems.

- **Statelessness**: Well-designed microservices are stateless and share nothing with no shared state or conversational state maintained by the services. In case there is a requirement to maintain state, they are maintained in a database, perhaps in memory.

- **Services are discoverable**: Microservices are discoverable. In a typical microservices environment, microservices self-advertise their existence and make themselves available for discovery. When services die, they automatically take themselves out from the microservices ecosystem.

- **Service interoperability**: Services are interoperable as they use standard protocols and message exchange standards. Messaging, HTTP, and so on are used as transport mechanisms. REST/JSON is the most popular method for developing interoperable services in the microservices world. In cases where further optimization is required on communications, other protocols such as Protocol Buffers, Thrift, Avro, or Zero MQ could be used. However, the use of these protocols may limit the overall interoperability of the services.

- **Service composeability**: Microservices are composeable. Service composeability is achieved either through service orchestration or service choreography.

 More detail on SOA principles can be found at:
`http://serviceorientation.com/serviceorientation/index`

Microservices are lightweight

Well-designed microservices are aligned to a single business capability, so they perform only one function. As a result, one of the common characteristics we see in most of the implementations are microservices with smaller footprints.

When selecting supporting technologies, such as web containers, we will have to ensure that they are also lightweight so that the overall footprint remains manageable. For example, Jetty or Tomcat are better choices as application containers for microservices compared to more complex traditional application servers such as WebLogic or WebSphere.

Container technologies such as Docker also help us keep the infrastructure footprint as minimal as possible compared to hypervisors such as VMWare or Hyper-V.

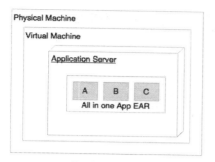

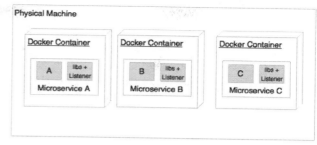

As shown in the preceding diagram, microservices are typically deployed in Docker containers, which encapsulate the business logic and needed libraries. This help us quickly replicate the entire setup on a new machine or on a completely different hosting environment or even to move across different cloud providers. As there is no physical infrastructure dependency, containerized microservices are easily portable.

Microservices with polyglot architecture

As microservices are autonomous and abstract everything behind service APIs, it is possible to have different architectures for different microservices. A few common characteristics that we see in microservices implementations are:

- Different services use different versions of the same technologies. One microservice may be written on Java 1.7, and another one could be on Java 1.8.

- Different languages are used to develop different microservices, such as one microservice is developed in Java and another one in Scala.

- Different architectures are used, such as one microservice using the Redis cache to serve data, while another microservice could use MySQL as a persistent data store.

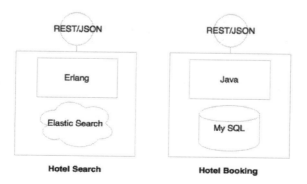

In the preceding example, as **Hotel Search** is expected to have high transaction volumes with stringent performance requirements, it is implemented using Erlang. In order to support predictive searching, Elasticsearch is used as the data store. At the same time, **Hotel Booking** needs more ACID transactional characteristics. Therefore, it is implemented using MySQL and Java. The internal implementations are hidden behind service endpoints defined as REST/JSON over HTTP.

Automation in a microservices environment

Most of the microservices implementations are automated to a maximum from development to production.

As microservices break monolithic applications into a number of smaller services, large enterprises may see a proliferation of microservices. A large number of microservices is hard to manage until and unless automation is in place. The smaller footprint of microservices also helps us automate the microservices development to the deployment life cycle. In general, microservices are automated end to end—for example, automated builds, automated testing, automated deployment, and elastic scaling.

As indicated in the preceding diagram, automations are typically applied during the development, test, release, and deployment phases:

- The development phase is automated using version control tools such as Git together with **Continuous Integration** (CI) tools such as Jenkins, Travis CI, and so on. This may also include code quality checks and automation of unit testing. Automation of a full build on every code check-in is also achievable with microservices.

- The testing phase will be automated using testing tools such as Selenium, Cucumber, and other AB testing strategies. As microservices are aligned to business capabilities, the number of test cases to automate is fewer compared to monolithic applications, hence regression testing on every build also becomes possible.

- Infrastructure provisioning is done through container technologies such as Docker, together with release management tools such as Chef or Puppet, and configuration management tools such as Ansible. Automated deployments are handled using tools such as Spring Cloud, Kubernetes, Mesos, and Marathon.

Microservices with a supporting ecosystem

Most of the large-scale microservices implementations have a supporting ecosystem in place. The ecosystem capabilities include DevOps processes, centralized log management, service registry, API gateways, extensive monitoring, service routing, and flow control mechanisms.

Microservices work well when supporting capabilities are in place, as represented in the preceding diagram.

Microservices are distributed and dynamic

Successful microservices implementations encapsulate logic and data within the service. This results in two unconventional situations: distributed data and logic and decentralized governance.

Compared to traditional applications, which consolidate all logic and data into one application boundary, microservices decentralize data and logic. Each service, aligned to a specific business capability, owns its data and logic.

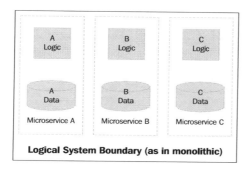

The dotted line in the preceding diagram implies the logical monolithic application boundary. When we migrate this to microservices, each microservice **A**, **B**, and **C** creates its own physical boundaries.

Microservices don't typically use centralized governance mechanisms the way they are used in SOA. One of the common characteristics of microservices implementations is that they do not relay on heavyweight enterprise-level products, such as **Enterprise Service Bus (ESB)**. Instead, the business logic and intelligence are embedded as a part of the services themselves.

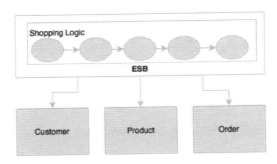

A typical SOA implementation is shown in the preceding diagram. Shopping logic is fully implemented in ESB by orchestrating different services exposed by Customer, Order, and Product. In the microservices approach, on the other hand, Shopping itself will run as a separate microservice, which interacts with Customer, Product, and Order in a fairly decoupled way.

SOA implementations heavily relay on static registry and repository configurations to manage services and other artifacts. Microservices bring a more dynamic nature into this. Hence, a static governance approach is seen as an overhead in maintaining up-to-date information. This is why most of the microservices implementations use automated mechanisms to build registry information dynamically from the runtime topologies.

Antifragility, fail fast, and self-healing

Antifragility is a technique successfully experimented at Netflix. It is one of the most powerful approaches to building fail-safe systems in modern software development.

 The antifragility concept is introduced by Nassim Nicholas Taleb in his book *Antifragile: Things That Gain from Disorder*.

In the antifragility practice, software systems are consistently challenged. Software systems evolve through these challenges and, over a period of time, get better and better at withstanding these challenges. Amazon's GameDay exercise and Netflix' Simian Army are good examples of such antifragility experiments.

Fail fast is another concept used to build fault-tolerant, resilient systems. This philosophy advocates systems that expect failures versus building systems that never fail. Importance should be given to how quickly the system can fail and if it fails, how quickly it can recover from this failure. With this approach, the focus is shifted from **Mean Time Between Failures (MTBF)** to **Mean Time To Recover (MTTR)**. A key advantage of this approach is that if something goes wrong, it kills itself, and downstream functions aren't stressed.

Self-healing is commonly used in microservices deployments, where the system automatically learns from failures and adjusts itself. These systems also prevent future failures.

Microservices examples

There is no "one size fits all" approach when implementing microservices. In this section, different examples are analyzed to crystalize the microservices concept.

An example of a holiday portal

In the first example, we will review a holiday portal, **Fly By Points**. Fly By Points collects points that are accumulated when a customer books a hotel, flight, or car through the online website. When the customer logs in to the Fly By Points website, he/she is able to see the points accumulated, personalized offers that can be availed of by redeeming the points, and upcoming trips if any.

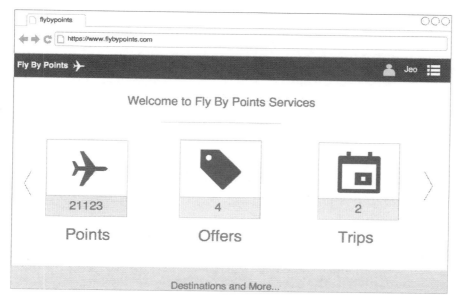

Let's assume that the preceding page is the home page after login. There are two upcoming trips for **Jeo**, four personalized offers, and 21,123 loyalty points. When the user clicks on each of the boxes, the details are queried and displayed.

The holiday portal has a Java Spring-based traditional monolithic application architecture, as shown in the following:

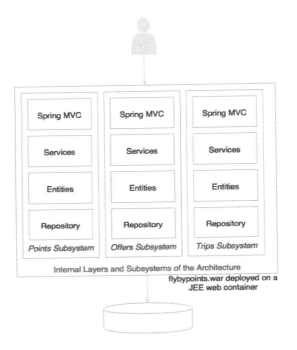

As shown in the preceding diagram, the holiday portal's architecture is web-based and modular, with a clear separation between layers. Following the usual practice, the holiday portal is also deployed as a single WAR file on a web server such as Tomcat. Data is stored on an all-encompassing backing relational database. This is a good fit for the purpose architecture when the complexities are few. As the business grows, the user base expands, and the complexity also increases. This results in a proportional increase in transaction volumes. At this point, enterprises should look to rearchitecting the monolithic application to microservices for better speed of delivery, agility, and manageability.

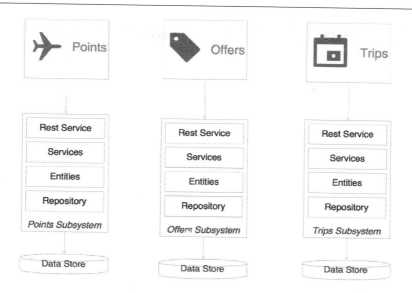

Examining the simple microservices version of this application, we can immediately note a few things in this architecture:

- Each subsystem has now become an independent system by itself, a microservice. There are three microservices representing three business functions: **Trips, Offers**, and **Points**. Each one has its internal data store and middle layer. The internal structure of each service remains the same.

- Each service encapsulates its own database as well as its own HTTP listener. As opposed to the previous model, there is no web server or WAR. Instead, each service has its own embedded HTTP listener, such as Jetty, Tomcat, and so on.

- Each microservice exposes a REST service to manipulate the resources/entity that belong to this service.

It is assumed that the presentation layer is developed using a client-side JavaScript MVC framework such as Angular JS. These client-side frameworks are capable of invoking REST calls directly.

When the web page is loaded, all the three boxes, Trips, Offers, and Points will be displayed with details such as points, the number of offers, and the number of trips. This will be done by each box independently making asynchronous calls to the respective backend microservices using REST. There is no dependency between the services at the service layer. When the user clicks on any of the boxes, the screen will be transitioned and will load the details of the item clicked on. This will be done by making another call to the respective microservice.

A microservice-based order management system

Let's examine another microservices example: an online retail website. In this case, we will focus more on the backend services, such as the Order Service which processes the Order Event generated when a customer places an order through the website:

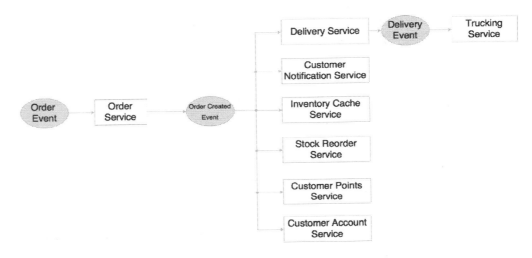

This microservices system is completely designed based on reactive programming practices.

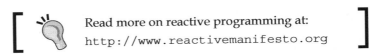

Read more on reactive programming at:
http://www.reactivemanifesto.org

When an event is published, a number of microservices are ready to kick-start upon receiving the event. Each one of them is independent and does not rely on other microservices. The advantage of this model is that we can keep adding or replacing microservices to achieve specific needs.

In the preceding diagram, there are eight microservices shown. The following activities take place upon the arrival of **Order Event**:

1. Order Service kicks off when Order Event is received. Order Service creates an order and saves the details to its own database.

2. If the order is successfully saved, Order Successful Event is created by Order Service and published.

3. A series of actions take place when Order Successful Event arrives.

4. Delivery Service accepts the event and places Delivery Record to deliver the order to the customer. This, in turn, generates Delivery Event and publishes the event.

5. Trucking Service picks up Delivery Event and processes it. For instance, Trucking Service creates a trucking plan.

6. Customer Notification Service sends a notification to the customer informing the customer that an order is placed.

7. Inventory Cache Service updates the inventory cache with the available product count.

8. Stock Reorder Service checks whether the stock limits are adequate and generates Replenish Event if required.

9. Customer Points Service recalculates the customer's loyalty points based on this purchase.

10. **Customer Account Service** updates the order history in the customer's account.

In this approach, each service is responsible for only one function. Services accept and generate events. Each service is independent and is not aware of its neighborhood. Hence, the neighborhood can organically grow as mentioned in the honeycomb analogy. New services can be added as and when necessary. Adding a new service does not impact any of the existing services.

An example of a travel agent portal

This third example is a simple travel agent portal application. In this example, we will see both synchronous REST calls as well as asynchronous events.

In this case, the portal is just a container application with multiple menu items or links in the portal. When specific pages are requested—for example, when the menu or a link is clicked on—they will be loaded from the specific microservices.

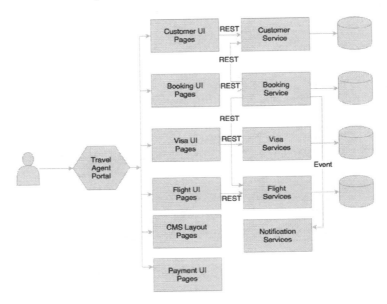

When a customer requests a booking, the following events take place internally:

1. The travel agent opens the flight UI, searches for a flight, and identifies the right flight for the customer. Behind the scenes, the flight UI is loaded from the Flight microservice. The flight UI only interacts with its own backend APIs within the Flight microservice. In this case, it makes a REST call to the Flight microservice to load the flights to be displayed.

2. The travel agent then queries the customer details by accessing the customer UI. Similar to the flight UI, the customer UI is loaded from the Customer microservice. Actions in the customer UI will invoke REST calls on the Customer microservice. In this case, customer details are loaded by invoking appropriate APIs on the Customer microservice.

3. Then, the travel agent checks the visa details for the customer's eligibility to travel to the selected country. This also follows the same pattern as mentioned in the previous two points.

4. Next, the travel agent makes a booking using the booking UI from the Booking microservice, which again follows the same pattern.

5. The payment pages are loaded from the Payment microservice. In general, the payment service has additional constraints such as PCIDSS compliance (protecting and encrypting data in motion and data at rest). The advantage of the microservices approach is that none of the other microservices need to be considered under the purview of PCIDSS as opposed to the monolithic application, where the complete application comes under the governing rules of PCIDSS. Payment also follows the same pattern as described earlier.

6. Once the booking is submitted, the Booking microservice calls the flight service to validate and update the flight booking. This orchestration is defined as part of the Booking microservice. Intelligence to make a booking is also held within the Booking microservice. As part of the booking process, it also validates, retrieves, and updates the Customer microservice.

7. Finally, the Booking microservice sends the Booking Event, which the Notification service picks up and sends a notification of to the customer.

The interesting factor here is that we can change the user interface, logic, and data of a microservice without impacting any other microservices.

This is a clean and neat approach. A number of portal applications can be built by composing different screens from different microservices, especially for different user communities. The overall behavior and navigation will be controlled by the portal application.

The approach has a number of challenges unless the pages are designed with this approach in mind. Note that the site layouts and static content will be loaded by the **Content Management System (CMS)** as layout templates. Alternately, this could be stored in a web server. The site layout may have fragments of UIs that will be loaded from the microservices at runtime.

Microservices benefits

Microservices offer a number of benefits over the traditional multitier, monolithic architectures. This section explains some key benefits of the microservices architecture approach.

Supports polyglot architecture

With microservices, architects and developers can choose fit for purpose architectures and technologies for each microservice. This gives the flexibility to design better-fit solutions in a more cost-effective way.

As microservices are autonomous and independent, each service can run with its own architecture or technology or different versions of technologies.

The following shows a simple, practical example of a polyglot architecture with microservices.

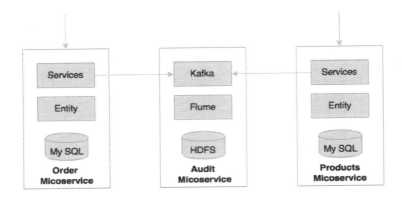

There is a requirement to audit all system transactions and record transaction details such as request and response data, the user who initiated the transaction, the service invoked, and so on.

As shown in the preceding diagram, while core services such as the Order and Products microservices use a relational data store, the Audit microservice persists data in Hadoop File System (HDFS). A relational data store is neither ideal nor cost effective in storing large data volumes such as in the case of audit data. In the monolithic approach, the application generally uses a shared, single database that stores Order, Products, and Audit data.

In this example, the audit service is a technical microservice using a different architecture. Similarly, different functional services could also use different architectures.

In another example, there could be a Reservation microservice running on Java 7, while a Search microservice could be running on Java 8. Similarly, an Order microservice could be written on Erlang, whereas a Delivery microservice could be on the Go language. None of these are possible with a monolithic architecture.

Enabling experimentation and innovation

Modern enterprises are thriving towards quick wins. Microservices are one of the key enablers for enterprises to do disruptive innovation by offering the ability to experiment and fail fast.

As services are fairly simple and smaller in size, enterprises can afford to experiment new processes, algorithms, business logics, and so on. With large monolithic applications, experimentation was not easy; nor was it straightforward or cost effective. Businesses had to spend huge money to build or change an application to try out something new. With microservices, it is possible to write a small microservice to achieve the targeted functionality and plug it into the system in a reactive style. One can then experiment with the new function for a few months, and if the new microservice does not work as expected, we can change or replace it with another one. The cost of change will be considerably less compared to that of the monolithic approach.

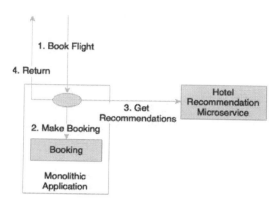

In another example of an airline booking website, the airline wants to show personalized hotel recommendations in their booking page. The recommendations must be displayed on the booking confirmation page.

As shown in the preceding diagram, it is convenient to write a microservice that can be plugged into the monolithic applications booking flow rather than incorporating this requirement in the monolithic application itself. The airline may choose to start with a simple recommendation service and keep replacing it with newer versions till it meets the required accuracy.

Elastically and selectively scalable

As microservices are smaller units of work, they enable us to implement selective scalability.

Scalability requirements may be different for different functions in an application. A monolithic application, packaged as a single WAR or an EAR, can only be scaled as a whole. An I/O-intensive function when streamed with high velocity data could easily bring down the service levels of the entire application.

In the case of microservices, each service could be independently scaled up or down. As scalability can be selectively applied at each service, the cost of scaling is comparatively less with the microservices approach.

In practice, there are many different ways available to scale an application and is largely subject to the architecture and behavior of the application. **Scale Cube** defines primarily three approaches to scaling an application:

- Scaling the x axis by horizontally cloning the application
- Scaling the y axis by splitting different functionality
- Scaling the z axis by partitioning or sharding the data

 Read more about Scale Cube in the following site: http://theartofscalability.com/

When y axis scaling is applied to monolithic applications, it breaks the monolithic to smaller units aligned with business functions. Many organizations successfully applied this technique to move away from monolithic applications. In principle, the resulting units of functions are in line with the microservices characteristics.

For instance, in a typical airline website, statistics indicate that the ratio of flight searching to flight booking could be as high as 500:1. This means one booking transaction for every 500 search transactions. In this scenario, the search needs 500 times more scalability than the booking function. This is an ideal use case for selective scaling.

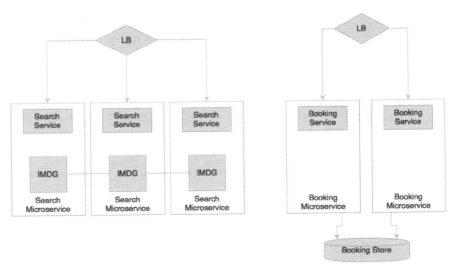

The solution is to treat search requests and booking requests differently. With a monolithic architecture, this is only possible with z scaling in the scale cube. However, this approach is expensive because in the z scale, the entire code base is replicated.

In the preceding diagram, Search and Booking are designed as different microservices so that Search can be scaled differently from Booking. In the diagram, Search has three instances, and Booking has two instances. Selective scalability is not limited to the number of instances, as shown in the diagram, but also in the way in which the microservices are architected. In the case of Search, an **in-memory data grid (IMDG)** such as Hazelcast can be used as the data store. This will further increase the performance and scalability of Search. When a new Search microservice instance is instantiated, an additional IMDG node is added to the IMDG cluster. Booking does not require the same level of scalability. In the case of Booking, both instances of the Booking microservice are connected to the same instance of the database.

Allowing substitution

Microservices are self-contained, independent deployment modules enabling the substitution of one microservice with another similar microservice.

Many large enterprises follow buy-versus-build policies to implement software systems. A common scenario is to build most of the functions in house and buy certain niche capabilities from specialists outside. This poses challenges in traditional monolithic applications as these application components are highly cohesive. Attempting to plug in third-party solutions to the monolithic applications results in complex integrations. With microservices, this is not an afterthought. Architecturally, a microservice can be easily replaced by another microservice developed either in-house or even extended by a microservice from a third party.

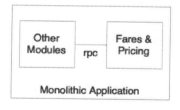 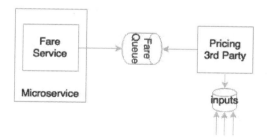

A pricing engine in the airline business is complex. Fares for different routes are calculated using complex mathematical formulas known as the pricing logic. Airlines may choose to buy a pricing engine from the market instead of building the product in house. In the monolithic architecture, Pricing is a function of Fares and Booking. In most cases Pricing, Fares, and Booking are hardwired, making it almost impossible to detach.

In a well-designed microservices system, Booking, Fares, and Pricing would be independent microservices. Replacing the Pricing microservice will have only a minimal impact on any other services as they are all loosely coupled and independent. Today, it could be a third-party service; tomorrow, it could be easily substituted by another third-party or home-grown service.

Enabling to build organic systems

Microservices help us build systems that are organic in nature. This is significantly important when migrating monolithic systems gradually to microservices.

Organic systems are systems that grow laterally over a period of time by adding more and more functions to it. In practice, an application grows unimaginably large in its lifespan, and in most cases, the manageability of the application reduces dramatically over this same period of time.

Microservices are all about independently manageable services. This enable us to keep adding more and more services as the need arises with minimal impact on the existing services. Building such systems does not need huge capital investments. Hence, businesses can keep building as part of their operational expenditure.

A loyalty system in an airline was built years ago, targeting individual passengers. Everything was fine until the airline started offering loyalty benefits to their corporate customers. Corporate customers are individuals grouped under corporations. As the current systems core data model is flat, targeting individuals, the corporate environment needs a fundamental change in the core data model, and hence huge reworking, to incorporate this requirement.

As shown in the preceding diagram, in a microservices-based architecture, customer information would be managed by the Customer microservice and loyalty by the Loyalty Points microservice.

In this situation, it is easy to add a new Corporate Customer microservice to manage corporate customers. When a corporation is registered, individual members will be pushed to the Customer microservice to manage them as usual. The Corporate Customer microservice provides a corporate view by aggregating data from the Customer microservice. It will also provide services to support corporate-specific business rules. With this approach, adding new services will have only a minimal impact on the existing services.

Helping reducing technology debt

As microservices are smaller in size and have minimal dependencies, they allow the migration of services that use end-of-life technologies with minimal cost.

Technology changes are one of the barriers in software development. In many traditional monolithic applications, due to the fast changes in technologies, today's next-generation applications could easily become legacy even before their release to production. Architects and developers tend to add a lot of protection against technology changes by adding layers of abstractions. However, in reality, this approach does not solve the issue but, instead, results in over-engineered systems. As technology upgrades are often risky and expensive with no direct returns to business, the business may not be happy to invest in reducing the technology debt of the applications.

With microservices, it is possible to change or upgrade technology for each service individually rather than upgrading an entire application.

Upgrading an application with, for instance, five million lines written on EJB 1.1 and Hibernate to the Spring, JPA, and REST services is almost similar to rewriting the entire application. In the microservices world, this could be done incrementally.

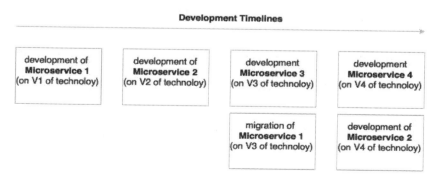

As shown in the preceding diagram, while older versions of the services are running on old versions of technologies, new service developments can leverage the latest technologies. The cost of migrating microservices with end-of-life technologies is considerably less compared to enhancing monolithic applications.

Allowing the coexistence of different versions

As microservices package the service runtime environment along with the service itself, this enables having multiple versions of the service to coexist in the same environment.

There will be situations where we will have to run multiple versions of the same service at the same time. Zero downtime promote, where one has to gracefully switch over from one version to another, is one example of a such a scenario as there will be a time window where both services will have to be up and running simultaneously. With monolithic applications, this is a complex procedure because upgrading new services in one node of the cluster is cumbersome as, for instance, this could lead to class loading issues. A canary release, where a new version is only released to a few users to validate the new service, is another example where multiple versions of the services have to coexist.

With microservices, both these scenarios are easily manageable. As each microservice uses independent environments, including service listeners such as Tomcat or Jetty embedded, multiple versions can be released and gracefully transitioned without many issues. When consumers look up services, they look for specific versions of services. For example, in a canary release, a new user interface is released to user A. When user A sends a request to the microservice, it looks up the canary release version, whereas all other users will continue to look up the last production version.

Care needs to be taken at the database level to ensure the database design is always backward compatible to avoid breaking the changes.

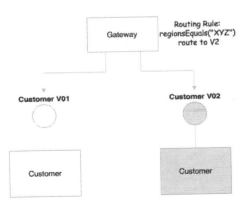

As shown in the preceding diagram, version 1 and 2 of the **Customer** service can coexist as they are not interfering with each other, given their respective deployment environments. Routing rules can be set at the gateway to divert traffic to specific instances, as shown in the diagram. Alternatively, clients can request specific versions as part of the request itself. In the diagram, the gateway selects the version based on the region from which the request is originated.

Supporting the building of self-organizing systems

Microservices help us build self-organizing systems. A self-organizing system support will automate deployment, be resilient, and exhibit self-healing and self-learning capabilities.

In a well-architected microservices system, a service is unaware of other services. It accepts a message from a selected queue and processes it. At the end of the process, it may send out another message, which triggers other services. This allows us to drop any service into the ecosystem without analyzing the impact on the overall system. Based on the input and output, the service will self-organize into the ecosystem. No additional code changes or service orchestration is required. There is no central brain to control and coordinate the processes.

Imagine an existing notification service that listens to an **INPUT** queue and sends notifications to an **SMTP** server, as shown in the following figure:

Let's assume, later, a personalization engine, responsible for changing the language of the message to the customer's native language, needs to be introduced to personalize messages before sending them to the customer, the personalization engine is responsible for changing the language of the message to the customer's native language.

With microservices, a new personalization microservice will be created to do this job. The input queue will be configured as INPUT in an external configuration server, and the personalization service will pick up the messages from the INPUT queue (earlier, this was used by the notification service) and send the messages to the OUTPUT queue after completing process. The notification services input queue will then send to OUTPUT. From the very next moment onward, the system automatically adopts this new message flow.

Supporting event-driven architecture

Microservices enable us to develop transparent software systems. Traditional systems communicate with each other through native protocols and hence behave like a black box application. Business events and system events, unless published explicitly, are hard to understand and analyze. Modern applications require data for business analysis, to understand dynamic system behaviors, and analyze market trends, and they also need to respond to real-time events. Events are useful mechanisms for data extraction.

A well-architected microservice always works with events for both input and output. These events can be tapped by any service. Once extracted, events can be used for a variety of use cases.

For example, the business wants to see the velocity of orders categorized by product type in real time. In a monolithic system, we need to think about how to extract these events. This may impose changes in the system.

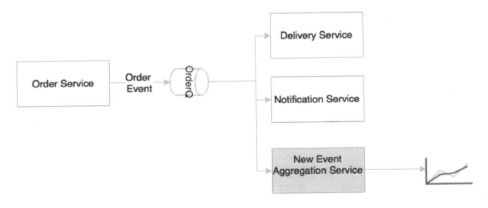

In the microservices world, **Order Event** is already published whenever an order is created. This means that it is just a matter of adding a new service to subscribe to the same topic, extract the event, perform the requested aggregations, and push another event for the dashboard to consume.

Enabling DevOps

Microservices are one of the key enablers of DevOps. DevOps is widely adopted as a practice in many enterprises, primarily to increase the speed of delivery and agility. A successful adoption of DevOps requires cultural changes, process changes, as well as architectural changes. DevOps advocates to have agile development, high-velocity release cycles, automatic testing, automatic infrastructure provisioning, and automated deployment.

Automating all these processes is extremely hard to achieve with traditional monolithic applications. Microservices are not the ultimate answer, but microservices are at the center stage in many DevOps implementations. Many DevOps tools and techniques are also evolving around the use of microservices.

Consider a monolithic application that takes hours to complete a full build and 20 to 30 minutes to start the application; one can see that this kind of application is not ideal for DevOps automation. It is hard to automate continuous integration on every commit. As large, monolithic applications are not automation friendly, continuous testing and deployments are also hard to achieve.

On the other hand, small footprint microservices are more automation-friendly and therefore can more easily support these requirements.

Microservices also enable smaller, focused agile teams for development. Teams will be organized based on the boundaries of microservices.

Relationship with other architecture styles

Now that we have seen the characteristics and benefits of microservices, in this section, we will explore the relationship of microservices with other closely related architecture styles such as SOA and Twelve-Factor Apps.

Relations with SOA

SOA and microservices follow similar concepts. Earlier in this chapter, we discussed that microservices are evolved from SOA, and many service characteristics are common in both approaches.

However, are they the same or are they different?

As microservices are evolved from SOA, many characteristics of microservices are similar to SOA. Let's first examine the definition of SOA.

The definition of SOA from *The Open Group* consortium is as follows:

> *"Service-Oriented Architecture (SOA) is an architectural style that supports service orientation. Service orientation is a way of thinking in terms of services and service-based development and the outcomes of services.*
>
> *A service:*
>
> *Is a logical representation of a repeatable business activity that has a specified outcome (e.g., check customer credit, provide weather data, consolidate drilling reports)*
>
> *It is self-contained.*
>
> *It may be composed of other services.*
>
> *It is a "black box" to consumers of the service."*

We observed similar aspects in microservices as well. So, in what way are microservices different? The answer is: it depends.

The answer to the previous question could be yes or no, depending upon the organization and its adoption of SOA. SOA is a broader term, and different organizations approached SOA differently to solve different organizational problems. The difference between microservices and SOA is in a way based on how an organization approaches SOA.

In order to get clarity, a few cases will be examined.

Service-oriented integration

Service-oriented integration refers to a service-based integration approach used by many organizations.

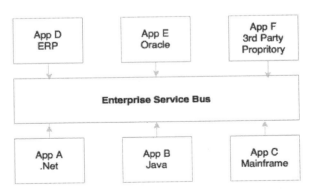

Many organizations would have used SOA primarily to solve their integration complexities, also known as integration spaghetti. Generally, this is termed as **Service-Oriented Integration (SOI)**. In such cases, applications communicate with each other through a common integration layer using standard protocols and message formats such as SOAP/XML-based web services over HTTP or JMS. These types of organizations focus on **Enterprise Integration Patterns (EIP)** to model their integration requirements. This approach strongly relies on heavyweight ESB such as TIBCO Business Works, WebSphere ESB, Oracle ESB, and the likes. Most ESB vendors also packed a set of related products such as rules engines, business process management engines, and so on as an SOA suite. Such organizations' integrations are deeply rooted into their products. They either write heavy orchestration logic in the ESB layer or the business logic itself in the service bus. In both cases, all enterprise services are deployed and accessed via ESB. These services are managed through an enterprise governance model. For such organizations, microservices are altogether different from SOA.

Legacy modernization

SOA is also used to build service layers on top of legacy applications.

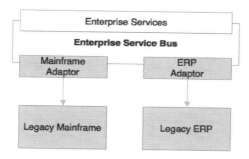

Another category of organizations would use SOA in transformation projects or legacy modernization projects. In such cases, the services are built and deployed in the ESB layer connecting to backend systems using ESB adapters. For these organizations, microservices are different from SOA.

Service-oriented application

Some organizations adopt SOA at an application level.

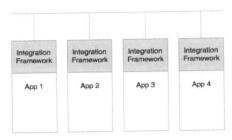

In this approach, lightweight integration frameworks, such as Apache Camel or Spring Integration, are embedded within applications to handle service-related cross-cutting capabilities such as protocol mediation, parallel execution, orchestration, and service integration. As some of the lightweight integration frameworks have native Java object support, such applications would even use native **Plain Old Java Objects (POJO)** services for integration and data exchange between services. As a result, all services have to be packaged as one monolithic web archive. Such organizations could see microservices as the next logical step of their SOA.

Monolithic migration using SOA

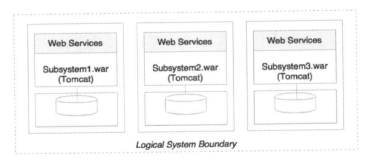

The last possibility is transforming a monolithic application into smaller units after hitting the breaking point with the monolithic system. They would break the application into smaller, physically deployable subsystems, similar to the y axis scaling approach explained earlier, and deploy them as web archives on web servers or as JARs deployed on some home-grown containers. These subsystems as service would use web services or other lightweight protocols to exchange data between services. They would also use SOA and service design principles to achieve this. For such organizations, they may tend to think that microservices are the same old wine in a new bottle.

Relations with Twelve-Factor apps

Cloud computing is one of the rapidly evolving technologies. Cloud computing promises many benefits, such as cost advantage, speed, agility, flexibility, and elasticity. There are many cloud providers offering different services. They lower the cost models to make it more attractive to the enterprises. Different cloud providers such as AWS, Microsoft, Rackspace, IBM, Google, and so on use different tools, technologies, and services. On the other hand, enterprises are aware of this evolving battlefield and, therefore, they are looking for options for de-risking from lockdown to a single vendor.

Many organizations do lift and shift their applications to the cloud. In such cases, the applications may not realize all the benefits promised by cloud platforms. Some applications need to undergo overhaul, whereas some may need minor tweaking before moving to cloud. This by and large depends upon how the application is architected and developed.

For example, if the application has its production database server URLs hardcoded as part of the applications WAR, it needs to be modified before moving the application to cloud. In the cloud, the infrastructure is transparent to the application, and especially, the physical IP addresses cannot be assumed.

How do we ensure that an application, or even microservices, can run seamlessly across multiple cloud providers and take advantages of cloud services such as elasticity?

It is important to follow certain principles while developing cloud native applications.

 Cloud native is a term used for developing applications that can work efficiently in a cloud environment, understanding and utilizing cloud behaviors such as elasticity, utilization based charging, fail aware, and so on.

Twelve-Factor App, forwarded by Heroku, is a methodology describing the characteristics expected from modern cloud-ready applications. Twelve-Factor App is equally applicable for microservices as well. Hence, it is important to understand Twelve-Factor App.

A single code base

The code base principle advises that each application has a single code base. There can be multiple instances of deployment of the same code base, such as development, testing, and production. Code is typically managed in a source control system such as Git, Subversion, and so on.

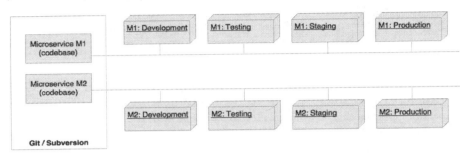

Extending the same philosophy for microservices, each microservice should have its own code base, and this code base is not shared with any other microservice. It also means that one microservice has exactly one code base.

Bundling dependencies

As per this principle, all applications should bundle their dependencies along with the application bundle. With build tools such as Maven and Gradle, we explicitly manage dependencies in a `pom.xml` or the `.gradle` file and link them using a central build artifact repository such as Nexus or Archiva. This ensures that the versions are managed correctly. The final executables will be packaged as a WAR file or an executable JAR file, embedding all the dependencies.

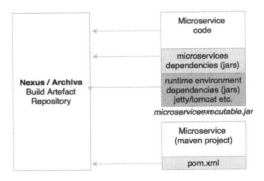

In the context of microservices, this is one of the fundamental principles to be followed. Each microservice should bundle all the required dependencies and execution libraries such as the HTTP listener and so on in the final executable bundle.

Externalizing configurations

This principle advises the externalization of all configuration parameters from the code. An application's configuration parameters vary between environments, such as support to the e-mail IDs or URL of an external system, username, passwords, queue name, and so on. These will be different for development, testing, and production. All service configurations should be externalized.

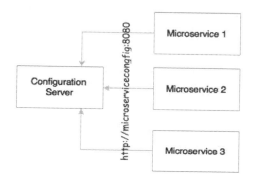

The same principle is obvious for microservices as well. The microservices configuration parameters should be loaded from an external source. This will also help to automate the release and deployment process as the only difference between these environments is the configuration parameters.

Backing services are addressable

All backing services should be accessible through an addressable URL. All services need to talk to some external resources during the life cycle of their execution. For example, they could be listening or sending messages to a messaging system, sending an e-mail, persisting data to database, and so on. All these services should be reachable through a URL without complex communication requirements.

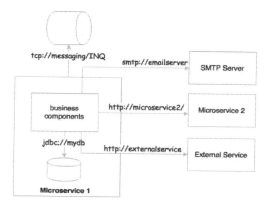

In the microservices world, microservices either talk to a messaging system to send or receive messages, or they could accept or send messages to other service APIs. In a regular case, these are either HTTP endpoints using REST and JSON or TCP- or HTTP-based messaging endpoints.

Isolation between build, release, and run

This principle advocates a strong isolation between the build, release, and run stages. The build stage refers to compiling and producing binaries by including all the assets required. The release stage refers to combining binaries with environment-specific configuration parameters. The run stage refers to running application on a specific execution environment. The pipeline is unidirectional, so it is not possible to propagate changes from the run stages back to the build stage. Essentially, it also means that it is not recommended to do specific builds for production; rather, it has to go through the pipeline.

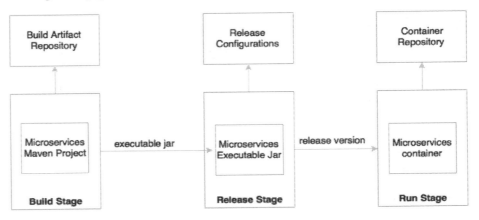

In microservices, the build will create executable JAR files, including the service runtime such as an HTTP listener. During the release phase, these executables will be combined with release configurations such as production URLs and so on and create a release version, most probably as a container similar to Docker. In the run stage, these containers will be deployed on production via a container scheduler.

Stateless, shared nothing processes

This principle suggests that processes should be stateless and share nothing. If the application is stateless, then it is fault tolerant and can be scaled out easily.

All microservices should be designed as stateless functions. If there is any requirement to store a state, it should be done with a backing database or in an in-memory cache.

Exposing services through port bindings

A Twelve-Factor application is expected to be self-contained. Traditionally, applications are deployed to a server: a web server or an application server such as Apache Tomcat or JBoss. A Twelve-Factor application does not rely on an external web server. HTTP listeners such as Tomcat or Jetty have to be embedded in the service itself.

Port binding is one of the fundamental requirements for microservices to be autonomous and self-contained. Microservices embed service listeners as a part of the service itself.

Concurrency to scale out

This principle states that processes should be designed to scale out by replicating the processes. This is in addition to the use of threads within the process.

In the microservices world, services are designed to scale out rather than scale up. The x axis scaling technique is primarily used for a scaling service by spinning up another identical service instance. The services can be elastically scaled or shrunk based on the traffic flow. Further to this, microservices may make use of parallel processing and concurrency frameworks to further speed up or scale up the transaction processing.

Disposability with minimal overhead

This principle advocates building applications with minimal startup and shutdown times with graceful shutdown support. In an automated deployment environment, we should be able bring up or bring down instances as quick as possible. If the application's startup or shutdown takes considerable time, it will have an adverse effect on automation. The startup time is proportionally related to the size of the application. In a cloud environment targeting auto-scaling, we should be able to spin up new instance quickly. This is also applicable when promoting new versions of services.

In the microservices context, in order to achieve full automation, it is extremely important to keep the size of the application as thin as possible, with minimal startup and shutdown time. Microservices also should consider a lazy loading of objects and data.

Development and production parity

This principle states the importance of keeping development and production environments as identical as possible. For example, let's consider an application with multiple services or processes, such as a job scheduler service, cache services, and one or more application services. In a development environment, we tend to run all of them on a single machine, whereas in production, we will facilitate independent machines to run each of these processes. This is primarily to manage the cost of infrastructure. The downside is that if production fails, there is no identical environment to re-produce and fix the issues.

Not only is this principle valid for microservices, but it is also applicable to any application development.

Externalizing logs

A Twelve-Factor application never attempts to store or ship log files. In a cloud, it is better to avoid local I/Os. If the I/Os are not fast enough in a given infrastructure, it could create a bottleneck. The solution to this is to use a centralized logging framework. Splunk, Greylog, Logstash, Logplex, and Loggly are some examples of log shipping and analysis tools. The recommended approach is to ship logs to a central repository by tapping the logback appenders and write to one of the shippers' endpoints.

In a microservices ecosystem, this is very important as we are breaking a system into a number of smaller services, which could result in decentralized logging. If they store logs in a local storage, it would be extremely difficult to correlate logs between services.

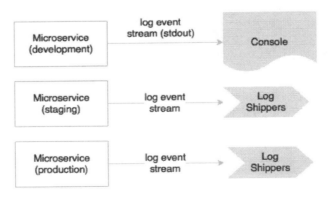

In development, the microservice may direct the log stream to `stdout`, whereas in production, these streams will be captured by the log shippers and sent to a central log service for storage and analysis.

Package admin processes

Apart from application services, most applications provide admin tasks as well. This principle advises to use the same release bundle as well as an identical environment for both application services and admin tasks. Admin code should also be packaged along with the application code.

Not only is this principle valid for microservices, but also it is applicable to any application development.

Microservice use cases

A microservice is not a silver bullet and will not solve all the architectural challenges of today's world. There is no hard-and-fast rule or rigid guideline on when to use microservices.

Microservices may not fit in each and every use case. The success of microservices largely depends on the selection of use cases. The first and the foremost activity is to do a litmus test of the use case against the microservices' benefits. The litmus test must cover all the microservices' benefits we discussed earlier in this chapter. For a given use case, if there are no quantifiable benefits or the cost outweighs the benefits, then the use case may not be the right choice for microservices.

Let's discuss some commonly used scenarios that are suitable candidates for a microservices architecture:

- Migrating a monolithic application due to improvements required in scalability, manageability, agility, or speed of delivery. Another similar scenario is rewriting an end-of-life heavily used legacy application. In both cases, microservices present an opportunity. Using a microservices architecture, it is possible to replatform a legacy application by slowly transforming functions to microservices. There are benefits in this approach. There is no humongous upfront investment required, no major disruption to business, and no severe business risks. As the service dependencies are known, the microservices dependencies can be well managed.

- Utility computing scenarios such as integrating an optimization service, forecasting service, price calculation service, prediction service, offer service, recommendation service, and so on are good candidates for microservices. These are independent stateless computing units that accept certain data, apply algorithms, and return the results. Independent technical services such as the communication service, the encryption service, authentication services, and so on are also good candidates for microservices.

- In many cases, we can build headless business applications or services that are autonomous in nature—for instance, the payment service, login service, flight search service, customer profile service, notification service, and so on. These are normally reused across multiple channels and, hence, are good candidates for building them as microservices.

- There could be micro or macro applications that serve a single purpose and performing a single responsibility. A simple time tracking application is an example of this category. All it does is capture the time, duration, and task performed. Common-use enterprise applications are also candidates for microservices.

- Backend services of a well-architected, responsive client-side MVC web application (the **Backend as a Service (BaaS)** scenario) load data on demand in response to the user navigation. In most of these scenarios, data could be coming from multiple logically different data sources as described in the *Fly By Points* example mentioned earlier.

- Highly agile applications, applications demanding speed of delivery or time to market, innovation pilots, applications selected for DevOps, applications of the System of Innovation type, and so on could also be considered as potential candidates for the microservices architecture.

- Applications that we could anticipate getting benefits from microservices such as polyglot requirements, applications that require **Command Query Responsibility segregations (CQRS)**, and so on are also potential candidates of the microservices architecture.

If the use case falls into any of these categories, it is a potential candidate for the microservices architecture.

There are few scenarios in which we should consider avoiding microservices:

- If the organization's policies are forced to use centrally managed heavyweight components such as ESB to host a business logic or if the organization has any other policies that hinder the fundamental principles of microservices, then microservices are not the right solution unless the organizational process is relaxed.

- If the organization's culture, processes, and so on are based on the traditional waterfall delivery model, lengthy release cycles, matrix teams, manual deployments and cumbersome release processes, no infrastructure provisioning, and so on, then microservices may not be the right fit. This is underpinned by Conway's Law. This states that there is a strong link between the organizational structure and software it creates.

Read more about the Conway's Law at:
`http://www.melconway.com/Home/Conways_Law.html`

Microservices early adopters

Many organizations have already successfully embarked on their journey to the microservices world. In this section, we will examine some of the frontrunners on the microservices space to analyze why they did what they did and how they did it. We will conduct some analysis at the end to draw some conclusions:

- **Netflix** (www.netflix.com): Netflix, an international on-demand media streaming company, is a pioneer in the microservices space. Netflix transformed their large pool of developers developing traditional monolithic code to smaller development teams producing microservices. These microservices work together to stream digital media to millions of Netflix customers. At Netflix, engineers started with monolithic, went through the pain, and then broke the application into smaller units that are loosely coupled and aligned to the business capability.

- **Uber** (www.uber.com): Uber, an international transportation network company, began in 2008 with a monolithic architecture with a single code base. All services were embedded into the monolithic application. When Uber expanded their business from one city to multiple cities, the challenges started. Uber then moved to SOA-based architecture by breaking the system into smaller independent units. Each module was given to different teams and empowered them to choose their language, framework, and database. Uber has many microservices deployed in their ecosystem using RPC and REST.

- **Airbnb** (www.airbnb.com): Airbnb, a world leader providing a trusted marketplace for accommodation, started with a monolithic application that performed all the required functions of the business. Airbnb faced scalability issues with increased traffic. A single code base became too complicated to manage, resulted in a poor separation of concerns, and ran into performance issues. Airbnb broke their monolithic application into smaller pieces with separate code bases running on separate machines with separate deployment cycles. Airbnb developed their own microservices or SOA ecosystem around these services.

- **Orbitz** (www.orbitz.com): Orbitz, an online travel portal, started with a monolithic architecture in the 2000s with a web layer, a business layer, and a database layer. As Orbitz expanded their business, they faced manageability and scalability issues with monolithic-tiered architecture. Orbitz then went through continuous architecture changes. Later, Orbitz broke down their monolithic to many smaller applications.

- **eBay** (www.ebay.com): eBay, one of the largest online retailers, started in the late 1990s with a monolithic Perl application and FreeBSD as the database. eBay went through scaling issues as the business grew. It was consistently investing in improving its architecture. In the mid 2000s, eBay moved to smaller decomposed systems based on Java and web services. They employed database partitions and functional segregation to meet the required scalability.

- **Amazon** (www.amazon.com): Amazon, one of the largest online retailer websites, was run on a big monolithic application written on C++ in 2001. The well-architected monolithic application was based on a tiered architecture with many modular components. However, all these components were tightly coupled. As a result, Amazon was not able to speed up their development cycle by splitting teams into smaller groups. Amazon then separated out the code as independent functional services, wrapped with web services, and eventually advanced to microservices.

- **Gilt** (www.gilt.com): Gilt, an online shopping website, began in 2007 with a tiered monolithic Rails application and a Postgres database at the back. Similarly to many other applications, as traffic volumes increased, the web application was not able to provide the required resiliency. Gilt went through an architecture overhaul by introducing Java and polyglot persistence. Later, Gilt moved to many smaller applications using the microservices concept.

- **Twitter** (www.twitter.com): Twitter, one of the largest social websites, began with a three-tiered monolithic rails application in the mid 2000s. Later, when Twitter experienced growth in its user base, they went through an architecture-refactoring cycle. With this refactoring, Twitter moved away from a typical web application to an API-based even driven core. Twitter uses Scala and Java to develop microservices with polyglot persistence.

- **Nike** (www.nike.com): Nike, the world leader in apparel and footwear, transformed their monolithic applications to microservices. Similarly to many other organizations, Nike too was run with age-old legacy applications that were hardly stable. In their journey, Nike moved to heavyweight commercial products with an objective to stabilize legacy applications but ended up in monolithic applications that were expensive to scale, had long release cycles, and needed too much manual work to deploy and manage applications. Later, Nike moved to a microservices-based architecture that brought down the development cycle considerably.

The common theme is monolithic migrations

When we analyze the preceding enterprises, there is one common theme. All these enterprises started with monolithic applications and transitioned to a microservices architecture by applying learning and pain points from their previous editions.

Even today, many start-ups begin with monolith as it is easy to start, conceptualize, and then slowly move to microservices when the demand arises. Monolithic to microservices migration scenarios have an added advantage: they have all the information upfront, readily available for refactoring.

Though, for all these enterprises, it is monolithic transformation, the catalysts were different for different organizations. Some of the common motivations are a lack of scalability, long development cycles, process automation, manageability, and changes in the business models.

While monolithic migrations are no-brainers, there are opportunities to build microservices from the ground up. More than building ground-up systems, look for opportunities to build smaller services that are quick wins for business — for example, adding a trucking service to an airline's end-to-end cargo management system or adding a customer scoring service to a retailer's loyalty system. These could be implemented as independent microservices exchanging messages with their respective monolithic applications.

Another point is that many organizations use microservices only for their business-critical customer engagement applications, leaving the rest of the legacy monolithic applications to take their own trajectory.

Another important observation is that most of the organizations examined previously are at different levels of maturity in their microservices journey. When eBay transitioned from a monolithic application in the early 2000s, they functionally split the application into smaller, independent, and deployable units. These logically divided units are wrapped with web services. While single responsibility and autonomy are their underpinning principles, the architectures are limited to the technologies and tools available at that point in time. Organizations such as Netflix and Airbnb built capabilities of their own to solve the specific challenges they faced. To summarize, all of these are not truly microservices, but are small, business-aligned services following the same characteristics.

There is no state called "definite or ultimate microservices". It is a journey and is evolving and maturing day by day. The mantra for architects and developers is the replaceability principle; build an architecture that maximizes the ability to replace its parts and minimizes the cost of replacing its parts. The bottom line is that enterprises shouldn't attempt to develop microservices by just following the hype.

Summary

In this chapter, you learned about the fundamentals of microservices with the help of a few examples.

We explored the evolution of microservices from traditional monolithic applications. We examined some of the principles and the mind shift required for modern application architectures. We also took a look at the characteristics and benefits of microservices and use cases. In this chapter, we established the microservices' relationship with service-oriented architecture and Twelve-Factor Apps. Lastly, we analyzed examples of a few enterprises from different industries.

We will develop a few sample microservices in the next chapter to bring more clarity to our learnings in this chapter.

2
Building Microservices with Spring Boot

Developing microservices is not so tedious anymore thanks to the powerful Spring Boot framework. Spring Boot is a framework to develop production-ready microservices in Java.

This chapter will move from the microservices theory explained in the previous chapter to hands-on practice by reviewing code samples. This chapter will introduce the Spring Boot framework and explain how Spring Boot can help build RESTful microservices in line with the principles and characteristics discussed in the previous chapter. Finally, some of the features offered by Spring Boot to make microservices production-ready will be reviewed.

By the end of this chapter, you will have learned about:

- Setting up the latest Spring development environment
- Developing RESTful services using the Spring framework
- Using Spring Boot to build fully qualified microservices
- Useful Spring Boot features to build production-ready microservices

Setting up a development environment

To crystalize microservices concepts, a couple of microservices will be built. For this, it is assumed that the following components are installed:

- **JDK 1.8**: http://www.oracle.com/technetwork/java/javase/downloads/jdk8-downloads-2133151.html
- **Spring Tool Suite 3.7.2 (STS)**: https://spring.io/tools/sts/all
- **Maven 3.3.1**: https://maven.apache.org/download.cgi

Alternately, other IDEs such as IntelliJ IDEA, NetBeans, or Eclipse could be used. Similarly, alternate build tools such as Gradle can be used. It is assumed that the Maven repository, class path, and other path variables are set properly to run STS and Maven projects.

This chapter is based on the following versions of Spring libraries:

- Spring Framework 4.2.6.RELEASE
- Spring Boot 1.3.5.RELEASE

> Detailed steps to download the code bundle are mentioned in the Preface of this book. Have a look.
>
> The code bundle for the book is also hosted on GitHub at https://github.com/PacktPublishing/Spring-Microservices. We also have other code bundles from our rich catalog of books and videos available at https://github.com/PacktPublishing/. Check them out!

Developing a RESTful service – the legacy approach

This example will review the traditional RESTful service development before jumping deep into Spring Boot.

STS will be used to develop this REST/JSON service.

> The full source code of this example is available as the legacyrest project in the code files of this book.

The following are the steps to develop the first RESTful service:

1. Start STS and set a workspace of choice for this project.
2. Navigate to **File | New | Project**.
3. Select **Spring Legacy Project** as shown in the following screenshot and click on **Next**:

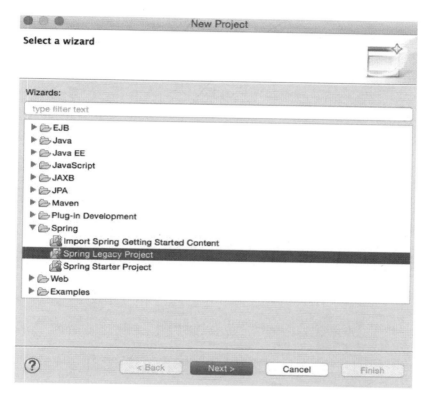

4. Select **Spring MVC Project** as shown in the following diagram and click on **Next**:

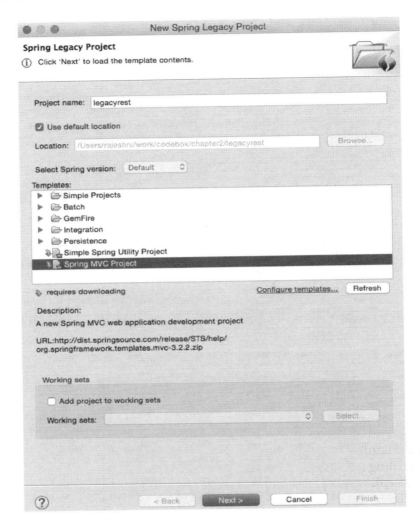

5. Select a top-level package name of choice. This example uses `org.rvslab.chapter2.legacyrest` as the top-level package.

6. Then, click on **Finish**.

7. This will create a project in the STS workspace with the name `legacyrest`. Before proceeding further, `pom.xml` needs editing.

8. Change the Spring version to `4.2.6.RELEASE`, as follows:

```
<org.springframework-version>4.2.6.RELEASE</org.springframework-version>
```

9. Add **Jackson** dependencies in the `pom.xml` file for JSON-to-POJO and POJO-to-JSON conversions. Note that the `2.*.*` version is used to ensure compatibility with Spring 4.

```
<dependency>
    <groupId>com.fasterxml.jackson.core</groupId>
    <artifactId>jackson-databind</artifactId>
    <version>2.6.4</version>
</dependency>
```

10. Some Java code needs to be added. In **Java Resources**, under **legacyrest**, expand the package and open the default **HomeController.java** file:

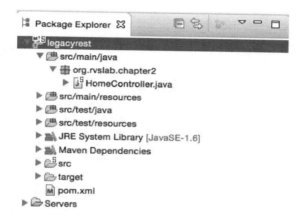

11. The default implementation is targeted more towards the MVC project. Rewriting `HomeController.java` to return a JSON value in response to the REST call will do the trick. The resulting `HomeController.java` file will look similar to the following:

```
@RestController
public class HomeController {
  @RequestMapping("/")
  public Greet sayHello(){
    return new Greet("Hello World!");
  }
}
```

```
class Greet {
  private String message;
  public Greet(String message) {
    this.message = message;
  }
  //add getter and setter
}
```

Examining the code, there are now two classes:

- Greet: This is a simple Java class with getters and setters to represent a data object. There is only one attribute in the Greet class, which is message.

- HomeController.java: This is nothing but a Spring controller REST endpoint to handle HTTP requests.

Note that the annotation used in HomeController is @RestController, which automatically injects @Controller and @ResponseBody and has the same effect as the following code:

```
@Controller
@ResponseBody
public class HomeController { }
```

12. The project can now be run by right-clicking on **legacyrest**, navigating to **Run As | Run On Server**, and then selecting the default server (**Pivotal tc Server Developer Edition v3.1**) that comes along with STS.

This should automatically start the server and deploy the web application on the TC server.

If the server started properly, the following message will appear in the console:

```
INFO : org.springframework.web.servlet.DispatcherServlet -
FrameworkServlet 'appServlet': initialization completed in 906 ms
May 08, 2016 8:22:48 PM org.apache.catalina.startup.Catalina start
INFO: Server startup in 2289 ms
```

13. If everything is fine, STS will open a browser window to `http://localhost:8080/legacyrest/` and display the JSON object as shown in the browser. Right-click on and navigate to **legacyrest | Properties | Web Project Settings** and review **Context Root** to identify the context root of the web application:

The alternate build option is to use Maven. Right-click on the project and navigate to **Run As | Maven install**. This will generate `chapter2-1.0.0-BUILD-SNAPSHOT.war` under the target folder. This war is deployable in any servlet container such as Tomcat, JBoss, and so on.

Moving from traditional web applications to microservices

Carefully examining the preceding RESTful service will reveal whether this really constitutes a microservice. At first glance, the preceding RESTful service is a fully qualified interoperable REST/JSON service. However, it is not fully autonomous in nature. This is primarily because the service relies on an underlying application server or web container. In the preceding example, a war was explicitly created and deployed on a Tomcat server.

This is a traditional approach to developing RESTful services as a web application. However, from the microservices point of view, one needs a mechanism to develop services as executables, self-contained JAR files with an embedded HTTP listener.

Spring Boot is a tool that allows easy development of such kinds of services. Dropwizard and WildFly Swarm are alternate server-less RESTful stacks.

Using Spring Boot to build RESTful microservices

Spring Boot is a utility framework from the Spring team to bootstrap Spring-based applications and microservices quickly and easily. The framework uses an opinionated approach over configurations for decision making, thereby reducing the effort required in writing a lot of boilerplate code and configurations. Using the 80-20 principle, developers should be able to kickstart a variety of Spring applications with many default values. Spring Boot further presents opportunities for the developers to customize applications by overriding the autoconfigured values.

Spring Boot not only increases the speed of development but also provides a set of production-ready ops features such as health checks and metrics collection. As Spring Boot masks many configuration parameters and abstracts many lower-level implementations, it minimizes the chance of error to a certain extent. Spring Boot recognizes the nature of the application based on the libraries available in the class path and runs the autoconfiguration classes packaged in these libraries.

Often, many developers mistakenly see Spring Boot as a code generator, but in reality, it is not. Spring Boot only autoconfigures build files — for example, POM files in the case of Maven. It also sets properties, such as data source properties, based on certain opinionated defaults. Take a look at the following code:

```
<dependency>
    <groupId>org.springframework.boot</groupId>
    <artifactId>spring-boot-starter-data-jpa</artifactId>
</dependency>
<dependency>
    <groupId>org.hsqldb</groupId>
    <artifactId>hsqldb</artifactId>
    <scope>runtime</scope>
</dependency>
```

For instance, in the preceding case, Spring Boot understands that the project is set to use the Spring Data JPA and HSQL databases. It automatically configures the driver class and other connection parameters.

One of the great outcomes of Spring Boot is that it almost eliminates the need to have traditional XML configurations. Spring Boot also enables microservices' development by packaging all the required runtime dependencies in a fat executable JAR file.

Getting started with Spring Boot

There are different ways that Spring Boot-based application development can be started:

- Using the Spring Boot CLI as a command-line tool
- Using IDEs such as STS to provide Spring Boot, which are supported out of the box
- Using the Spring Initializr project at `http://start.spring.io`

All these three options will be explored in this chapter, developing a variety of sample services.

Developing the Spring Boot microservice using the CLI

The easiest way to develop and demonstrate Spring Boot's capabilities is using the Spring Boot CLI, a command-line tool. Perform the following steps:

1. Install the Spring Boot command-line tool by downloading the `spring-boot-cli-1.3.5.RELEASE-bin.zip` file from `http://repo.spring.io/release/org/springframework/boot/spring-boot-cli/1.3.5.RELEASE/spring-boot-cli-1.3.5.RELEASE-bin.zip`.

2. Unzip the file into a directory of your choice. Open a terminal window and change the terminal prompt to the `bin` folder.

   Ensure that the `bin` folder is added to the system path so that Spring Boot can be run from any location.

3. Verify the installation with the following command. If successful, the Spring CLI version will be printed in the console:

   ```
   $spring --version
   Spring CLI v1.3.5.RELEASE
   ```

4. As the next step, a quick REST service will be developed in Groovy, which is supported out of the box in Spring Boot. To do so, copy and paste the following code using any editor of choice and save it as `myfirstapp.groovy` in any folder:

```
@RestController
class HelloworldController {
    @RequestMapping("/")
    String sayHello() {
        "Hello World!"
    }
}
```

5. In order to run this Groovy application, go to the folder where `myfirstapp.groovy` is saved and execute the following command. The last few lines of the server start-up log will be similar to the following:

```
$spring run myfirstapp.groovy


2016-05-09 18:13:55.351  INFO 35861 --- [nio-8080-exec-1]
o.s.web.servlet.DispatcherServlet        : FrameworkServlet
'dispatcherServlet': initialization started
2016-05-09 18:13:55.375  INFO 35861 --- [nio-8080-exec-1]
o.s.web.servlet.DispatcherServlet        : FrameworkServlet
'dispatcherServlet': initialization completed in 24 ms
```

6. Open a browser window and go to `http://localhost:8080`; the browser will display the following message:

Hello World!

There is no war file created, and no Tomcat server was run. Spring Boot automatically picked up Tomcat as the webserver and embedded it into the application. This is a very basic, minimal microservice. The `@RestController` annotation, used in the previous code, will be examined in detail in the next example.

Developing the Spring Boot Java microservice using STS

In this section, developing another Java-based REST/JSON Spring Boot service using STS will be demonstrated.

The full source code of this example is available as the `chapter2.bootrest` project in the code files of this book.

1. Open STS, right-click within the **Project Explorer** window, navigate to **New | Project**, and select **Spring Starter Project**, as shown in the following screenshot, and click on **Next**:

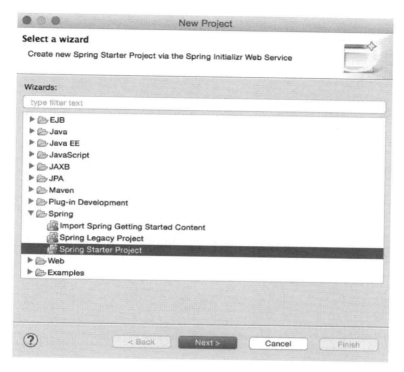

Spring Starter Project is a basic template wizard that provides a number of other starter libraries to select from.

2. Type the project name as `chapter2.bootrest` or any other name of your choice. It is important to choose the packaging as JAR. In traditional web applications, a war file is created and then deployed to a servlet container, whereas Spring Boot packages all the dependencies to a self-contained, autonomous JAR file with an embedded HTTP listener.

3. Select 1.8 under **Java Version**. Java 1.8 is recommended for Spring 4 applications. Change the other Maven properties such as **Group**, **Artifact**, and **Package**, as shown in the following screenshot:

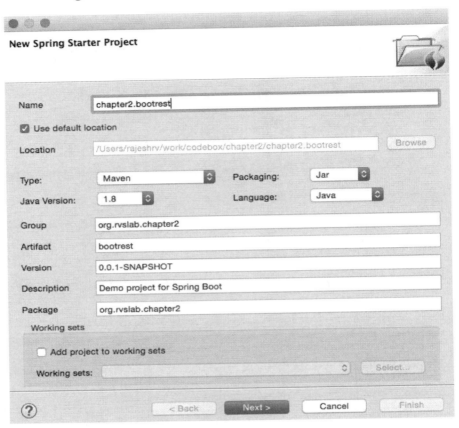

4. Once completed, click on **Next**.

5. The wizard will show the library options. In this case, as the REST service is developed, select **Web** under **Web**. This is an interesting step that tells Spring Boot that a Spring MVC web application is being developed so that Spring Boot can include the necessary libraries, including Tomcat as the HTTP listener and other configurations, as required:

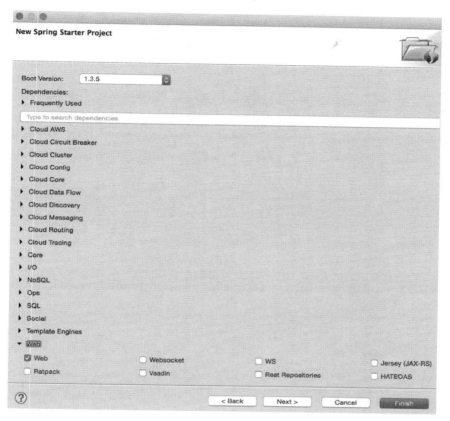

6. Click on **Finish**.

This will generate a project named `chapter2.bootrest` in **Project Explorer** in STS:

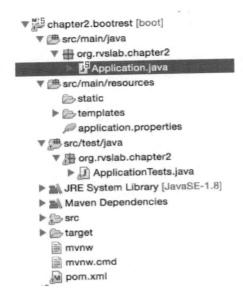

7. Take a moment to examine the generated application. Files that are of interest are:

   ° `pom.xml`

   ° `Application.java`

   ° `Application.properties`

   ° `ApplicationTests.java`

Examining the POM file

The parent element is one of the interesting aspects in the `pom.xml` file. Take a look at the following:

```
<parent>
  <groupId>org.springframework.boot</groupId>
    <artifactId>spring-boot-starter-parent</artifactId>
    <version>1.3.4.RELEASE</version>
</parent>
```

The `spring-boot-starter-parent` pattern is a **bill of materials (BOM)**, a pattern used by Maven's dependency management. BOM is a special kind of POM file used to manage different library versions required for a project. The advantage of using the `spring-boot-starter-parent` POM file is that developers need not worry about finding the right compatible versions of different libraries such as Spring, Jersey, JUnit, Logback, Hibernate, Jackson, and so on. For instance, in our first legacy example, a specific version of the Jackson library was added to work with Spring 4. In this example, these are taken care of by the `spring-boot-starter-parent` pattern.

The starter POM file has a list of Boot dependencies, sensible resource filtering, and sensible plug-in configurations required for the Maven builds.

> Refer to `https://github.com/spring-projects/spring-boot/blob/1.3.x/spring-boot-dependencies/pom.xml` to take a look at the different dependencies provided in the starter parent (version 1.3.x). All these dependencies can be overridden if required.

The starter POM file itself does not add JAR dependencies to the project. Instead, it will only add library versions. Subsequently, when dependencies are added to the POM file, they refer to the library versions from this POM file. A snapshot of some of the properties are as shown as follows:

```
<spring-boot.version>1.3.5.BUILD-SNAPSHOT</spring-boot.version>
<hibernate.version>4.3.11.Final</hibernate.version>
<jackson.version>2.6.6</jackson.version>
<jersey.version>2.22.2</jersey.version>
<logback.version>1.1.7</logback.version>
<spring.version>4.2.6.RELEASE</spring.version>
<spring-data-releasetrain.version>Gosling-SR4</spring-data-
releasetrain.version>
<tomcat.version>8.0.33</tomcat.version>
```

Reviewing the dependency section, one can see that this is a clean and neat POM file with only two dependencies, as follows:

```
<dependencies>
   <dependency>
   <groupId>org.springframework.boot</groupId>
   <artifactId>spring-boot-starter-web</artifactId>
   </dependency>
```

```
    <dependency>
    <groupId>org.springframework.boot</groupId>
    <artifactId>spring-boot-starter-test</artifactId>
    <scope>test</scope>
    </dependency>
</dependencies>
```

As web is selected, `spring-boot-starter-web` adds all dependencies required for a Spring MVC project. It also includes dependencies to Tomcat as an embedded HTTP listener. This provides an effective way to get all the dependencies required as a single bundle. Individual dependencies could be replaced with other libraries, for example replacing Tomcat with Jetty.

Similar to web, Spring Boot comes up with a number of `spring-boot-starter-*` libraries, such as `amqp`, `aop`, `batch`, `data-jpa`, `thymeleaf`, and so on.

The last thing to be reviewed in the `pom.xml` file is the Java 8 property. By default, the parent POM file adds Java 6. It is recommended to override the Java version to 8 for Spring:

```
<java.version>1.8</java.version>
```

Examining Application.java

Spring Boot, by default, generated a `org.rvslab.chapter2.Application.java` class under `src/main/java` to bootstrap, as follows:

```
@SpringBootApplication
public class Application {
    public static void main(String[] args) {
        SpringApplication.run(Application.class, args);
    }
}
```

There is only a `main` method in `Application`, which will be invoked at startup as per the Java convention. The `main` method bootstraps the Spring Boot application by calling the `run` method on `SpringApplication`. `Application.class` is passed as a parameter to tell Spring Boot that this is the primary component.

More importantly, the magic is done by the `@SpringBootApplication` annotation. The `@SpringBootApplication` annotation is a top-level annotation that encapsulates three other annotations, as shown in the following code snippet:

```
@Configuration
@EnableAutoConfiguration
@ComponentScan
public class Application {
```

The `@Configuration` annotation hints that the contained class declares one or more `@Bean` definitions. The `@Configuration` annotation is meta-annotated with `@Component`; therefore, it is a candidate for component scanning.

The `@EnableAutoConfiguration` annotation tells Spring Boot to automatically configure the Spring application based on the dependencies available in the class path.

Examining application.properties

A default `application.properties` file is placed under `src/main/resources`. It is an important file to configure any required properties for the Spring Boot application. At the moment, this file is kept empty and will be revisited with some test cases later in this chapter.

Examining ApplicationTests.java

The last file to be examined is `ApplicationTests.java` under `src/test/java`. This is a placeholder to write test cases against the Spring Boot application.

To implement the first RESTful service, add a REST endpoint, as follows:

1. One can edit `Application.java` under `src/main/java` and add a RESTful service implementation. The RESTful service is exactly the same as what was done in the previous project. Append the following code at the end of the `Application.java` file:

```
@RestController
class GreetingController{
  @RequestMapping("/")
  Greet greet(){
    return new Greet("Hello World!");
  }
```

```
}
class Greet {
  private String message;
public Greet() {}

  public Greet(String message) {
    this.message = message;
  }
//add getter and setter
}
```

2. To run, navigate to **Run As | Spring Boot App**. Tomcat will be started on the
   8080 port:

```
 /\\ / ___'_ __ _ _(_)_ __ __ _ \ \ \ \
( ( )\___ | '_ | '_| | '_ \/ _` | \ \ \ \
 \\/  ___)| |_)| | | | | || (_| |  ) ) ) )
  '  |____| .__|_| |_|_| |_\__, | / / / /
 =========|_|==============|___/=/_/_/_/
 :: Spring Boot ::        (v1.3.5.RELEASE)

2016-05-11 16:49:10.236  INFO 41130 --- [           main]
org.rvslab.chapter2.Application          : Starting Application on rvslab.local with
PID 41130 (/Users/rajeshrv/work/codebox/chapter2/chapter2.bootrest/target/classes
```

We can notice from the log that:

- ° Spring Boot get its own process ID (in this case, it is 41130)
- ° Spring Boot is automatically started with the Tomcat server at the
     localhost, port 8080.

3. Next, open a browser and point to http://localhost:8080. This will show
   the JSON response as shown in the following screenshot:

```
{"message":"Hello World!"}
```

A key difference between the legacy service and this one is that the Spring Boot
service is self-contained. To make this clearer, run the Spring Boot application
outside STS. Open a terminal window, go to the project folder, and run Maven,
as follows:

```
$ maven install
```

This will generate a fat JAR file under the target folder of the project. Running the application from the command line shows:

```
$java -jar target/bootrest-0.0.1-SNAPSHOT.jar
```

As one can see, `bootrest-0.0.1-SNAPSHOT.jar` is self-contained and could be run as a standalone application. At this point, the JAR is as thin as 13 MB. Even though the application is no more than just "Hello World", the Spring Boot service just developed, practically follows the principles of microservices.

Testing the Spring Boot microservice

There are multiple ways to test REST/JSON Spring Boot microservices. The easiest way is to use a web browser or a curl command pointing to the URL, as follows:

```
curl http://localhost:8080
```

There are number of tools available to test RESTful services, such as Postman, Advanced REST client, SOAP UI, Paw, and so on.

In this example, to test the service, the default test class generated by Spring Boot will be used.

Adding a new test case to `ApplicatonTests.java` results in:

```
@RunWith(SpringJUnit4ClassRunner.class)
@SpringApplicationConfiguration(classes = Application.class)
@WebIntegrationTest
public class ApplicationTests {
  @Test
  public void testVanillaService() {
    RestTemplate restTemplate = new RestTemplate();
    Greet greet = restTemplate.getForObject
      ("http://localhost:8080", Greet.class);
    Assert.assertEquals("Hello World!", greet.getMessage());
  }
}
```

Note that `@WebIntegrationTest` is added and `@WebAppConfiguration` removed at the class level. The `@WebIntegrationTest` annotation is a handy annotation that ensures that the tests are fired against a fully up-and-running server. Alternately, a combination of `@WebAppConfiguration` and `@IntegrationTest` will give the same result.

Also note that `RestTemplate` is used to call the RESTful service. `RestTemplate` is a utility class that abstracts the lower-level details of the HTTP client.

To test this, one can open a terminal window, go to the project folder, and run `mvn install`.

Developing the Spring Boot microservice using Spring Initializr – the HATEOAS example

In the next example, Spring Initializr will be used to create a Spring Boot project. Spring Initializr is a drop-in replacement for the STS project wizard and provides a web UI to configure and generate a Spring Boot project. One of the advantages of Spring Initializr is that it can generate a project through the website that then can be imported into any IDE.

In this example, the concept of **HATEOAS** (short for **Hypertext As The Engine Of Application State**) for REST-based services and the **HAL (Hypertext Application Language)** browser will be examined.

HATEOAS is a REST service pattern in which navigation links are provided as part of the payload metadata. The client application determines the state and follows the transition URLs provided as part of the state. This methodology is particularly useful in responsive mobile and web applications in which the client downloads additional data based on user navigation patterns.

The HAL browser is a handy API browser for `hal+json` data. HAL is a format based on JSON that establishes conventions to represent hyperlinks between resources. HAL helps APIs be more explorable and discoverable.

The full source code of this example is available as the `chapter2.boothateoas` project in the code files of this book.

Here are the concrete steps to develop a HATEOAS sample using Spring Initilizr:

1. In order to use Spring Initilizr, go to `https://start.spring.io`:

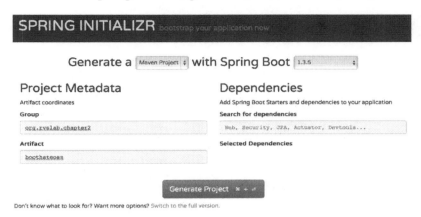

2. Fill the details, such as whether it is a Maven project, Spring Boot version, group, and artifact ID, as shown earlier, and click on **Switch to the full version** link under the **Generate Project** button. Select **Web**, **HATEOAS**, and **Rest Repositories HAL Browser**. Make sure that the Java version is 8 and the package type is selected as **JAR**:

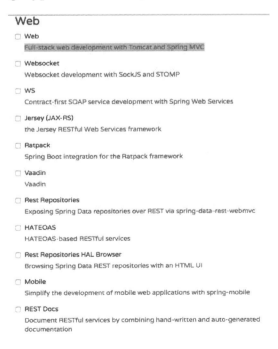

3. Once selected, hit the **Generate Project** button. This will generate a Maven project and download the project as a ZIP file into the download directory of the browser.

4. Unzip the file and save it to a directory of your choice.

5. Open STS, go to the **File** menu and click on **Import**:

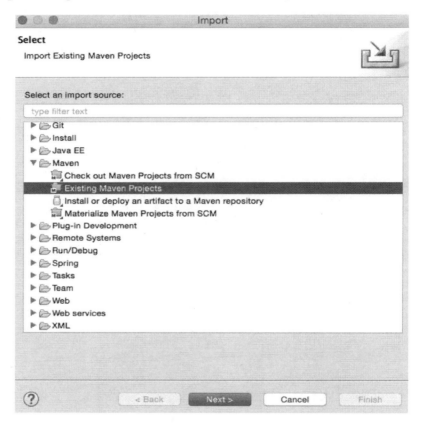

6. Navigate to **Maven | Existing Maven Projects** and click on **Next**.

7. Click on **Browse** next to **Root Directory** and select the unzipped folder. Click on **Finish**. This will load the generated Maven project into STS' **Project Explorer**.

8. Edit the `Application.java` file to add a new REST endpoint, as follows:

```
@RequestMapping("/greeting")
@ResponseBody
public HttpEntity<Greet> greeting(@RequestParam(value = "name",
required = false, defaultValue = "HATEOAS") String name) {
        Greet greet = new Greet("Hello " + name);
        greet.add(linkTo(methodOn(GreetingController.
          class).greeting(name)).withSelfRel());

        return new ResponseEntity<Greet>(greet,
          HttpStatus.OK);
}
```

9. Note that this is the same `GreetingController` class as in the previous example. However, a method was added this time named `greeting`. In this new method, an additional optional request parameter is defined and defaulted to HATEOAS. The following code adds a link to the resulting JSON code. In this case, it adds the link to the same API:

```
greet.add(linkTo(methodOn(GreetingController.class).
greeting(name)).withSelfRel());
```

In order to do this, we need to extend the `Greet` class from `ResourceSupport`, as shown here. The rest of the code remains the same:

```
class Greet extends ResourceSupport{
```

10. The `add` method is a method in `ResourceSupport`. The `linkTo` and `methodOn` methods are static methods of `ControllerLinkBuilder`, a utility class for creating links on controller classes. The `methodOn` method will do a dummy method invocation, and `linkTo` will create a link to the controller class. In this case, we will use `withSelfRel` to point it to itself.

11. This will essentially produce a link, `/greeting?name=HATEOAS`, by default. A client can read the link and initiate another call.

12. Run this as a Spring Boot app. Once the server startup is complete, point the browser to `http://localhost:8080`.

13. This will open the HAL browser window. In the **Explorer** field, type /greeting?name=World! and click on the **Go** button. If everything is fine, the HAL browser will show the response details as shown in the following screenshot:

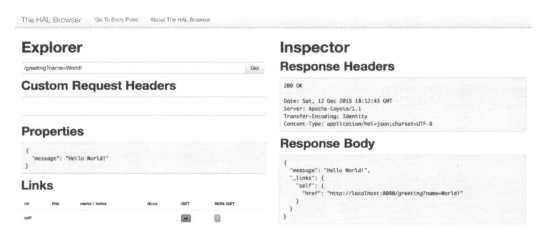

As shown in the screenshot, the **Response Body** section has the result with a link with href pointing back to the same service. This is because we pointed the reference to itself. Also, review the **Links** section. The little green box against **self** is the navigable link.

It does not make much sense in this simple example, but this could be handy in larger applications with many related entities. Using the links provided, the client can easily navigate back and forth between these entities with ease.

What's next?

A number of basic Spring Boot examples have been reviewed so far. The rest of this chapter will examine some of the Spring Boot features that are important from a microservices development perspective. In the upcoming sections, we will take a look at how to work with dynamically configurable properties, change the default embedded web server, add security to the microservices, and implement cross-origin behavior when dealing with microservices.

 The full source code of this example is available as the chapter2.boot-advanced project in the code files of this book.

The Spring Boot configuration

In this section, the focus will be on the configuration aspects of Spring Boot. The `chapter2.bootrest` project, already developed, will be modified in this section to showcase configuration capabilities. Copy and paste `chapter2.bootrest` and rename the project as `chapter2.boot-advanced`.

Understanding the Spring Boot autoconfiguration

Spring Boot uses convention over configuration by scanning the dependent libraries available in the class path. For each `spring-boot-starter-*` dependency in the POM file, Spring Boot executes a default `AutoConfiguration` class. `AutoConfiguration` classes use the `*AutoConfiguration` lexical pattern, where `*` represents the library. For example, the autoconfiguration of JPA repositories is done through `JpaRepositoriesAutoConfiguration`.

Run the application with `--debug` to see the autoconfiguration report. The following command shows the autoconfiguration report for the `chapter2.boot-advanced` project:

```
$java -jar target/bootadvanced-0.0.1-SNAPSHOT.jar --debug
```

Here are some examples of the autoconfiguration classes:

- `ServerPropertiesAutoConfiguration`
- `RepositoryRestMvcAutoConfiguration`
- `JpaRepositoriesAutoConfiguration`
- `JmsAutoConfiguration`

It is possible to exclude the autoconfiguration of certain libraries if the application has special requirements and you want to get full control of the configurations. The following is an example of excluding `DataSourceAutoConfiguration`:

```
@EnableAutoConfiguration(exclude={DataSourceAutoConfiguration.class})
```

Overriding default configuration values

It is also possible to override default configuration values using the `application.properties` file. STS provides an easy-to-autocomplete, contextual help on `application.properties`, as shown in the following screenshot:

```
server.port 9090

spring.j
        spring.jackson.date-format : String
        spring.jackson.deserialization : Map<com.fasterxml.jackson.databind.DeserializationFeatu
        spring.jackson.generator : Map<com.fasterxml.jackson.core.JsonGenerator.Feature[AUTO_
        spring.jackson.joda-date-time-format : String
        spring.jackson.locale : Locale
        spring.jackson.mapper : Map<com.fasterxml.jackson.databind.MapperFeature[USE_ANNO
        spring.jackson.parser : Map<com.fasterxml.jackson.core.JsonParser.Feature[AUTO_CLOS
        spring.jackson.property-naming-strategy : String
        spring.jackson.serialization : Map<com.fasterxml.jackson.databind.SerializationFeature[WF
        spring.jackson.serialization-inclusion : com.fasterxml.jackson.annotation.JsonInclude$Incl
        spring.jackson.time-zone : TimeZone
        spring.jersey.application-path : String
        spring.jersey.filter.order : int
        spring.jersey.init : Map<String, String>
        spring.jersey.type : org.springframework.boot.autoconfigure.jersey.JerseyProperties$Type[
        spring.jms.jndi-name : String
```

In the preceding screenshot, `server.port` is edited to be set as `9090`. Running this application again will start the server on port `9090`.

Changing the location of the configuration file

In order to align with the Twelve-Factor app, configuration parameters need to be externalized from the code. Spring Boot externalizes all configurations into `application.properties`. However, it is still part of the application's build. Furthermore, properties can be read from outside the package by setting the following properties:

```
spring.config.name= # config file name
spring.config.location= # location of config file
```

Here, `spring.config.location` could be a local file location.

The following command starts the Spring Boot application with an externally provided configuration file:

```
$java -jar target/bootadvanced-0.0.1-SNAPSHOT.jar --spring.config.
name=bootrest.properties
```

Reading custom properties

At startup, `SpringApplication` loads all the properties and adds them to the Spring `Environment` class. Add a custom property to the `application.properties` file. In this case, the custom property is named `bootrest.customproperty`. Autowire the Spring `Environment` class into the `GreetingController` class. Edit the `GreetingController` class to read the custom property from `Environment` and add a log statement to print the custom property to the console.

Perform the following steps to do this:

1. Add the following property to the `application.properties` file:

   ```
   bootrest.customproperty=hello
   ```

2. Then, edit the `GreetingController` class as follows:

   ```
   @Autowired
   Environment env;

   Greet greet(){
       logger.info("bootrest.customproperty "+
         env.getProperty("bootrest.customproperty"));
       return new Greet("Hello World!");
   }
   ```

3. Rerun the application. The log statement prints the custom variable in the console, as follows:

   ```
   org.rvslab.chapter2.GreetingController   : bootrest.customproperty
   hello
   ```

Using a .yaml file for configuration

As an alternate to `application.properties`, one may use a `.yaml` file. YAML provides a JSON-like structured configuration compared to the flat properties file.

To see this in action, simply replace `application.properties` with `application.yaml` and add the following property:

```
server
  port: 9080
```

Rerun the application to see the port printed in the console.

Using multiple configuration profiles

Furthermore, it is possible to have different profiles such as development, testing, staging, production, and so on. These are logical names. Using these, one can configure different values for the same properties for different environments. This is quite handy when running the Spring Boot application against different environments. In such cases, there is no rebuild required when moving from one environment to another.

Update the `.yaml` file as follows. The Spring Boot group profiles properties based on the dotted separator:

```
spring:
    profiles: development
server:
    port: 9090
---

spring:
    profiles: production
server:
    port: 8080
```

Run the Spring Boot application as follows to see the use of profiles:

mvn -Dspring.profiles.active=production install

mvn -Dspring.profiles.active=development install

Active profiles can be specified programmatically using the `@ActiveProfiles` annotation, which is especially useful when running test cases, as follows:

```
@ActiveProfiles("test")
```

Other options to read properties

The properties can be loaded in a number of ways, such as the following:

- Command-line parameters (`-Dhost.port =9090`)
- Operating system environment variables
- JNDI (`java:comp/env`)

Changing the default embedded web server

Embedded HTTP listeners can easily be customized as follows. By default, Spring Boot supports Tomcat, Jetty, and Undertow. In the following example, Tomcat is replaced with Undertow:

```xml
<dependency>
    <groupId>org.springframework.boot</groupId>
    <artifactId>spring-boot-starter-web</artifactId>
    <exclusions>
        <exclusion>
            <groupId>org.springframework.boot</groupId>
            <artifactId>spring-boot-starter-tomcat</artifactId>
        </exclusion>
    </exclusions>
</dependency>
<dependency>
    <groupId>org.springframework.boot</groupId>
    <artifactId>spring-boot-starter-undertow</artifactId>
</dependency>
```

Implementing Spring Boot security

It is important to secure microservices. In this section, some basic measures to secure Spring Boot microservices will be reviewed using `chapter2.bootrest` to demonstrate the security features.

Securing microservices with basic security

Adding basic authentication to Spring Boot is pretty simple. Add the following dependency to `pom.xml`. This will include the necessary Spring security library files:

```xml
<dependency>
  <groupId>org.springframework.boot</groupId>
  <artifactId>spring-boot-starter-security</artifactId>
</dependency>
```

Open `Application.java` and add `@EnableGlobalMethodSecurity` to the `Application` class. This annotation will enable method-level security:

```
@EnableGlobalMethodSecurity
@SpringBootApplication
public class Application {
    public static void main(String[] args) {
        SpringApplication.run(Application.class, args);
    }
}
```

The default basic authentication assumes the user as being `user`. The default password will be printed in the console at startup. Alternately, the username and password can be added in `application.properties`, as shown here:

```
security.user.name=guest
security.user.password=guest123
```

Add a new test case in `ApplicationTests` to test the secure service results, as in the following:

```
@Test
public void testSecureService() {
    String plainCreds = "guest:guest123";
    HttpHeaders headers = new HttpHeaders();
    headers.add("Authorization", "Basic " + new String(Base64.
encode(plainCreds.getBytes()))) ;
    HttpEntity<String> request = new HttpEntity<String>(headers);
    RestTemplate restTemplate = new RestTemplate();

    ResponseEntity<Greet> response = restTemplate.exchange("http://
localhost:8080", HttpMethod.GET, request, Greet.class);
    Assert.assertEquals("Hello World!", response.getBody().
getMessage());
  }
```

As shown in the code, a new `Authorization` request header with Base64 encoding the username-password string is created.

Rerun the application using Maven. Note that the new test case passed, but the old test case failed with an exception. The earlier test case now runs without credentials, and as a result, the server rejected the request with the following message:

org.springframework.web.client.HttpClientErrorException: 401 Unauthorized

Securing a microservice with OAuth2

In this section, we will take a look at the basic Spring Boot configuration for OAuth2. When a client application requires access to a protected resource, the client sends a request to an authorization server. The authorization server validates the request and provides an access token. This access token is validated for every client-to-server request. The request and response sent back and forth depends on the grant type.

 Read more about OAuth and grant types at http://oauth.net.

The resource owner password credentials grant approach will be used in this example:

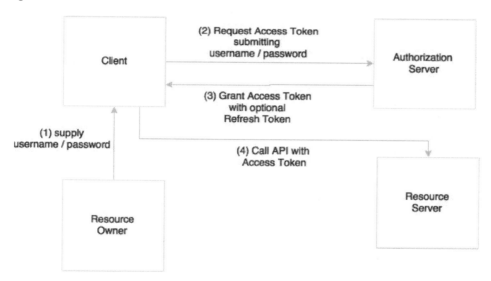

In this case, as shown in the preceding diagram, the resource owner provides the client with a username and password. The client then sends a token request to the authorization server by providing the credential information. The authorization server authorizes the client and returns with an access token. On every subsequent request, the server validates the client token.

To implement OAuth2 in our example, perform the following steps:

1. As a first step, update pom.xml with the OAuth2 dependency, as follows:

```
<dependency>
  <groupId>org.springframework.security.oauth</groupId>
  <artifactId>spring-security-oauth2</artifactId>
  <version>2.0.9.RELEASE</version>
</dependency>
```

2. Next, add two new annotations, @EnableAuthorizationServer and @EnableResourceServer, to the Application.java file. The @EnableAuthorizationServer annotation creates an authorization server with an in-memory repository to store client tokens and provide clients with a username, password, client ID, and secret. The @EnableResourceServer annotation is used to access the tokens. This enables a spring security filter that is authenticated via an incoming OAuth2 token.

   In our example, both the authorization server and resource server are the same. However, in practice, these two will run separately. Take a look at the following code:

```
@EnableResourceServer
@EnableAuthorizationServer
@SpringBootApplication
public class Application {
```

3. Add the following properties to the application.properties file:

```
security.user.name=guest
security.user.password=guest123
security.oauth2.client.clientId: trustedclient
security.oauth2.client.clientSecret: trustedclient123
security.oauth2.client.authorized-grant-types: authorization_
code,refresh_token,password
security.oauth2.client.scope: openid
```

4. Then, add another test case to test OAuth2, as follows:

```
@Test
public void testOAuthService() {
        ResourceOwnerPasswordResourceDetails resource = new
ResourceOwnerPasswordResourceDetails();
        resource.setUsername("guest");
        resource.setPassword("guest123");
            resource.setAccessTokenUri("http://localhost:8080/oauth/
token");
        resource.setClientId("trustedclient");
        resource.setClientSecret("trustedclient123");
        resource.setGrantType("password");

        DefaultOAuth2ClientContext clientContext = new
DefaultOAuth2ClientContext();
        OAuth2RestTemplate restTemplate = new
OAuth2RestTemplate(resource, clientContext);

        Greet greet = restTemplate.getForObject("http://
localhost:8080", Greet.class);

        Assert.assertEquals("Hello World!", greet.getMessage());
    }
```

As shown in the preceding code, a special REST template,
OAuth2RestTemplate, is created by passing the resource details
encapsulated in a resource details object. This REST template handles the
OAuth2 processes underneath. The access token URI is the endpoint for
the token access.

5. Rerun the application using mvn install. The first two test cases will
   fail, and the new one will succeed. This is because the server only accepts
   OAuth2-enabled requests.

These are quick configurations provided by Spring Boot out of the box but
are not good enough to be production grade. We may need to customize
ResourceServerConfigurer and AuthorizationServerConfigurer to make
them production-ready. This notwithstanding, the approach remains the same.

Enabling cross-origin access for microservices

Browsers are generally restricted when client-side web applications running from one origin request data from another origin. Enabling cross-origin access is generally termed as **CORS (Cross-Origin Resource Sharing)**.

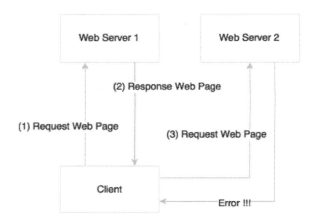

This example shows how to enable cross-origin requests. With microservices, as each service runs with its own origin, it will easily get into the issue of a client-side web application consuming data from multiple origins. For instance, a scenario where a browser client accessing Customer from the Customer microservice and Order History from the Order microservices is very common in the microservices world.

Spring Boot provides a simple declarative approach to enabling cross-origin requests. The following example shows how to enable a microservice to enable cross-origin requests:

```
@RestController
class GreetingController{
  @CrossOrigin
  @RequestMapping("/")
  Greet greet(){
    return new Greet("Hello World!");
  }
}
```

By default, all the origins and headers are accepted. We can further customize the cross-origin annotations by giving access to specific origins, as follows. The `@CrossOrigin` annotation enables a method or class to accept cross-origin requests:

```
@CrossOrigin("http://mytrustedorigin.com")
```

Global CORS can be enabled using the `WebMvcConfigurer` bean and customizing the `addCorsMappings(CorsRegistry registry)` method.

Implementing Spring Boot messaging

In an ideal case, all microservice interactions are expected to happen asynchronously using publish-subscribe semantics. Spring Boot provides a hassle-free mechanism to configure messaging solutions:

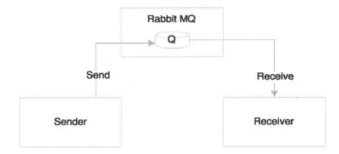

In this example, we will create a Spring Boot application with a sender and receiver, both connected though an external queue. Perform the following steps:

 The full source code of this example is available as the `chapter2.bootmessaging` project in the code files of this book.

1. Create a new project using STS to demonstrate this capability. In this example, instead of selecting **Web**, select **AMQP** under **I/O**:

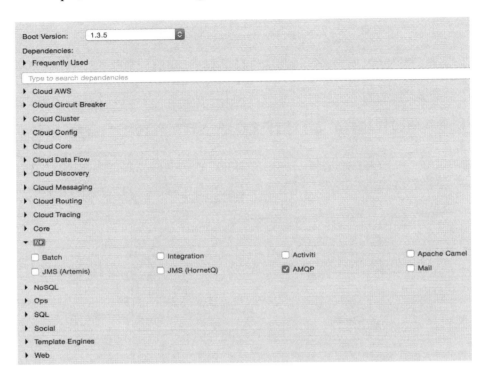

2. Rabbit MQ will also be needed for this example. Download and install the latest version of Rabbit MQ from `https://www.rabbitmq.com/download.html`.

   Rabbit MQ 3.5.6 is used in this book.

3. Follow the installation steps documented on the site. Once ready, start the RabbitMQ server via the following command:

   ```
   $./rabbitmq-server
   ```

4. Make the configuration changes to the `application.properties` file to reflect the RabbitMQ configuration. The following configuration uses the default port, username, and password of RabbitMQ:

   ```
   spring.rabbitmq.host=localhost
   spring.rabbitmq.port=5672
   spring.rabbitmq.username=guest
   spring.rabbitmq.password=guest
   ```

5. Add a message sender component and a queue named `TestQ` of the `org.springframework.amqp.core.Queue` type to the `Application.java` file under `src/main/java`. `RabbitMessagingTemplate` is a convenient way to send messages, which will abstract all the messaging semantics. Spring Boot provides all boilerplate configurations to send messages:

```
@Component
class Sender {
  @Autowired
  RabbitMessagingTemplate template;
  @Bean
  Queue queue() {
    return new Queue("TestQ", false);
  }
  public void send(String message){
    template.convertAndSend("TestQ", message);
  }
}
```

6. To receive the message, all that needs to be used is a `@RabbitListener` annotation. Spring Boot autoconfigures all the required boilerplate configurations:

```
@Component
class Receiver {
    @RabbitListener(queues = "TestQ")
    public void processMessage(String content) {
        System.out.println(content);
    }
}
```

7. The last piece of this exercise is to wire the sender to our main application and implement the `run` method of `CommandLineRunner` to initiate the message sending. When the application is initialized, it invokes the `run` method of `CommandLineRunner`, as follows:

```
@SpringBootApplication
public class Application implements CommandLineRunner{

    @Autowired
    Sender sender;

    public static void main(String[] args) {
```

```
        SpringApplication.run(Application.class, args);
    }

    @Override
    public void run(String... args) throws Exception {
        sender.send("Hello Messaging..!!!");
    }
}
```

8. Run the application as a Spring Boot application and verify the output. The following message will be printed in the console:

```
Hello Messaging..!!!
```

Developing a comprehensive microservice example

So far, the examples we have considered are no more than just a simple "Hello world." Putting together what we have learned, this section demonstrates an end-to-end Customer Profile microservice implementation. The Customer Profile microservices will demonstrate interaction between different microservices. It also demonstrates microservices with business logic and primitive data stores.

In this example, two microservices, the Customer Profile and Customer Notification services, will be developed:

As shown in the diagram, the Customer Profile microservice exposes methods to **create, read, update, and delete (CRUD)** a customer and a registration service to register a customer. The registration process applies certain business logic, saves the customer profile, and sends a message to the Customer Notification microservice. The Customer Notification microservice accepts the message sent by the registration service and sends an e-mail message to the customer using an SMTP server. Asynchronous messaging is used to integrate Customer Profile with the Customer Notification service.

The Customer microservices class domain model diagram is as shown here:

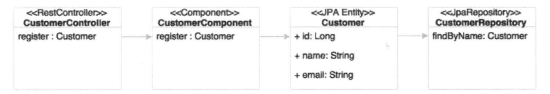

`CustomerController` in the diagram is the REST endpoint, which invokes a component class, `CustomerComponent`. The component class/bean handles all the business logic. `CustomerRepository` is a Spring data JPA repository defined to handle the persistence of the `Customer` entity.

 The full source code of this example is available as the `chapter2.bootcustomer` and `chapter2. bootcustomernotification` projects in the code files of this book.

1. Create a new Spring Boot project and call it `chapter2.bootcustomer`, the same way as earlier. Select the options as in the following screenshot in the starter module selection screen:

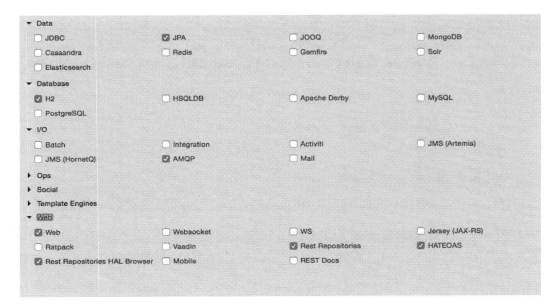

This will create a web project with JPA, the REST repository, and H2 as a database. H2 is a tiny in-memory embedded database with which it is easy to demonstrate database features. In the real world, it is recommended to use an appropriate enterprise-grade database. This example uses JPA to define persistence entities and the REST repository to expose REST-based repository services.

The project structure will be similar to the following screenshot:

2. Start building the application by adding an Entity class named `Customer`. For simplicity, there are only three fields added to the `Customer` Entity class: the autogenerated `id` field, `name`, and `email`. Take a look at the following code:

```
@Entity
class Customer {
  @Id
  @GeneratedValue(strategy = GenerationType.AUTO)
  private Long id;
  private String name;
  private String email;
```

3. Add a repository class to handle the persistence handling of Customer. `CustomerRepository` extends the standard JPA repository. This means that all CRUD methods and default finder methods are automatically implemented by the Spring Data JPA repository, as follows:

```
@RepositoryRestResource
interface CustomerRespository extends JpaRepository
<Customer,Long>{
  Optional<Customer> findByName(@Param("name") String name);
}
```

In this example, we added a new method to the repository class, findByName, which essentially searches the customer based on the customer name and returns a Customer object if there is a matching name.

4. The @RepositoryRestResource annotation enables the repository access through RESTful services. This will also enable HATEOAS and HAL by default. As for CRUD methods there is no additional business logic required, we will leave it as it is without controller or component classes. Using HATEOAS will help us navigate through Customer Repository methods effortlessly.

   Note that there is no configuration added anywhere to point to any database. As H2 libraries are in the class path, all the configuration is done by default by Spring Boot based on the H2 autoconfiguration.

5. Update the Application.java file by adding CommandLineRunner to initialize the repository with some customer records, as follows:

```
@SpringBootApplication
public class Application {
    public static void main(String[] args) {
        SpringApplication.run(Application.class, args);
    }

    @Bean
  CommandLineRunner init(CustomerRespository repo) {
  return (evt) -> {
    repo.save(new Customer("Adam","adam@boot.com"));
    repo.save(new Customer("John","john@boot.com"));
  repo.save(new Customer("Smith","smith@boot.com"));
    repo.save(new Customer("Edgar","edgar@boot.com"));
    repo.save(new Customer("Martin","martin@boot.com"));
    repo.save(new Customer("Tom","tom@boot.com"));
    repo.save(new Customer("Sean","sean@boot.com"));
  };
  }
}
```

6. CommandLineRunner, defined as a bean, indicates that it should run when it is contained in SpringApplication. This will insert six sample customer records into the database at startup.

7. At this point, run the application as Spring Boot App. Open the HAL browser and point the browser to http://localhost:8080.

8. In the **Explorer** section, point to `http://localhost:8080/customers` and click on **Go**. This will list all the customers in the **Response Body** section of the HAL browser.

9. In the **Explorer** section, enter `http://localhost:8080/customers?size=2 &page=1&sort=name` and click on **Go**. This will automatically execute paging and sorting on the repository and return the result.

   As the page size is set to 2 and the first page is requested, it will come back with two records in a sorted order.

10. Review the **Links** section. As shown in the following screenshot, it will facilitate navigating **first**, **next**, **prev**, and **last**. These are done using the HATEOAS links automatically generated by the repository browser:

Links

rel	title	name / index	docs	GET	NON-GET
first				→	!
prev				→	!
self				→	!
next				→	!
last				→	!
profile				→	!
search				→	!

11. Also, one can explore the details of a customer by selecting the appropriate link, such as `http://localhost:8080/customers/2`.

12. As the next step, add a controller class, `CustomerController`, to handle service endpoints. There is only one endpoint in this class, `/register`, which is used to register a customer. If successful, it returns the `Customer` object as the response, as follows:

```
@RestController
class CustomerController{

    @Autowired
    CustomerRegistrar customerRegistrar;

    @RequestMapping( path="/register", method = RequestMethod.POST)
    Customer register(@RequestBody Customer customer){
        return customerRegistrar.register(customer);
    }
}
```

13. A `CustomerRegistrar` component is added to handle the business logic. In this case, there is only minimal business logic added to the component. In this component class, while registering a customer, we will just check whether the customer name already exists in the database or not. If it does not exist, then we will insert a new record, and otherwise, we will send an error message back, as follows:

```
@Component
class CustomerRegistrar {

    CustomerRespository customerRespository;

    @Autowired
    CustomerRegistrar(CustomerRespository customerRespository){
        this.customerRespository = customerRespository;
    }

    Customer register(Customer customer){
        Optional<Customer> existingCustomer = customerRespository.
findByName(customer.getName());
        if (existingCustomer.isPresent()){
            throw new RuntimeException("is already exists");
        } else {
            customerRespository.save(customer);
        }
        return customer;
    }
}
```

14. Restart the Boot application and test using the HAL browser via the URL `http://localhost:8080`.

15. Point the **Explorer** field to `http://localhost:8080/customers`. Review the results in the **Links** section:

Links

16. Click on the **NON-GET** option against **self**. This will open a form to create a new customer:

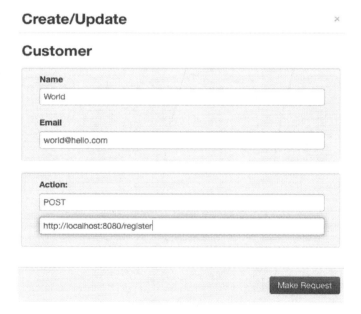

17. Fill the form and change the **Action** as shown in the diagram. Click on the **Make Request** button. This will call the register service and register the customer. Try giving a duplicate name to test the negative case.

18. Let's complete the last part in the example by integrating the Customer Notification service to notify the customer. When registration is successful, send an e-mail to the customer by asynchronously calling the Customer Notification microservice.

19. First update `CustomerRegistrar` to call the second service. This is done through messaging. In this case, we injected a `Sender` component to send a notification to the customer by passing the customer's e-mail address to the sender, as follows:

```
@Component
@Lazy
class CustomerRegistrar {

    CustomerRespository customerRespository;
    Sender sender;

    @Autowired
    CustomerRegistrar(CustomerRespository customerRespository,
Sender sender){
        this.customerRespository = customerRespository;
        this.sender = sender;
    }

    Customer register(Customer customer){
        Optional<Customer> existingCustomer = customerRespository.
findByName(customer.getName());
        if (existingCustomer.isPresent()){
            throw new RuntimeException("is already exists");
        } else {
            customerRespository.save(customer);
            sender.send(customer.getEmail());
        }
        return customer;
    }
}
```

20. The sender component will be based on RabbitMQ and AMQP. In this example, `RabbitMessagingTemplate` is used as explored in the last messaging example; take a look at the following:

```
@Component
@Lazy
class Sender {

    @Autowired
```

```
RabbitMessagingTemplate template;

@Bean
Queue queue() {
  return new Queue("CustomerQ", false);
}

public void send(String message){
  template.convertAndSend("CustomerQ", message);
}
}
```

The @Lazy annotation is a useful one and it helps to increase the boot startup time. These beans will be initialized only when the need arises.

21. We will also update the `application.property` file to include Rabbit MQ-related properties, as follows:

```
spring.rabbitmq.host=localhost
spring.rabbitmq.port=5672
spring.rabbitmq.username=guest
spring.rabbitmq.password=guest
```

22. We are ready to send the message. To consume the message and send e-mails, we will create a notification service. For this, let's create another Spring Boot service, `chapter2.bootcustomernotification`. Make sure that the **AMQP** and **Mail** starter libraries are selected when creating the Spring Boot service. Both **AMQP** and **Mail** are under **I/O**.

23. The package structure of the `chapter2.bootcustomernotification` project is as shown here:

24. Add a `Receiver` class. The `Receiver` class waits for a message on customer. This will receive a message sent by the Customer Profile service. On the arrival of a message, it sends an e-mail, as follows:

```
@Component
class Receiver {
  @Autowired
  Mailer mailer;

  @Bean
  Queue queue() {
    return new Queue("CustomerQ", false);
  }

  @RabbitListener(queues = "CustomerQ")
    public void processMessage(String email) {
       System.out.println(email);
       mailer.sendMail(email);
    }
}
```

25. Add another component to send an e-mail to the customer. We will use `JavaMailSender` to send an e-mail via the following code:

```
@Component
class Mailer {
  @Autowired
  private JavaMailSender javaMailService;
    public void sendMail(String email){
       SimpleMailMessage mailMessage=new
         SimpleMailMessage();
       mailMessage.setTo(email);
       mailMessage.setSubject("Registration");
       mailMessage.setText("Successfully Registered");
       javaMailService.send(mailMessage);
    }
}
```

Behind the scenes, Spring Boot automatically configures all the parameters required by `JavaMailSender`.

26. To test SMTP, a test setup for SMTP is required to ensure that the mails are going out. In this example, FakeSMTP will be used. You can download FakeSMTP from `http://nilhcem.github.io/FakeSMTP`.

Once you download `fakeSMTP-2.0.jar`, run the SMTP server by executing the following command:

```
$ java -jar fakeSMTP-2.0.jar
```

This will open a GUI to monitor e-mail messages. Click on the **Start Server** button next to the listening port textbox.

28. Update `application.properties` with the following configuration parameters to connect to RabbitMQ as well as to the mail server:

```
spring.rabbitmq.host=localhost
spring.rabbitmq.port=5672
spring.rabbitmq.username=guest
spring.rabbitmq.password=guest

spring.mail.host=localhost
spring.mail.port=2525
```

29. We are ready to test our microservices end to end. Start both the Spring Boot apps. Open the browser and repeat the customer creation steps through the HAL browser. In this case, immediately after submitting the request, we will be able to see the e-mail in the SMTP GUI.

Internally, the Customer Profile service asynchronously calls the Customer Notification service, which, in turn, sends the e-mail message to the SMTP server:

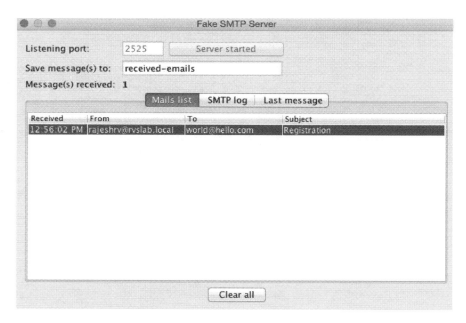

Spring Boot actuators

The previous sections explored most of the Spring Boot features required to develop a microservice. In this section, some of the production-ready operational aspects of Spring Boot will be explored.

Spring Boot actuators provide an excellent out-of-the-box mechanism to monitor and manage Spring Boot applications in production:

 The full source code of this example is available as the `chapter2.bootactuator` project in the code files of this book.

1. Create another **Spring Starter Project** and name it `chapter2.bootactuator`. This time, select **Web** and **Actuators** under **Ops**. Similar to the `chapter2.bootrest` project, add a `GreeterController` endpoint with the `greet` method.

2. Start the application as Spring Boot app.

3. Point the browser to `localhost:8080/actuator`. This will open the HAL browser. Then, review the **Links** section.

   A number of links are available under the **Links** section. These are automatically exposed by the Spring Boot actuator:

Links

rel	title	name / index	docs	GET	NON-GET
self				→	□
dump				→	□
configprops				→	□
env				→	□
mappings				→	□
info				→	□
health				→	□
autoconfig				→	□
metrics				→	□
trace				→	□
beans				→	□

Some of the important links are listed as follows:

- `dump`: This performs a thread dump and displays the result
- `mappings`: This lists all the HTTP request mappings
- `info`: This displays information about the application
- `health`: This displays the application's health conditions
- `autoconfig`: This displays the autoconfiguration report
- `metrics`: This shows different metrics collected from the application

Monitoring using JConsole

Alternately, we can use the JMX console to see the Spring Boot information. Connect to the remote Spring Boot instance from JConsole. The Boot information will be shown as follows:

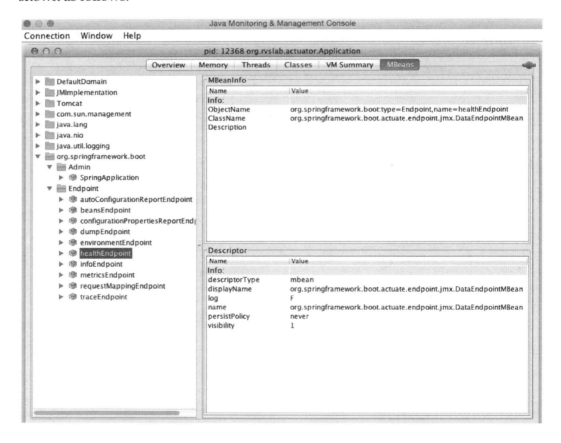

Monitoring using SSH

Spring Boot provides remote access to the Boot application using SSH. The following command connects to the Spring Boot application from a terminal window:

```
$ ssh -p 2000 user@localhost
```

The password can be customized by adding the `shell.auth.simple.user.password` property in the `application.properties` file. The updated `application.properties` file will look similar to the following:

```
shell.auth.simple.user.password=admin
```

When connected with the preceding command, similar actuator information can be accessed. Here is an example of the metrics information accessed through the CLI:

- `help`: This lists out all the options available
- `dashboard`: This is one interesting feature that shows a lot of system-level information

Configuring application information

The following properties can be set in `application.properties` to customize application-related information. After adding, restart the server and visit the `/info` endpoint of the actuator to take a look at the updated information, as follows:

```
info.app.name=Boot actuator
info.app.description= My Greetings Service
info.app.version=1.0.0
```

Adding a custom health module

Adding a new custom module to the Spring Boot application is not so complex. To demonstrate this feature, assume that if a service gets more than two transactions in a minute, then the server status will be set as Out of Service.

In order to customize this, we have to implement the `HealthIndicator` interface and override the `health` method. The following is a quick and dirty implementation to do the job:

```
class TPSCounter {
  LongAdder count;
  int threshold = 2;
```

```
Calendar expiry = null;

TPSCounter(){
  this.count = new LongAdder();
  this.expiry = Calendar.getInstance();
  this.expiry.add(Calendar.MINUTE, 1);
}

boolean isExpired(){
  return Calendar.getInstance().after(expiry);
}

boolean isWeak(){
  return (count.intValue() > threshold);
}

void increment(){
   count.increment();
}
}
```

The preceding class is a simple POJO class that maintains the transaction counts in the window. The isWeak method checks whether the transaction in a particular window reached its threshold. The isExpired method checks whether the current window is expired or not. The increment method simply increases the counter value.

For the next step, implement our custom health indicator class, TPSHealth. This is done by extending HealthIndicator, as follows:

```
@Component
class TPSHealth implements HealthIndicator {
  TPSCounter counter;

@Override
    public Health health() {
        boolean health = counter.isWeak(); // perform some specific
health check
        if (health) {
            return Health.outOfService().withDetail("Too many
requests", "OutofService").build();
        }
        return Health.up().build();
    }
```

```
    void updateTx(){
    if(counter == null || counter.isExpired()){
      counter = new TPSCounter();

    }
    counter.increment();
    }
  }
```

The `health` method checks whether the counter is weak or not. A weak counter means the service is handling more transactions than it can handle. If it is weak, it marks the instance as Out of Service.

Finally, we will autowire `TPSHealth` into the `GreetingController` class and then call `health.updateTx()` in the `greet` method, as follows:

```
Greet greet(){
    logger.info("Serving Request....!!!");
    health.updateTx();
    return new Greet("Hello World!");
}
```

Go to the `/health` end point in the HAL browser and take a look at the status of the server.

Now, open another browser, point to `http://localhost:8080`, and fire the service twice or thrice. Go back to the `/health` endpoint and refresh to see the status. It should be changed to Out of Service.

In this example, as there is no action taken other than collecting the health status, even though the status is Out of Service, new service calls will still go through. However, in the real world, a program should read the `/health` endpoint and block further requests from going to this instance.

Building custom metrics

Similar to health, customization of the metrics is also possible. The following example shows how to add counter service and gauge service, just for demonstration purposes:

```
@Autowired
CounterService counterService;

@Autowired
GaugeService gaugeService;
```

Add the following methods in the greet method:

```
this.counterService.increment("greet.txnCount");
this.gaugeService.submit("greet.customgauge", 1.0);
```

Restart the server and go to /metrics to see the new gauge and counter added already reflected there.

Documenting microservices

The traditional approach of API documentation is either by writing service specification documents or using static service registries. With a large number of microservices, it would be hard to keep the documentation of APIs in sync.

Microservices can be documented in many ways. This section will explore how microservices can be documented using the popular Swagger framework. The following example will use Springfox libraries to generate REST API documentation. Springfox is a set of Java- and Spring-friendly libraries.

Create a new **Spring Starter Project** and select **Web** in the library selection window. Name the project chapter2.swagger.

The full source code of this example is available as the chapter2.swagger project in the code files of this book.

As Springfox libraries are not part of the Spring suite, edit pom.xml and add Springfox Swagger library dependencies. Add the following dependencies to the project:

```
<dependency>
    <groupId>io.springfox</groupId>
    <artifactId>springfox-swagger2</artifactId>
    <version>2.3.1</version>
</dependency>
<dependency>
    <groupId>io.springfox</groupId>
    <artifactId>springfox-swagger-ui</artifactId>
    <version>2.3.1</version>
</dependency>
```

Create a REST service similar to the services created earlier, but also add the
@EnableSwagger2 annotation, as follows:

```
@SpringBootApplication
@EnableSwagger2
public class Application {
```

This is all that's required for a basic Swagger documentation. Start the application
and point the browser to `http://localhost:8080/swagger-ui.html`. This will
open the Swagger API documentation page:

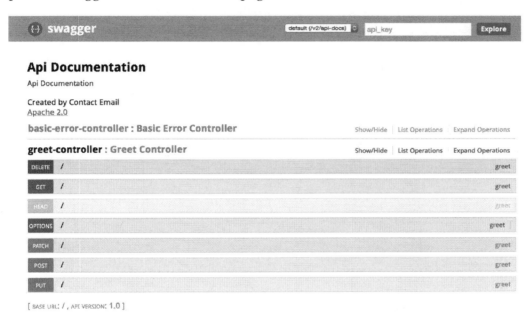

As shown in the diagram, the Swagger lists out the possible operations on **Greet
Controller**. Click on the **GET** operation. This expands the **GET** row, which provides
an option to try out the operation.

Summary

In this chapter, you learned about Spring Boot and its key features to build production-ready applications.

We explored the previous-generation web applications and then how Spring Boot makes developers' lives easier to develop fully qualified microservices. We also discussed the asynchronous message-based interaction between services. Further, we explored how to achieve some of the key capabilities required for microservices, such as security, HATEOAS, cross-origin, configurations, and so on with practical examples. We also took a look at how Spring Boot actuators help the operations teams and also how we can customize it to our needs. Finally, documenting microservices APIs was also explored.

In the next chapter, we will take a deeper look at some of the practical issues that may arise when implementing microservices. We will also discuss a capability model that essentially helps organizations when dealing with large microservices implementations.

3
Applying Microservices Concepts

Microservices are good, but can also be an evil if they are not properly conceived. Wrong microservice interpretations could lead to irrecoverable failures.

This chapter will examine the technical challenges around practical implementations of microservices. It will also provide guidelines around critical design decisions for successful microservices development. The solutions and patterns for a number of commonly raised concerns around microservices will also be examined. This chapter will also review the challenges in enterprise scale microservices development, and how to overcome those challenges. More importantly, a capability model for a microservices ecosystem will be established at the end.

In this chapter you will learn about the following:

- Trade-offs between different design choices and patterns to be considered when developing microservices
- Challenges and anti-patterns in developing enterprise grade microservices
- A capability model for a microservices ecosystem

Patterns and common design decisions

Microservices have gained enormous popularity in recent years. They have evolved as the preferred choice of architects, putting SOA into the backyards. While acknowledging the fact that microservices are a vehicle for developing scalable cloud native systems, successful microservices need to be carefully designed to avoid catastrophes. Microservices are not the one-size-fits-all, universal solution for all architecture problems.

Generally speaking, microservices are a great choice for building a lightweight, modular, scalable, and distributed system of systems. Over-engineering, wrong use cases, and misinterpretations could easily turn the system into a disaster. While selecting the right use cases is paramount in developing a successful microservice, it is equally important to take the right design decisions by carrying out an appropriate trade-off analysis. A number of factors are to be considered when designing microservices, as detailed in the following sections.

Establishing appropriate microservice boundaries

One of the most common questions relating to microservices is regarding the size of the service. How big (mini-monolithic) or how small (nano service) can a microservice be, or is there anything like right-sized services? Does size really matter?

A quick answer could be "one REST endpoint per microservice", or "less than 300 lines of code", or "a component that performs a single responsibility". But before we pick up any of these answers, there is lot more analysis to be done to understand the boundaries for our services.

Domain-driven design (DDD) defines the concept of a **bounded context**. A bounded context is a subdomain or a subsystem of a larger domain or system that is responsible for performing a particular function.

[Read more about DDD at `http://domainlanguage.com/ddd/`.]

The following diagram is an example of the domain model:

In a finance back office, system invoices, accounting, billing, and the like represent different bounded contexts. These bounded contexts are strongly isolated domains that are closely aligned with business capabilities. In the financial domain, the invoices, accounting, and billing are different business capabilities often handled by different subunits under the finance department.

A bounded context is a good way to determine the boundaries of microservices. Each bounded context could be mapped to a single microservice. In the real world, communication between bounded contexts are typically less coupled, and often, disconnected.

Even though real world organizational boundaries are the simplest mechanisms for establishing a bounded context, these may prove wrong in some cases due to inherent problems within the organization's structures. For example, a business capability may be delivered through different channels such as front offices, online, roaming agents, and so on. In many organizations, the business units may be organized based on delivery channels rather than the actual underlying business capabilities. In such cases, organization boundaries may not provide accurate service boundaries.

A top-down domain decomposition could be another way to establish the right bounded contexts.

There is no silver bullet to establish microservices boundaries, and often, this is quite challenging. Establishing boundaries is much easier in the scenario of monolithic application to microservices migration, as the service boundaries and dependencies are known from the existing system. On the other hand, in a green field microservices development, the dependencies are hard to establish upfront.

The most pragmatic way to design microservices boundaries is to run the scenario at hand through a number of possible options, just like a service litmus test. Keep in mind that there may be multiple conditions matching a given scenario that will lead to a trade-off analysis.

The following scenarios could help in defining the microservice boundaries.

Autonomous functions

If the function under review is autonomous by nature, then it can be taken as a microservices boundary. Autonomous services typically would have fewer dependencies on external functions. They accept input, use its internal logic and data for computation, and return a result. All utility functions such as an encryption engine or a notification engine are straightforward candidates.

A delivery service that accepts an order, processes it, and then informs the trucking service is another example of an autonomous service. An online flight search based on cached seat availability information is yet another example of an autonomous function.

Size of a deployable unit

Most of the microservices ecosystems will take advantage of automation, such as automatic integration, delivery, deployment, and scaling. Microservices covering broader functions result in larger deployment units. Large deployment units pose challenges in automatic file copy, file download, deployment, and start up times. For instance, the size of a service increases with the density of the functions that it implements.

A good microservice ensures that the size of its deployable units remains manageable.

Most appropriate function or subdomain

It is important to analyze what would be the most useful component to detach from the monolithic application. This is particularly applicable when breaking monolithic applications into microservices. This could be based on parameters such as resource-intensiveness, cost of ownership, business benefits, or flexibility.

In a typical hotel booking system, approximately 50-60% of the requests are search-based. In this case, moving out the search function could immediately bring in flexibility, business benefits, cost reduction, resource free up, and so on.

Polyglot architecture

One of the key characteristics of microservices is its support for polyglot architecture. In order to meet different non-functional and functional requirements, components may require different treatments. It could be different architectures, different technologies, different deployment topologies, and so on. When components are identified, review them against the requirement for polyglot architectures.

In the hotel booking scenario mentioned earlier, a Booking microservice may need transactional integrity, whereas a Search microservice may not. In this case, the Booking microservice may use an ACID compliance database such as MySQL, whereas the Search microservice may use an eventual consistent database such as Cassandra.

Selective scaling

Selective scaling is related to the previously discussed polyglot architecture. In this context, all functional modules may not require the same level of scalability. Sometimes, it may be appropriate to determine boundaries based on scalability requirements.

For example, in the hotel booking scenario, the Search microservice has to scale considerably more than many of the other services such as the Booking microservice or the Notification microservice due to the higher velocity of search requests. In this case, a separate Search microservice could run on top of an Elasticsearch or an in-memory data grid for better response.

Small, agile teams

Microservices enable Agile development with small, focused teams developing different parts of the pie. There could be scenarios where parts of the systems are built by different organizations, or even across different geographies, or by teams with varying skill sets. This approach is a common practice, for example, in manufacturing industries.

In the microservices world, each of these teams builds different microservices, and then assembles them together. Though this is not the desired way to break down the system, organizations may end up in such situations. Hence, this approach cannot be completely ruled out.

In an online product search scenario, a service could provide personalized options based on what the customer is looking for. This may require complex machine learning algorithms, and hence need a specialist team. In this scenario, this function could be built as a microservice by a separate specialist team.

Single responsibility

In theory, the single responsibility principle could be applied at a method, at a class, or at a service. However, in the context of microservices, it does not necessarily map to a single service or endpoint.

A more practical approach could be to translate single responsibility into single business capability or a single technical capability. As per the *single responsibility* principle, one responsibility cannot be shared by multiple microservices. Similarly, one microservice should not perform multiple responsibilities.

There could, however, be special cases where a single business capability is divided across multiple services. One of such cases is managing the customer profile, where there could be situations where you may use two different microservices for managing reads and writes using a **Command Query Responsibility Segregation (CQRS)** approach to achieve some of the quality attributes.

Replicability or changeability

Innovation and speed are of the utmost importance in IT delivery. Microservices boundaries should be identified in such a way that each microservice is easily detachable from the overall system, with minimal cost of re-writing. If part of the system is just an experiment, it should ideally be isolated as a microservice.

An organization may develop a recommendation engine or a customer ranking engine as an experiment. If the business value is not realized, then throw away that service, or replace it with another one.

Many organizations follow the startup model, where importance is given to meeting functions and quick delivery. These organizations may not worry too much about the architecture and technologies. Instead, the focus will be on what tools or technologies can deliver solutions faster. Organizations increasingly choose the approach of developing **Minimum Viable Products** (**MVPs**) by putting together a few services, and allowing the system to evolve. Microservices play a vital role in such cases where the system evolves, and services gradually get rewritten or replaced.

Coupling and cohesion

Coupling and cohesion are two of the most important parameters for deciding service boundaries. Dependencies between microservices have to be evaluated carefully to avoid highly coupled interfaces. A functional decomposition, together with a modeled dependency tree, could help in establishing a microservices boundary. Avoiding too chatty services, too many synchronous request-response calls, and cyclic synchronous dependencies are three key points, as these could easily break the system. A successful equation is to keep high cohesion within a microservice, and loose coupling between microservices. In addition to this, ensure that transaction boundaries are not stretched across microservices. A first class microservice will react upon receiving an event as an input, execute a number of internal functions, and finally send out another event. As part of the compute function, it may read and write data to its own local store.

Think microservice as a product

DDD also recommends mapping a bounded context to a product. As per DDD, each bounded context is an ideal candidate for a product. Think about a microservice as a product by itself. When microservice boundaries are established, assess them from a product's point of view to see whether they really stack up as product. It is much easier for business users to think boundaries from a product point of view. A product boundary may have many parameters, such as a targeted community, flexibility in deployment, sell-ability, reusability, and so on.

Designing communication styles

Communication between microservices can be designed either in synchronous (request-response) or asynchronous (fire and forget) styles.

Synchronous style communication

The following diagram shows an example request/response style service:

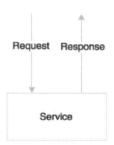

In synchronous communication, there is no shared state or object. When a caller requests a service, it passes the required information and waits for a response. This approach has a number of advantages.

An application is stateless, and from a high availability standpoint, many active instances can be up and running, accepting traffic. Since there are no other infrastructure dependencies such as a shared messaging server, there are management fewer overheads. In case of an error at any stage, the error will be propagated back to the caller immediately, leaving the system in a consistent state, without compromising data integrity.

The downside in a synchronous request-response communication is that the user or the caller has to wait until the requested process gets completed. As a result, the calling thread will wait for a response, and hence, this style could limit the scalability of the system.

A synchronous style adds hard dependencies between microservices. If one service in the service chain fails, then the entire service chain will fail. In order for a service to succeed, all dependent services have to be up and running. Many of the failure scenarios have to be handled using timeouts and loops.

Asynchronous style communication

The following diagram is a service designed to accept an asynchronous message as input, and send the response asynchronously for others to consume:

The asynchronous style is based on reactive event loop semantics which decouple microservices. This approach provides higher levels of scalability, because services are independent, and can internally spawn threads to handle an increase in load. When overloaded, messages will be queued in a messaging server for later processing. That means that if there is a slowdown in one of the services, it will not impact the entire chain. This provides higher levels of decoupling between services, and therefore maintenance and testing will be simpler.

The downside is that it has a dependency to an external messaging server. It is complex to handle the fault tolerance of a messaging server. Messaging typically works with an active/passive semantics. Hence, handling continuous availability of messaging systems is harder to achieve. Since messaging typically uses persistence, a higher level of I/O handling and tuning is required.

How to decide which style to choose?

Both approaches have their own merits and constraints. It is not possible to develop a system with just one approach. A combination of both approaches is required based on the use cases. In principle, the asynchronous approach is great for building true, scalable microservice systems. However, attempting to model everything as asynchronous leads to complex system designs.

How does the following example look in the context where an end user clicks on a UI to get profile details?

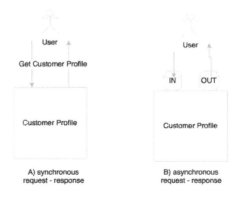

This is perhaps a simple query to the backend system to get a result in a request-response model. This can also be modeled in an asynchronous style by pushing a message to an input queue, and waiting for a response in an output queue till a response is received for the given correlation ID. However, though we use asynchronous messaging, the user is still blocked for the entire duration of the query.

Another use case is that of a user clicking on a UI to search hotels, which is depicted in the following diagram:

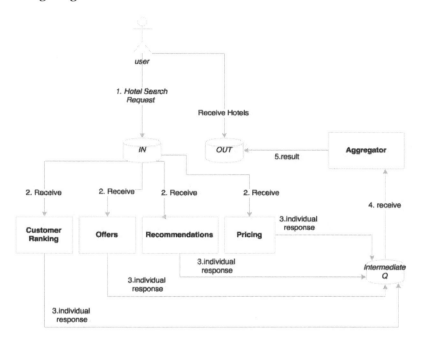

This is very similar to the previous scenario. However, in this case, we assume that this business function triggers a number of activities internally before returning the list of hotels back to the user. For example, when the system receives this request, it calculates the customer ranking, gets offers based on the destination, gets recommendations based on customer preferences, optimizes the prices based on customer values and revenue factors, and so on. In this case, we have an opportunity to do many of these activities in parallel so that we can aggregate all these results before presenting them to the customer. As shown in the preceding diagram, virtually any computational logic could be plugged in to the search pipeline listening to the **IN** queue.

An effective approach in this case is to start with a synchronous request response, and refactor later to introduce an asynchronous style when there is value in doing that.

The following example shows a fully asynchronous style of service interactions:

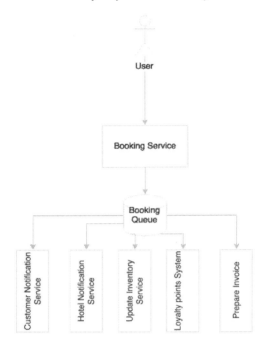

The service is triggered when the user clicks on the booking function. It is again, by nature, a synchronous style communication. When booking is successful, it sends a message to the customer's e-mail address, sends a message to the hotel's booking system, updates the cached inventory, updates the loyalty points system, prepares an invoice, and perhaps more. Instead of pushing the user into a long wait state, a better approach is to break the service into pieces. Let the user wait till a booking record is created by the Booking Service. On successful completion, a booking event will be published, and return a confirmation message back to the user. Subsequently, all other activities will happen in parallel, asynchronously.

In all three examples, the user has to wait for a response. With the new web application frameworks, it is possible to send requests asynchronously, and define the callback method, or set an observer for getting a response. Therefore, the users won't be fully blocked from executing other activities.

In general, an asynchronous style is always better in the microservices world, but identifying the right pattern should be purely based on merits. If there are no merits in modeling a transaction in an asynchronous style, then use the synchronous style till you find an appealing case. Use reactive programming frameworks to avoid complexity when modeling user-driven requests, modeled in an asynchronous style.

Orchestration of microservices

Composability is one of the service design principles. This leads to confusion around who is responsible for the composing services. In the SOA world, ESBs are responsible for composing a set of finely-grained services. In some organizations, ESBs play the role of a proxy, and service providers themselves compose and expose coarse-grained services. In the SOA world, there are two approaches for handling such situations.

The first approach is orchestration, which is depicted in the following diagram:

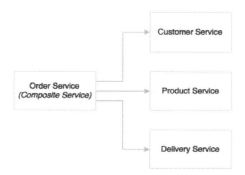

In the orchestration approach, multiple services are stitched together to get a complete function. A central brain acts as the orchestrator. As shown in the diagram, the order service is a composite service that will orchestrate other services. There could be sequential as well as parallel branches from the master process. Each task will be fulfilled by an atomic task service, typically a web service. In the SOA world, ESBs play the role of orchestration. The orchestrated service will be exposed by ESBs as a composite service.

The second approach is choreography, which is shown in the following diagram:

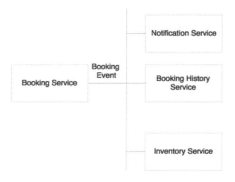

In the choreography approach, there is no central brain. An event, a booking event in this case, is published by a producer, a number of consumers wait for the event, and independently apply different logics on the incoming event. Sometimes, events could even be nested where the consumers can send another event which will be consumed by another service. In the SOA world, the caller pushes a message to the ESB, and the downstream flow will be automatically determined by the consuming services.

Microservices are autonomous. This essentially means that in an ideal situation, all required components to complete their function should be within the service. This includes the database, orchestration of its internal services, intrinsic state management, and so on. The service endpoints provide coarse-grained APIs. This is perfectly fine as long as there are no external touch points required. But in reality, microservices may need to talk to other microservices to fulfil their function.

In such cases, choreography is the preferred approach for connecting multiple microservices together. Following the autonomy principle, a component sitting outside a microservice and controlling the flow is not the desired option. If the use case can be modeled in choreographic style, that would be the best possible way to handle the situation.

But it may not be possible to model choreography in all cases. This is depicted in the following diagram:

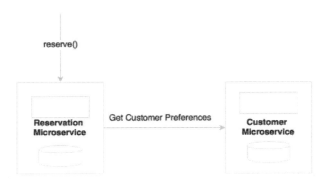

In the preceding example, Reservation and Customer are two microservices, with clearly segregated functional responsibilities. A case could arise when Reservation would want to get Customer preferences while creating a reservation. These are quite normal scenarios when developing complex systems.

Can we move Customer to Reservation so that Reservation will be complete by itself? If Customer and Reservation are identified as two microservices based on various factors, it may not be a good idea to move Customer to Reservation. In such a case, we will meet another monolithic application sooner or later.

Can we make the Reservation to Customer call asynchronous? This example is shown in the following diagram:

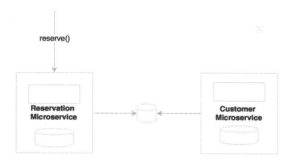

Customer preference is required for Reservation to progress, and hence, it may require a synchronous blocking call to Customer. Retrofitting this by modeling asynchronously does not really make sense.

Can we take out just the orchestration bit, and create another composite microservice, which then composes Reservation and Customer?

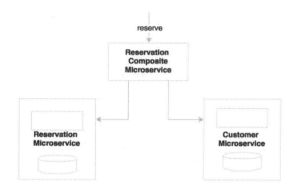

This is acceptable in the approach for composing multiple components within a microservice. But creating a composite microservice may not be a good idea. We will end up creating many microservices with no business alignment, which would not be autonomous, and could result in many fine-grained microservices.

Can we duplicate customer preference by keeping a slave copy of the preference data into Reservation?

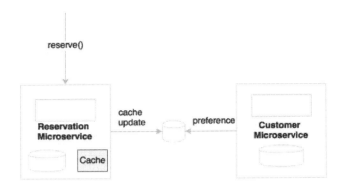

Changes will be propagated whenever there is a change in the master. In this case, Reservation can use customer preference without fanning out a call. It is a valid thought, but we need to carefully analyze this. Today we replicate customer preference, but in another scenario, we may want to reach out to customer service to see whether the customer is black-listed from reserving. We have to be extremely careful in deciding what data to duplicate. This could add to the complexity.

How many endpoints in a microservice?

In many situations, developers are confused with the number of endpoints per microservice. The question really is whether to limit each microservice with one endpoint or multiple endpoints:

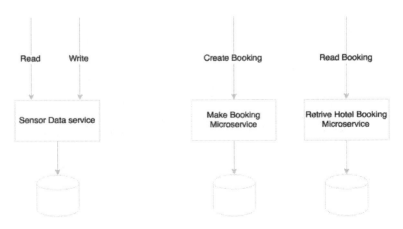

The number of endpoints is not really a decision point. In some cases, there may be only one endpoint, whereas in some other cases, there could be more than one endpoint in a microservice. For instance, consider a sensor data service which collects sensor information, and has two logical endpoints: create and read. But in order to handle CQRS, we may create two separate physical microservices as shown in the case of **Booking** in the preceding diagram. Polyglot architecture could be another scenario where we may split endpoints into different microservices.

Considering a notification engine, notifications will be send out in response to an event. The process of notification such as preparation of data, identification of a person, and delivery mechanisms, are different for different events. Moreover, we may want to scale each of these processes differently at different time windows. In such situations, we may decide to break each notification endpoint in to a separate microservice.

In yet another example, a Loyalty Points microservice may have multiple services such as accrue, redeem, transfer, and balance. We may not want to treat each of these services differently. All of these services are connected and use the points table for data. If we go with one endpoint per service, we will end up in a situation where many fine-grained services access data from the same data store or replicated copies of the same data store.

In short, the number of endpoints is not a design decision. One microservice may host one or more endpoints. Designing appropriate bounded context for a microservice is more important.

One microservice per VM or multiple?

One microservice could be deployed in multiple **Virtual Machines** (**VMs**) by replicating the deployment for scalability and availability. This is a no brainer. The question is whether multiple microservices could be deployed in one virtual machine? There are pros and cons for this approach. This question typically arises when the services are simple, and the traffic volume is less.

Consider an example where we have a couple of microservices, and the overall transaction per minute is less than 10. Also assume that the smallest possible VM size available is 2-core 8 GB RAM. A further assumption is that in such cases, a 2-core 8 GB VM can handle 10-15 transactions per minute without any performance concerns. If we use different VMs for each microservice, it may not be cost effective, and we will end up paying more for infrastructure and license, since many vendors charge based on the number of cores.

The simplest way to approach this problem is to ask a few questions:

- Does the VM have enough capacity to run both services under peak usage?
- Do we want to treat these services differently to achieve SLAs (selective scaling)? For example, for scalability, if we have an all-in-one VM, we will have to replicate VMs which replicate all services.
- Are there any conflicting resource requirements? For example, different OS versions, JDK versions, and others.

If all your answers are *No*, then perhaps we can start with collocated deployment, until we encounter a scenario to change the deployment topology. However, we will have to ensure that these services are not sharing anything, and are running as independent OS processes.

Having said that, in an organization with matured virtualized infrastructure or cloud infrastructure, this may not be a huge concern. In such environments, the developers need not worry about where the services are running. Developers may not even think about capacity planning. Services will be deployed in a compute cloud. Based on the infrastructure availability, SLAs and the nature of the service, the infrastructure self-manages deployments. AWS Lambda is a good example of such a service.

Rules engine – shared or embedded?

Rules are an essential part of any system. For example, an offer eligibility service may execute a number of rules before making a yes or no decision. Either we hand code rules, or we may use a rules engine. Many enterprises manage rules centrally in a rules repository as well as execute them centrally. These enterprise rule engines are primarily used for providing the business an opportunity to author and manage rules as well as reuse rules from the central repository. **Drools** is one of the popular open source rules engines. IBM, FICO, and Bosch are some of the pioneers in the commercial space. These rule engines improve productivity, enable reuse of rules, facts, vocabularies, and provide faster rule execution using the rete algorithm.

In the context of microservices, a central rules engine means fanning out calls from microservices to the central rules engine. This also means that the service logic is now in two places, some within the service, and some external to the service. Nevertheless, the objective in the context of microservices is to reduce external dependencies:

If the rules are simple enough, few in numbers, only used within the boundaries of a service, and not exposed to business users for authoring, then it may be better to hand-code business rules than rely on an enterprise rule engine:

If the rules are complex, limited to a service context, and not given to business users, then it is better to use an embedded rules engine within the service:

If the rules are managed and authored by business, or if the rules are complex, or if we are reusing rules from other service domains, then a central authoring repository with a locally embedded execution engine could be a better choice.

Note that this has to be carefully evaluated since all vendors may not support the local rule execution approach, and there could be technology dependencies such as running rules only within a specific application server, and so on.

Role of BPM and workflows

Business Process Management (BPM) and **Intelligent Business Process Management (iBPM)** are tool suites for designing, executing, and monitoring business processes.

Typical use cases for BPM are:

- Coordinating a long-running business process, where some processes are realized by existing assets, whereas some other areas may be niche, and there is no concrete implementation of the processes being in place. BPM allows composing both types, and provides an end-to-end automated process. This often involves systems and human interactions.

- Process-centric organizations, such as those that have implemented Six Sigma, want to monitor their processes for continuous improvement on efficiency.

- Process re-engineering with a top-down approach by redefining the business process of an organization.

There could be two scenarios where BPM fits in the microservices world:

The first scenario is business process re-engineering, or threading an end-to-end long running business process, as stated earlier. In this case, BPM operates at a higher level, where it may automate a cross-functional, long-running business process by stitching a number of coarse-grained microservices, existing legacy connectors, and human interactions. As shown in the preceding diagram, the loan approval BPM invokes microservices as well as legacy application services. It also integrates human tasks.

In this case, microservices are headless services that implement a subprocess. From the microservices' perspective, BPM is just another consumer. Care needs to be taken in this approach to avoid accepting a shared state from a BPM process as well as moving business logic to BPM:

The second scenario is monitoring processes, and optimizing them for efficiency. This goes hand in hand with a completely automated, asynchronously choreographed microservices ecosystem. In this case, microservices and BPM work as independent ecosystems. Microservices send events at various timeframes such as the start of a process, state changes, end of a process, and so on. These events are used by the BPM engine to plot and monitor process states. We may not require a full-fledged BPM solution for this, as we are only mocking a business process to monitor its efficiency. In this case, the order delivery process is not a BPM implementation, but it is more of a monitoring dashboard that captures and displays the progress of the process.

To summarize, BPM could still be used at a higher level for composing multiple microservices in situations where end-to-end cross-functional business processes are modeled by automating systems and human interactions. A better and simpler approach is to have a business process dashboard to which microservices feed state change events as mentioned in the second scenario.

Can microservices share data stores?

In principle, microservices should abstract presentation, business logic, and data stores. If the services are broken as per the guidelines, each microservice logically could use an independent database:

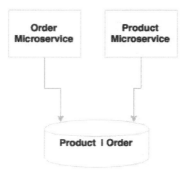

In the preceding diagram, both **Product** and **Order** microservices share one database and one data model. Shared data models, shared schema, and shared tables are recipes for disasters when developing microservices. This may be good at the beginning, but when developing complex microservices, we tend to add relationships between data models, add join queries, and so on. This can result in tightly coupled physical data models.

If the services have only a few tables, it may not be worth investing a full instance of a database like an Oracle database instance. In such cases, a schema level segregation is good enough to start with:

There could be scenarios where we tend to think of using a shared database for multiple services. Taking an example of a customer data repository or master data managed at the enterprise level, the customer registration and customer segmentation microservices logically share the same customer data repository:

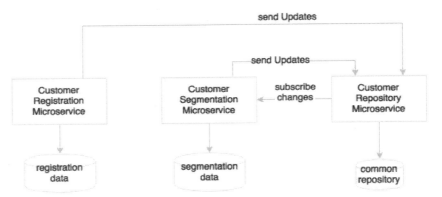

As shown in the preceding diagram, an alternate approach in this scenario is to separate the transactional data store for microservices from the enterprise data repository by adding a local transactional data store for these services. This will help the services to have flexibility in remodeling the local data store optimized for its purpose. The enterprise customer repository sends change events when there is any change in the customer data repository. Similarly, if there is any change in any of the transactional data stores, the changes have to be sent to the central customer repository.

Setting up transaction boundaries

Transactions in operational systems are used to maintain the consistency of data stored in an RDBMS by grouping a number of operations together into one atomic block. They either commit or rollback the entire operation. Distributed systems follow the concept of distributed transactions with a two-phase commit. This is particularly required if heterogeneous components such as an RPC service, JMS, and so on participate in a transaction.

Is there a place for transactions in microservices? Transactions are not bad, but one should use transactions carefully, by analyzing what we are trying do.

For a given microservice, an RDBMS like MySQL may be selected as a backing store to ensure 100% data integrity, for example, a stock or inventory management service where data integrity is key. It is appropriate to define transaction boundaries within the microsystem using local transactions. However, distributed global transactions should be avoided in the microservices context. Proper dependency analysis is required to ensure that transaction boundaries do not span across two different microservices as much as possible.

Altering use cases to simplify transactional requirements

Eventual consistency is a better option than distributed transactions that span across multiple microservices. Eventual consistency reduces a lot of overheads, but application developers may need to re-think the way they write application code. This could include remodeling functions, sequencing operations to minimize failures, batching insert and modify operations, remodeling data structure, and finally, compensating operations that negate the effect.

A classical problem is that of the last room selling scenario in a hotel booking use case. What if there is only one room left, and there are multiple customers booking this singe available room? A business model change sometimes makes this scenario less impactful. We could set an "under booking profile", where the actual number of bookable rooms can go below the actual number of rooms (*bookable* = *available* - 3) in anticipation of some cancellations. Anything in this range will be accepted as "subject to confirmation", and customers will be charged only if payment is confirmed. Bookings will be confirmed in a set time window.

Now consider the scenario where we are creating customer profiles in a NoSQL database like CouchDB. In more traditional approaches with RDBMS, we insert a customer first, and then insert the customer's address, profile details, then preferences, all in one transaction. When using NoSQL, we may not do the same steps. Instead, we may prepare a JSON object with all the details, and insert this into CouchDB in one go. In this second case, no explicit transaction boundaries are required.

Distributed transaction scenarios

The ideal scenario is to use local transactions within a microservice if required, and completely avoid distributed transactions. There could be scenarios where at the end of the execution of one service, we may want to send a message to another microservice. For example, say a tour reservation has a wheelchair request. Once the reservation is successful, we will have to send a message for the wheelchair booking to another microservice that handles ancillary bookings. The reservation request itself will run on a local transaction. If sending this message fails, we are still in the transaction boundary, and we can roll back the entire transaction. What if we create a reservation and send the message, but after sending the message, we encounter an error in the reservation, the reservation transaction fails, and subsequently, the reservation record is rolled back? Now we end up in a situation where we've unnecessarily created an orphan wheelchair booking:

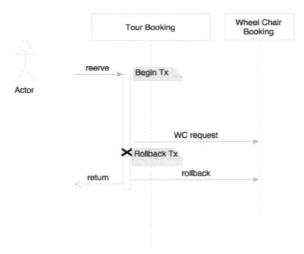

There are a couple of ways we can address this scenario. The first approach is to delay sending the message till the end. This ensures that there are less chances for any failure after sending the message. Still, if failure occurs after sending the message, then the exception handling routine is run, that is, we send a compensating message to reverse the wheelchair booking.

Service endpoint design consideration

One of the important aspects of microservices is service design. Service design has two key elements: contract design and protocol selection.

Contract design

The first and foremost principle of service design is simplicity. The services should be designed for consumers to consume. A complex service contract reduces the usability of the service. The **KISS (Keep It Simple Stupid)** principle helps us to build better quality services faster, and reduces the cost of maintenance and replacement. The **YAGNI (You Ain't Gonna Need It)** is another principle supporting this idea. Predicting future requirements and building systems are, in reality, not future-proofed. This results in large upfront investment as well as higher cost of maintenance.

Evolutionary design is a great concept. Do just enough design to satisfy today's wants, and keep changing and refactoring the design to accommodate new features as and when they are required. Having said that, this may not be simple unless there is a strong governance in place.

Consumer Driven Contracts (CDC) is a great idea that supports evolutionary design. In many cases, when the service contract gets changed, all consuming applications have to undergo testing. This makes change difficult. CDC helps in building confidence in consumer applications. CDC advocates each consumer to provide their expectation to the provider in the form of test cases so that the provider uses them as integration tests whenever the service contract is changed.

Postel's law is also relevant in this scenario. Postel's law primarily addresses TCP communications; however, this is also equally applicable to service design. When it comes to service design, service providers should be as flexible as possible when accepting consumer requests, whereas service consumers should stick to the contract as agreed with the provider.

Protocol selection

In the SOA world, HTTP/SOAP, and messaging were kinds of default service protocols for service interactions. Microservices follow the same design principles for service interaction. Loose coupling is one of the core principles in the microservices world too.

Microservices fragment applications into many physically independent deployable services. This not only increases the communication cost, it is also susceptible to network failures. This could also result in poor performance of services.

Message-oriented services

If we choose an asynchronous style of communication, the user is disconnected, and therefore, response times are not directly impacted. In such cases, we may use standard JMS or AMQP protocols for communication with JSON as payload. Messaging over HTTP is also popular, as it reduces complexity. Many new entrants in messaging services support HTTP-based communication. Asynchronous REST is also possible, and is handy when calling long-running services.

HTTP and REST endpoints

Communication over HTTP is always better for interoperability, protocol handling, traffic routing, load balancing, security systems, and the like. Since HTTP is stateless, it is more compatible for handling stateless services with no affinity. Most of the development frameworks, testing tools, runtime containers, security systems, and so on are friendlier towards HTTP.

With the popularity and acceptance of REST and JSON, it is the default choice for microservice developers. The HTTP/REST/JSON protocol stack makes building interoperable systems very easy and friendly. HATEOAS is one of the design patterns emerging for designing progressive rendering and self-service navigations. As discussed in the previous chapter, HATEOAS provides a mechanism to link resources together so that the consumer can navigate between resources. RFC 5988 – Web Linking is another upcoming standard.

Optimized communication protocols

If the service response times are stringent, then we need to pay special attention to the communication aspects. In such cases, we may choose alternate protocols such as Avro, Protocol Buffers, or Thrift for communicating between services. But this limits the interoperability of services. The trade-off is between performance and interoperability requirements. Custom binary protocols need careful evaluation as they bind native objects on both sides—consumer and producer. This could run into release management issues such as class version mismatch in Java-based RPC style communications.

API documentations

Last thing: a good API is not only simple, but should also have enough documentation for the consumers. There are many tools available today for documenting REST-based services like Swagger, RAML, and API Blueprint.

Handling shared libraries

The principle behind microservices is that they should be autonomous and self-contained. In order to adhere to this principle, there may be situations where we will have to duplicate code and libraries. These could be either technical libraries or functional components.

For example, the eligibility for a flight upgrade will be checked at the time of check-in as well as when boarding. If check-in and boarding are two different microservices, we may have to duplicate the eligibility rules in both the services. This was the trade-off between adding a dependency versus code duplication.

It may be easy to embed code as compared to adding an additional dependency, as it enables better release management and performance. But this is against the DRY principle.

DRY principle
Every piece of knowledge must have a single, unambiguous, authoritative representation within a system.

The downside of this approach is that in case of a bug or an enhancement on the shared library, it has to be upgraded in more than one place. This may not be a severe setback as each service can contain a different version of the shared library:

An alternative option of developing the shared library as another microservice itself needs careful analysis. If it is not qualified as a microservice from the business capability point of view, then it may add more complexity than its usefulness. The trade-off analysis is between overheads in communication versus duplicating the libraries in multiple services.

User interfaces in microservices

The microservices principle advocates a microservice as a vertical slice from the database to presentation:

In reality, we get requirements to build quick UI and mobile applications mashing up the existing APIs. This is not uncommon in the modern scenario, where a business wants quick turnaround time from IT:

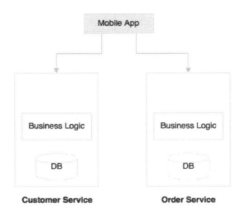

Penetration of mobile applications is one of the causes of this approach. In many organizations, there will be mobile development teams sitting close to the business team, developing rapid mobile applications by combining and mashing up APIs from multiple sources, both internal and external. In such situations, we may just expose services, and leave it for the mobile teams to realize in the way the business wants. In this case, we will build headless microservices, and leave it to the mobile teams to build a presentation layer.

Another category of problem is that the business may want to build consolidated web applications targeted to communities:

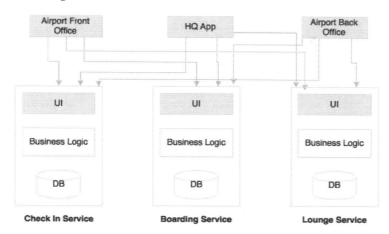

For example, the business may want to develop a departure control application targeting airport users. A departure control web application may have functions such as check-in, lounge management, boarding, and so on. These may be designed as independent microservices. But from the business standpoint, it all needs to be clubbed into a single web application. In such cases, we will have to build web applications by mashing up services from the backend.

One approach is to build a container web application or a placeholder web application, which links to multiple microservices at the backend. In this case, we develop full stack microservices, but the screens coming out of this could be embedded in to another placeholder web application. One of the advantages of this approach is that you can have multiple placeholder web applications targeting different user communities, as shown in the preceding diagram. We may use an API gateway to avoid those crisscross connections. We will explore the API gateway in the next section.

Use of API gateways in microservices

With the advancement of client-side JavaScript frameworks like AngularJS, the server is expected to expose RESTful services. This could lead to two issues. The first issue is the mismatch in contract expectations. The second issue is multiple calls to the server to render a page.

We start with the contract mismatch case. For example, `GetCustomer` may return a JSON with many fields:

```
Customer {
  Name:
  Address:
  Contact:
}
```

In the preceding case, `Name`, `Address`, and `Contact` are nested JSON objects. But a mobile client may expect only basic information such as first name, and last name. In the SOA world, an ESB or a mobile middleware did this job of transformation of data for the client. The default approach in microservices is to get all the elements of `Customer`, and then the client takes up the responsibility to filter the elements. In this case, the overhead is on the network.

There are several approaches we can think about to solve this case:

```
Customer {
  Id: 1
  Name: /customer/name/1
  Address: /customer/address/1
  Contact: /customer/contact/1
}
```

In the first approach, minimal information is sent with links as explained in the section on HATEOAS. In the preceding case, for customer ID 1, there are three links, which will help the client to access specific data elements. The example is a simple logical representation, not the actual JSON. The mobile client in this case will get basic customer information. The client further uses the links to get the additional required information.

The second approach is used when the client makes the REST call; it also sends the required fields as part of the query string. In this scenario, the client sends a request with `firstname` and `lastname` as the query string to indicate that the client only requires these two fields. The downside is that it ends up in complex server-side logic as it has to filter based on the fields. The server has to send different elements based on the incoming query.

The third approach is to introduce a level of indirection. In this, a gateway component sits between the client and the server, and transforms data as per the consumer's specification. This is a better approach as we do not compromise on the backend service contract. This leads to what is called UI services. In many cases, the API gateway acts as a proxy to the backend, exposing a set of consumer-specific APIs:

 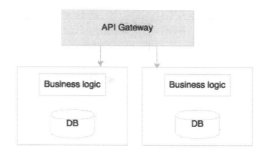

A) API gateway is part of the micro service

B) Common API gateway

There are two ways we can deploy an API gateway. The first one is one API gateway per microservice as shown in diagram **A**. The second approach (diagram **B**) is to have a common API gateway for multiple services. The choice really depends on what we are looking for. If we are using an API gateway as a reverse proxy, then off-the-shelf gateways such as Apigee, Mashery, and the like could be used as a shared platform. If we need fine-grained control over traffic shaping and complex transformations, then per service custom API gateways may be more useful.

A related problem is that we will have to make many calls from the client to the server. If we refer to our holiday example in *Chapter 1, Demystifying Microservices,* you know that for rendering each widget, we had to make a call to the server. Though we transfer only data, it can still add a significant overhead on the network. This approach is not fully wrong, as in many cases, we use responsive design and progressive design. The data will be loaded on demand, based on user navigations. In order to do this, each widget in the client should make independent calls to the server in a lazy mode. If bandwidth is an issue, then an API gateway is the solution. An API gateway acts as a middleman to compose and transform APIs from multiple microservices.

Use of ESB and iPaaS with microservices

Theoretically, SOA is not all about ESBs, but the reality is that ESBs have always been at the center of many SOA implementations. What would be the role of an ESB in the microservices world?

In general, microservices are fully cloud native systems with smaller footprints. The lightweight characteristics of microservices enable automation of deployments, scaling, and so on. On the contrary, enterprise ESBs are heavyweight in nature, and most of the commercial ESBs are not cloud friendly. The key features of an ESB are protocol mediation, transformation, orchestration, and application adaptors. In a typical microservices ecosystem, we may not need any of these features.

The limited ESB capabilities that are relevant for microservices are already available with more lightweight tools such as an API gateway. Orchestration is moved from the central bus to the microservices themselves. Therefore, there is no centralized orchestration capability expected in the case of microservices. Since the services are set up to accept more universal message exchange styles using REST/JSON calls, no protocol mediation is required. The last piece of capability that we get from ESBs are the adaptors to connect back to the legacy systems. In the case of microservices, the service itself provides a concrete implementation, and hence, there are no legacy connectors required. For these reasons, there is no natural space for ESBs in the microservices world.

Many organizations established ESBs as the backbone for their application integrations (EAI). Enterprise architecture policies in such organizations are built around ESBs. There could be a number of enterprise-level policies such as auditing, logging, security, validation, and so on that would have been in place when integrating using ESB. Microservices, however, advocate a more decentralized governance. ESBs will be an overkill if integrated with microservices.

Not all services are microservices. Enterprises have legacy applications, vendor applications, and so on. Legacy services use ESBs to connect with microservices. ESBs still hold their place for legacy integration and vendor applications to integrate at the enterprise level.

With the advancement of clouds, the capabilities of ESBs are not sufficient to manage integration between clouds, cloud to on-premise, and so on. **Integration Platform as a Service (iPaaS)** is evolving as the next generation application integration platform, which further reduces the role of ESBs. In typical deployments, iPaaS invokes API gateways to access microservices.

Service versioning considerations

When we allow services to evolve, one of the important aspect to consider is service versioning. Service versioning should be considered upfront, and not as an afterthought. Versioning helps us to release new services without breaking the existing consumers. Both the old version and the new version will be deployed side by side.

Semantic versions are widely used for service versioning. A semantic version has three components: **major**, **minor**, and **patch**. Major is used when there is a breaking change, minor is used when there is a backward compatible change, and patch is used when there is a backward compatible bug fix.

Versioning could get complicated when there is more than one service in a microservice. It is always simple to version services at the service level compared to the operations level. If there is a change in one of the operations, the service is upgraded and deployed to V2. The version change is applicable to all operations in the service. This is the notion of immutable services.

There are three different ways in which we can version REST services:

- URI versioning
- Media type versioning
- Custom header

In URI versioning, the version number is included in the URL itself. In this case, we just need to be worried about the major versions only. Hence, if there is a minor version change or a patch, the consumers do not need to worry about the changes. It is a good practice to alias the latest version to a non-versioned URI, which is done as follows:

```
/api/v3/customer/1234
/api/customer/1234   - aliased to v3.

@RestController("CustomerControllerV3")
@RequestMapping("api/v3/customer")
public class CustomerController {

}
```

A slightly different approach is to use the version number as part of the URL parameter:

```
api/customer/100?v=1.5
```

In case of media type versioning, the version is set by the client on the HTTP `Accept` header as follows:

```
Accept:  application/vnd.company.customer-v3+json
```

A less effective approach for versioning is to set the version in the custom header:

```
@RequestMapping(value = "/{id}", method = RequestMethod.GET, headers =
{"version=3"})
public Customer getCustomer(@PathVariable("id") long id) {
    //other code goes here.
}
```

In the URI approach, it is simple for the clients to consume services. But this has some inherent issues such as the fact that versioning-nested URI resources could be complex. Indeed, migrating clients is slightly complex as compared to media type approaches, with caching issues for multiple versions of the services, and others. However, these issues are not significant enough for us to not go with a URI approach. Most of the big Internet players such as Google, Twitter, LinkedIn, and Salesforce are following the URI approach.

Design for cross origin

With microservices, there is no guarantee that the services will run from the same host or same domain. Composite UI web applications may call multiple microservices for accomplishing a task, and these could come from different domains and hosts.

CORS allows browser clients to send requests to services hosted on different domains. This is essential in a microservices-based architecture.

One approach is to enable all microservices to allow cross origin requests from other trusted domains. The second approach is to use an API gateway as a single trusted domain for the clients.

Handling shared reference data

When breaking large applications, one of the common issues which we see is the management of master data or reference data. Reference data is more like shared data required between different microservices. City master, country master, and so on will be used in many services such as flight schedules, reservations, and others.

There are a few ways in which we can solve this. For instance, in the case of relatively static, never changing data, then every service can hardcode this data within all the microservices themselves:

Another approach, as shown in the preceding diagram, is to build it as another microservice. This is good, clean, and neat, but the downside is that every service may need to call the master data multiple times. As shown in the diagram for the **Search** and **Booking** example, there are transactional microservices, which use the **Geography** microservice to access shared data:

Another option is to replicate the data with every microservice. There is no single owner, but each service has its required master data. When there is an update, all the services are updated. This is extremely performance friendly, but one has to duplicate the code in all the services. It is also complex to keep data in sync across all microservices. This approach makes sense if the code base and data is simple or the data is more static.

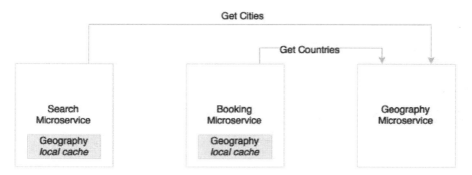

Yet another approach is similar to the first approach, but each service has a local near cache of the required data, which will be loaded incrementally. A local embedded cache such as Ehcache or data grids like Hazelcast or Infinispan could also be used based on the data volumes. This is the most preferred approach for a large number of microservices that have dependency on the master data.

Microservices and bulk operations

Since we have broken monolithic applications into smaller, focused services, it is no longer possible to use join queries across microservice data stores. This could lead to situations where one service may need many records from other services to perform its function.

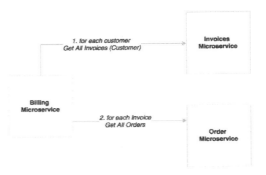

For example, a monthly billing function needs the invoices of many customers to process the billing. To make it a bit more complicated, invoices may have many orders. When we break billing, invoices, and orders into three different microservices, the challenge that arises is that the **Billing** service has to query the **Invoices** service for each customer to get all the invoices, and then for each invoice, call the **Order** service for getting the orders. This is not a good solution, as the number of calls that goes to other microservices are high:

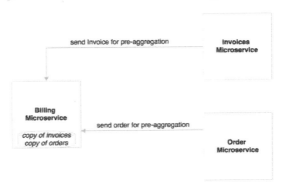

There are two ways we can think about for solving this. The first approach is to pre-aggregate data as and when it is created. When an order is created, an event is sent out. Upon receiving the event, the **Billing** microservice keeps aggregating data internally for monthly processing. In this case, there is no need for the **Billing** microservice to go out for processing. The downside of this approach is that there is duplication of data.

A second approach, when pre-aggregation is not possible, is to use batch APIs. In such cases, we call `GetAllInvoices`, then we use multiple batches, and each batch further uses parallel threads to get orders. Spring Batch is useful in these situations.

Microservices challenges

In the previous section, you learned about the right design decisions to be taken, and the trade-offs to be applied. In this section, we will review some of the challenges with microservices, and how to address them for a successful microservice development.

Data islands

Microservices abstract their own local transactional store, which is used for their own transactional purposes. The type of store and the data structure will be optimized for the services offered by the microservice.

For example, if we want to develop a customer relationship graph, we may use a graph database like Neo4j, OrientDB, and the like. A predictive text search to find out a customer based on any related information such as passport number, address, e-mail, phone, and so on could be best realized using an indexed search database like Elasticsearch or Solr.

This will place us into a unique situation of fragmenting data into heterogeneous data islands. For example, Customer, Loyalty Points, Reservations, and others are different microservices, and hence, use different databases. What if we want to do a near real-time analysis of all high value customers by combining data from all three data stores? This was easy with a monolithic application, because all the data was present in a single database:

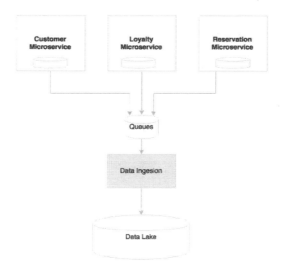

In order to satisfy this requirement, a data warehouse or a data lake is required. Traditional data warehouses like Oracle, Teradata, and others are used primarily for batch reporting. But with NoSQL databases (like Hadoop) and microbatching techniques, near real-time analytics is possible with the concept of data lakes. Unlike the traditional warehouses that are purpose-built for batch reporting, data lakes store raw data without assuming how the data is going to be used. Now the question really is how to port the data from microservices into data lakes.

Data porting from microservices to a data lake or a data warehouse can be done in many ways. Traditional ETL could be one of the options. Since we allow backdoor entry with ETL, and break the abstraction, this is not considered an effective way for data movement. A better approach is to send events from microservices as and when they occur, for example, customer registration, customer update events, and so on. Data ingestion tools consume these events, and propagate the state change to the data lake appropriately. The data ingestion tools are highly scalable platforms such as Spring Cloud Data Flow, Kafka, Flume, and so on.

Logging and monitoring

Log files are a good piece of information for analysis and debugging. Since each microservice is deployed independently, they emit separate logs, maybe to a local disk. This results in fragmented logs. When we scale services across multiple machines, each service instance could produce separate log files. This makes it extremely difficult to debug and understand the behavior of the services through log mining.

Examining **Order**, **Delivery**, and **Notification** as three different microservices, we find no way to correlate a customer transaction that runs across all three of them:

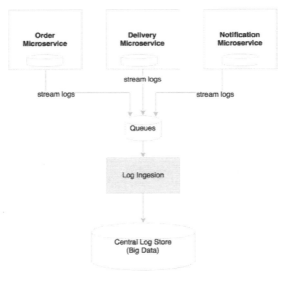

When implementing microservices, we need a capability to ship logs from each service to a centrally managed log repository. With this approach, services do not have to rely on the local disk or local I/Os. A second advantage is that the log files are centrally managed, and are available for all sorts of analysis such as historical, real time, and trending. By introducing a correlation ID, end-to-end transactions can be easily tracked.

With a large number of microservices, and with multiple versions and service instances, it would be difficult to find out which service is running on which server, what's the health of these services, the service dependencies, and so on. This was much easier with monolithic applications that are tagged against a specific or a fixed set of servers.

Apart from understanding the deployment topology and health, it also poses a challenge in identifying service behaviors, debugging, and identifying hotspots. Strong monitoring capabilities are required to manage such an infrastructure.

We will cover the logging and monitoring aspects in *Chapter 7, Logging and Monitoring Microservices*.

Dependency management

Dependency management is one of the key issues in large microservice deployments. How do we identify and reduce the impact of a change? How do we know whether all the dependent services are up and running? How will the service behave if one of the dependent services is not available?

Too many dependencies could raise challenges in microservices. Four important design aspects are stated as follows:

- Reducing dependencies by properly designing service boundaries.
- Reducing impacts by designing dependencies as loosely coupled as possible. Also, designing service interactions through asynchronous communication styles.
- Tackling dependency issues using patterns such as circuit breakers.
- Monitoring dependencies using visual dependency graphs.

Organization culture

One of the biggest challenges in microservices implementation is the organization culture. To harness the speed of delivery of microservices, the organization should adopt Agile development processes, continuous integration, automated QA checks, automated delivery pipelines, automated deployments, and automatic infrastructure provisioning.

Organizations following a waterfall development or heavyweight release management processes with infrequent release cycles are a challenge for microservices development. Insufficient automation is also a challenge for microservices deployment.

In short, Cloud and DevOps are supporting facets of microservice development. These are essential for successful microservices implementation.

Governance challenges

Microservices impose decentralized governance, and this is quite in contrast with the traditional SOA governance. Organizations may find it hard to come up with this change, and that could negatively impact the microservices development.

There are number of challenges that comes with a decentralized governance model. How do we understand who is consuming a service? How do we ensure service reuse? How do we define which services are available in the organization? How do we ensure enforcement of enterprise polices?

The first thing is to have a set of standards, best practices, and guidelines on how to implement better services. These should be available to the organization in the form of standard libraries, tools, and techniques. This ensures that the services developed are top quality, and that they are developed in a consistent manner.

The second important consideration is to have a place where all stakeholders can not only see all the services, but also their documentations, contracts, and service-level agreements. Swagger and API Blueprint are commonly used for handling these requirements.

Operation overheads

Microservices deployment generally increases the number of deployable units and virtual machines (or containers). This adds significant management overheads and increases the cost of operations.

With a single application, a dedicated number of containers or virtual machines in an on-premise data center may not make much sense unless the business benefit is very high. The cost generally goes down with economies of scale. A large number of microservices that are deployed in a shared infrastructure which is fully automated makes more sense, since these microservices are not tagged against any specific VMs or containers. Capabilities around infrastructure automation, provisioning, containerized deployment, and so on are essential for large scale microservices deployments. Without this automation, it would result in a significant operation overhead and increased cost.

With many microservices, the number of **configurable items** (CIs) becomes too high, and the number of servers in which these CIs are deployed might also be unpredictable. This makes it extremely difficult to manage data in a traditional **Configuration Management Database** (CMDB). In many cases, it is more useful to dynamically discover the current running topology than a statically configured CMDB-style deployment topology.

Testing microservices

Microservices also pose a challenge for the testability of services. In order to achieve a full-service functionality, one service may rely on another service, and that, in turn, on another service — either synchronously or asynchronously. The issue is how do we test an end-to-end service to evaluate its behavior? The dependent services may or may not be available at the time of testing.

Service virtualization or service mocking is one of the techniques used for testing services without actual dependencies. In testing environments, when the services are not available, mock services can simulate the behavior of the actual service. The microservices ecosystem needs service virtualization capabilities. However, this may not give full confidence, as there may by many corner cases that mock services do not simulate, especially when there are deep dependencies.

Another approach, as discussed earlier, is to use a consumer driven contract. The translated integration test cases can cover more or less all corner cases of the service invocation.

Test automation, appropriate performance testing, and continuous delivery approaches such as A/B testing, future flags, canary testing, blue-green deployments, and red-black deployments, all reduce the risks of production releases.

Infrastructure provisioning

As briefly touched on under operation overheads, manual deployment could severely challenge the microservices rollouts. If a deployment has manual elements, the deployer or operational administrators should know the running topology, manually reroute traffic, and then deploy the application one by one till all services are upgraded. With many server instances running, this could lead to significant operational overheads. Moreover, the chances of errors are high in this manual approach.

Microservices require a supporting elastic cloud-like infrastructure which can automatically provision VMs or containers, automatically deploy applications, adjust traffic flows, replicate new version to all instances, and gracefully phase out older versions. The automation also takes care of scaling up elastically by adding containers or VMs on demand, and scaling down when the load falls below threshold.

In a large deployment environment with many microservices, we may also need additional tools to manage VMs or containers that can further initiate or destroy services automatically.

The microservices capability model

Before we conclude this chapter, we will review a capability model for microservices based on the design guidelines and common pattern and solutions described in this chapter.

The following diagram depicts the microservices capability model:

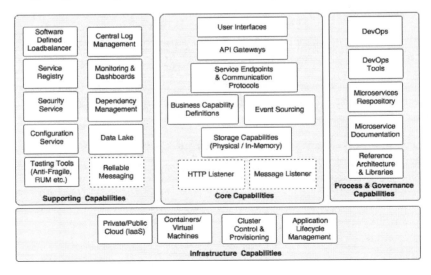

The capability model is broadly classified in to four areas:

- **Core capabilities**: These are part of the microservices themselves
- **Supporting capabilities**: These are software solutions supporting core microservice implementations
- **Infrastructure capabilities**: These are infrastructure level expectations for a successful microservices implementation
- **Governance capabilities**: These are more of process, people, and reference information

Core capabilities

The core capabilities are explained as follows:

- **Service listeners** (HTTP/messaging): If microservices are enabled for a HTTP-based service endpoint, then the HTTP listener is embedded within the microservices, thereby eliminating the need to have any external application server requirement. The HTTP listener is started at the time of the application startup. If the microservice is based on asynchronous communication, then instead of an HTTP listener, a message listener is started. Optionally, other protocols could also be considered. There may not be any listeners if the microservice is a scheduled service. Spring Boot and Spring Cloud Streams provide this capability.

- **Storage capability**: The microservices have some kind of storage mechanisms to store state or transactional data pertaining to the business capability. This is optional, depending on the capabilities that are implemented. The storage could be either a physical storage (RDBMS such as MySQL; NoSQL such as Hadoop, Cassandra, Neo 4J, Elasticsearch, and so on), or it could be an in-memory store (cache like Ehcache, data grids like Hazelcast, Infinispan, and so on)

- **Business capability definition**: This is the core of microservices, where the business logic is implemented. This could be implemented in any applicable language such as Java, Scala, Conjure, Erlang, and so on. All required business logic to fulfill the function will be embedded within the microservices themselves.

- **Event sourcing**: Microservices send out state changes to the external world without really worrying about the targeted consumers of these events. These events could be consumed by other microservices, audit services, replication services, or external applications, and the like. This allows other microservices and applications to respond to state changes.

- **Service endpoints and communication protocols**: These define the APIs for external consumers to consume. These could be synchronous endpoints or asynchronous endpoints. Synchronous endpoints could be based on REST/JSON or any other protocols such as Avro, Thrift, Protocol Buffers, and so on. Asynchronous endpoints are through Spring Cloud Streams backed by RabbitMQ, other messaging servers, or other messaging style implementations such as ZeroMQ.

- **API gateway**: The API gateway provides a level of indirection by either proxying service endpoints or composing multiple service endpoints. The API gateway is also useful for policy enforcements. It may also provide real time load balancing capabilities. There are many API gateways available in the market. Spring Cloud Zuul, Mashery, Apigee, and 3scale are some examples of the API gateway providers.

- **User interfaces**: Generally, user interfaces are also part of microservices for users to interact with the business capabilities realized by the microservices. These could be implemented in any technology, and are channel- and device-agnostic.

Infrastructure capabilities

Certain infrastructure capabilities are required for a successful deployment, and managing large scale microservices. When deploying microservices at scale, not having proper infrastructure capabilities can be challenging, and can lead to failures:

- **Cloud**: Microservices implementation is difficult in a traditional data center environment with long lead times to provision infrastructures. Even a large number of infrastructures dedicated per microservice may not be very cost effective. Managing them internally in a data center may increase the cost of ownership and cost of operations. A cloud-like infrastructure is better for microservices deployment.

- **Containers or virtual machines**: Managing large physical machines is not cost effective, and they are also hard to manage. With physical machines, it is also hard to handle automatic fault tolerance. Virtualization is adopted by many organizations because of its ability to provide optimal use of physical resources. It also provides resource isolation. It also reduces the overheads in managing large physical infrastructure components. Containers are the next generation of virtual machines. VMWare, Citrix, and so on provide virtual machine technologies. Docker, Drawbridge, Rocket, and LXD are some of the containerizer technologies.

- **Cluster control and provisioning**: Once we have a large number of containers or virtual machines, it is hard to manage and maintain them automatically. Cluster control tools provide a uniform operating environment on top of the containers, and share the available capacity across multiple services. Apache Mesos and Kubernetes are examples of cluster control systems.

- **Application lifecycle management**: Application lifecycle management tools help to invoke applications when a new container is launched, or kill the application when the container shuts down. Application life cycle management allows for script application deployments and releases. It automatically detects failure scenario, and responds to those failures thereby ensuring the availability of the application. This works in conjunction with the cluster control software. Marathon partially addresses this capability.

Supporting capabilities

Supporting capabilities are not directly linked to microservices, but they are essential for large scale microservices development:

- **Software defined load balancer**: The load balancer should be smart enough to understand the changes in the deployment topology, and respond accordingly. This moves away from the traditional approach of configuring static IP addresses, domain aliases, or cluster addresses in the load balancer. When new servers are added to the environment, it should automatically detect this, and include them in the logical cluster by avoiding any manual interactions. Similarly, if a service instance is unavailable, it should take it out from the load balancer. A combination of Ribbon, Eureka, and Zuul provide this capability in Spring Cloud Netflix.

- **Central log management**: As explored earlier in this chapter, a capability is required to centralize all logs emitted by service instances with the correlation IDs. This helps in debugging, identifying performance bottlenecks, and predictive analysis. The result of this is fed back into the life cycle manager to take corrective actions.

- **Service registry**: A service registry provides a runtime environment for services to automatically publish their availability at runtime. A registry will be a good source of information to understand the services topology at any point. Eureka from Spring Cloud, Zookeeper, and Etcd are some of the service registry tools available.

- **Security service**: A distributed microservices ecosystem requires a central server for managing service security. This includes service authentication and token services. OAuth2-based services are widely used for microservices security. Spring Security and Spring Security OAuth are good candidates for building this capability.

- **Service configuration**: All service configurations should be externalized as discussed in the Twelve-Factor application principles. A central service for all configurations is a good choice. Spring Cloud Config server, and Archaius are out-of-the-box configuration servers.

- **Testing tools (anti-fragile, RUM, and so on)**: Netflix uses Simian Army for anti-fragile testing. Matured services need consistent challenges to see the reliability of the services, and how good fallback mechanisms are. Simian Army components create various error scenarios to explore the behavior of the system under failure scenarios.

- **Monitoring and dashboards**: Microservices also require a strong monitoring mechanism. This is not just at the infrastructure-level monitoring but also at the service level. Spring Cloud Netflix Turbine, Hysterix Dashboard, and the like provide service level information. End-to-end monitoring tools like AppDynamic, New Relic, Dynatrace, and other tools like statd, Sensu, and Spigo could add value to microservices monitoring.

- **Dependency and CI management**: We also need tools to discover runtime topologies, service dependencies, and to manage configurable items. A graph-based CMDB is the most obvious tool to manage these scenarios.

- **Data lake**: As discussed earlier in this chapter, we need a mechanism to combine data stored in different microservices, and perform near real-time analytics. A data lake is a good choice for achieving this. Data ingestion tools like Spring Cloud Data Flow, Flume, and Kafka are used to consume data. HDFS, Cassandra, and the like are used for storing data.

- **Reliable messaging**: If the communication is asynchronous, we may need a reliable messaging infrastructure service such as RabbitMQ or any other reliable messaging service. Cloud messaging or messaging as a service is a popular choice in Internet scale message-based service endpoints.

Process and governance capabilities

The last piece in the puzzle is the process and governance capabilities that are required for microservices:

- **DevOps**: The key to successful implementation of microservices is to adopt DevOps. DevOps compliment microservices development by supporting Agile development, high velocity delivery, automation, and better change management.

- **DevOps tools**: DevOps tools for Agile development, continuous integration, continuous delivery, and continuous deployment are essential for successful delivery of microservices. A lot of emphasis is required on automated functioning, real user testing, synthetic testing, integration, release, and performance testing.

- **Microservices repository**: A microservices repository is where the versioned binaries of microservices are placed. These could be a simple Nexus repository or a container repository such as a Docker registry.

- **Microservice documentation**: It is important to have all microservices properly documented. Swagger or API Blueprint are helpful in achieving good microservices documentation.

- **Reference architecture and libraries**: The reference architecture provides a blueprint at the organization level to ensure that the services are developed according to certain standards and guidelines in a consistent manner. Many of these could then be translated to a number of reusable libraries that enforce service development philosophies.

Summary

In this chapter, you learned about handling practical scenarios that will arise in microservices development.

You learned various solution options and patterns that could be applied to solve common microservices problems. We reviewed a number of challenges when developing large scale microservices, and how to address those challenges effectively.

We also built a capability reference model for a microservices-based ecosystem. The capability model helps in addressing gaps when building Internet scale microservices. The capability model learned in this chapter will be the backbone for this book. The remaining chapters will deep dive into the capability model.

In the next chapter, we will take a real-world problem and model it using the microservices architecture to see how to translate our learnings into practice.

Microservices Evolution – A Case Study

Like SOA, a microservices architecture can be interpreted differently by different organizations, based on the problem in hand. Unless a sizable, real world problem is examined in detail, microservices concepts are hard to understand.

This chapter will introduce BrownField Airline (BF), a fictitious budget airline, and their journey from a monolithic **Passenger Sales and Service (PSS)** application to a next generation microservices architecture. This chapter examines the PSS application in detail, and explains the challenges, approach, and transformation steps of a monolithic system to a microservices-based architecture, adhering to the principles and practices that were explained in the previous chapter.

The intention of this case study is to get us as close as possible to a live scenario so that the architecture concepts can be set in stone.

By the end of this chapter, you will have learned about the following:

- A real world case for migrating monolithic systems to microservices-based ones, with the BrownField Airline's PSS application as an example
- Various approaches and transition strategies for migrating a monolithic application to microservices
- Designing a new futuristic microservices system to replace the PSS application using Spring Framework components

Reviewing the microservices capability model

The examples in this chapter explore the following microservices capabilities from the microservices capability model discussed in *Chapter 3, Applying Microservices Concepts*:

- **HTTP Listener**
- **Message Listener**
- **Storage Capabilities (Physical/In-Memory)**
- **Business Capability Definitions**
- **Service Endpoints & Communication Protocols**
- **User Interfaces**
- **Security Service**
- **Microservice Documentation**

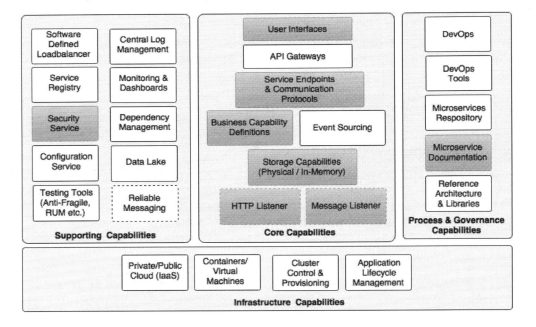

In *Chapter 2, Building Microservices with Spring Boot*, we explored all these capabilities in isolation including how to secure Spring Boot microservices. This chapter will build a comprehensive microservices example based on a real world case study.

The full source code of this chapter is available under the
`Chapter 4` projects in the code files.

Understanding the PSS application

BrownField Airline is one of the fastest growing low-cost, regional airlines, flying directly to more than 100 destinations from its hub. As a start-up airline, BrownField Airline started its operations with few destinations and few aircrafts. BrownField developed its home-grown PSS application to handle their passenger sales and services.

Business process view

This use case is considerably simplified for discussion purposes. The process view in the following diagram shows BrownField Airline's end-to-end passenger services operations covered by the current PSS solution:

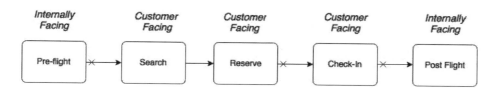

The current solution is automating certain customer-facing functions as well as certain internally facing functions. There are two internally facing functions, **Pre-flight** and **Post-flight**. **Pre-flight** functions include the planning phase, used for preparing flight schedules, plans, aircrafts, and so on. **Post-flight** functions are used by the back office for revenue management, accounting, and so on. The **Search** and **Reserve** functions are part of the online seat reservation process, and the **Check-in** function is the process of accepting passengers at the airport. The **Check-in** function is also accessible to the end users over the Internet for online check-in.

The cross marks at the beginning of the arrows in the preceding diagram indicate that they are disconnected, and occur at different timelines. For example, passengers are allowed to book 360 days in advance, whereas the check-in generally happens 24 hours before flight departure.

Functional view

The following diagram shows the functional building blocks of BrownField Airline's PSS landscape. Each business process and its related subfunctions are represented in a row:

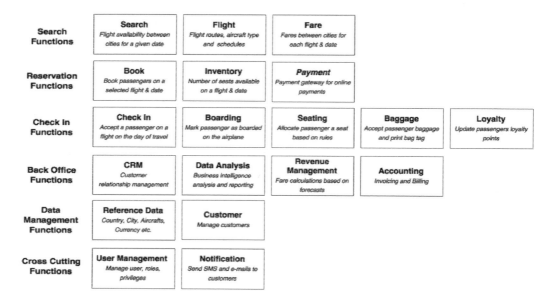

Each subfunction shown in the preceding diagram explains its role in the overall business process. Some subfunctions participate in more than one business process. For example, inventory is used in both search as well as in booking. To avoid any complication, this is not shown in the diagram. Data management and cross-cutting subfunctions are used across many business functions.

Architectural view

In order to effectively manage the end-to-end passenger operations, BrownField had developed an in-house PSS application, almost ten years back. This well-architected application was developed using Java and JEE technologies combined with the best-of-the-breed open source technologies available at the time.

The overall architecture and technologies are shown in the following diagram:

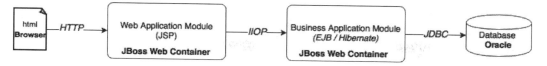

The architecture has well-defined boundaries. Also, different concerns are separated into different layers. The web application was developed as an *N*-tier, component-based modular system. The functions interact with each other through well-defined service contracts defined in the form of EJB endpoints.

Design view

The application has many logical functional groupings or subsystems. Further, each subsystem has many components organized as depicted in the next diagram:

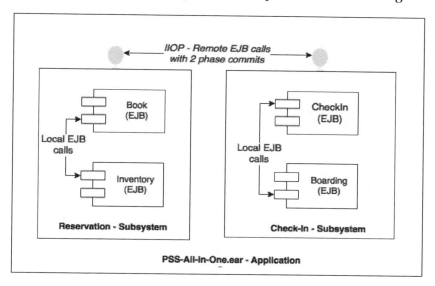

Subsystems interact with each other through remote EJB calls using the IIOP protocol. The transactional boundaries span across subsystems. Components within the subsystems communicate with each other through local EJB component interfaces. In theory, since subsystems use remote EJB endpoints, they could run on different physically separated application servers. This was one of the design goals.

Implementation view

The implementation view in the following diagram showcases the internal organization of a subsystem and its components. The purpose of the diagram is also to show the different types of artifacts:

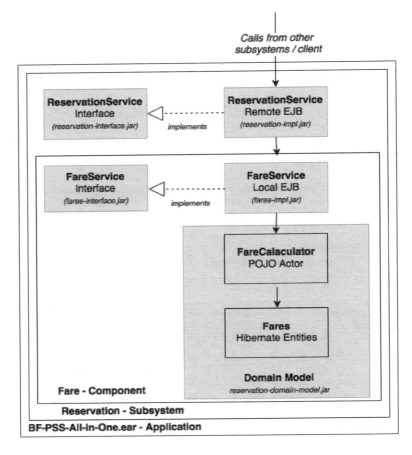

In the preceding diagram, the gray-shaded boxes are treated as different Maven projects, and translate into physical artifacts. Subsystems and components are designed adhering to the *program to an interface* principle. Interfaces are packaged as separate JAR files so that clients are abstracted from the implementations. The complexity of the business logic is buried in the domain model. Local EJBs are used as component interfaces. Finally, all subsystems are packaged into a single all-in-one EAR, and deployed in the application server.

Deployment view

The application's initial deployment was simple and straightforward as shown in the next diagram:

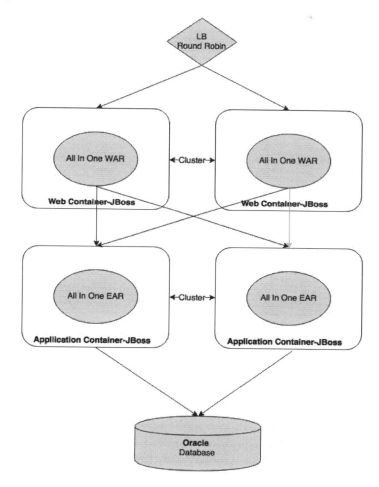

The web modules and business modules were deployed into separate application server clusters. The application was scaled horizontally by adding more and more application servers to the cluster.

Zero downtime deployments were handled by creating a standby cluster, and gracefully diverting the traffic to that cluster. The standby cluster is destroyed once the primary cluster is patched with the new version and brought back to service. Most of the database changes were designed for backward compatibility, but breaking changes were promoted with application outages.

Death of the monolith

The PSS application was performing well, successfully supporting all business requirements as well as the expected service levels. The system had no issues in scaling with the organic growth of the business in the initial years.

The business has seen tremendous growth over a period of time. The fleet size increased significantly, and new destinations got added to the network. As a result of this rapid growth, the number of bookings has gone up, resulting in a steep increase in transaction volumes, up to 200 - to 500 - fold of what was originally estimated.

Pain points

The rapid growth of the business eventually put the application under pressure. Odd stability issues and performance issues surfaced. New application releases started breaking the working code. Moreover, the cost of change and the speed of delivery started impacting the business operations profoundly.

An end-to-end architecture review was ordered, and it exposed the weaknesses of the system as well as the root causes of many failures, which were as follows:

- **Stability**: The stability issues are primarily due to stuck threads, which limit the application server's capability to accept more transactions. The stuck threads are mainly due to database table locks. Memory issues are another contributor to the stability issues. There were also issues in certain resource intensive operations that were impacting the whole application.

- **Outages**: The outage window increased largely because of the increase in server startup time. The root cause of this issue boiled down to the large size of the EAR. Message pile up during any outage windows causes heavy usage of the application immediately after an outage window. Since everything is packaged in a single EAR, any small application code change resulted in full redeployment. The complexity of the zero downtime deployment model described earlier, together with the server startup times increased both the number of outages and their duration.

- **Agility**: The complexity of the code also increased considerably over time, partially due to the lack of discipline in implementing the changes. As a result, changes became harder to implement. Also, the impact analysis became too complex to perform. As a result, inaccurate impact analysis often led to fixes that broke the working code. The application build time went up severely, from a few minutes to hours, causing unacceptable drops in development productivity. The increase in build time also led to difficulty in build automation, and eventually stopped **continuous integration** (CI) and unit testing.

Stop gap fix

Performance issues were partially addressed by applying the Y-axis scale method in the scale cube, as described in *Chapter 1, Demystifying Microservices*. The all-encompassing EAR is deployed into multiple disjoint clusters. A software proxy was installed to selectively route the traffic to designated clusters as shown in the following diagram:

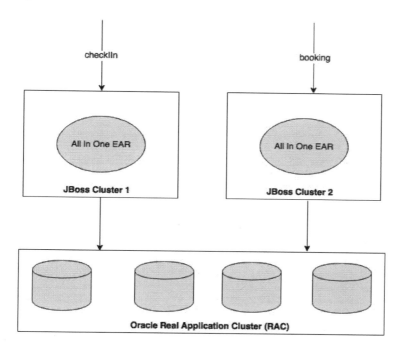

This helped BrownField's IT to scale the application servers. Therefore, the stability issues were controlled. However, this soon resulted in a bottleneck at the database level. Oracle's **Real Application Cluster (RAC)** was implemented as a solution to this problem at the database layer.

This new scaling model reduced the stability issues, but at a premium of increased complexity and cost of ownership. The technology debt also increased over a period of time, leading to a state where a complete rewrite was the only option for reducing this technology debt.

Retrospection

Although the application was well-architected, there was a clear segregation between the functional components. They were loosely coupled, programmed to interfaces, with access through standards-based interfaces, and had a rich domain model.

The obvious question is, how come such a well-architected application failed to live up to the expectations? What else could the architects have done?

It is important to understand what went wrong over a period of time. In the context of this book, it is also important to understand how microservices can avoid the recurrence of these scenarios. We will examine some of these scenarios in the subsequent sections.

Shared data

Almost all functional modules require reference data such as the airline's details, airplane details, a list of airports and cities, countries, currencies, and so on. For example, fare is calculated based on the point of origin (city), a flight is between an origin and a destination (airports), check-in is at the origin airport (airport), and so on. In some functions, the reference data is a part of the information model, whereas in some other functions, it is used for validation purposes.

Much of this reference data is neither fully static nor fully dynamic. Addition of a country, city, airport, or the like could happen when the airline introduces new routes. Aircraft reference data could change when the airline purchases a new aircraft, or changes an existing airplane's seat configuration.

One of the common usage scenarios of reference data is to filter the operational data based on certain reference data. For instance, say a user wishes to see all the flights to a country. In this case, the flow of events could be as follows: find all the cities in the selected country, then all airports in the cities, and then fire a request to get all the flights to the list of resulting airports identified in that country.

The architects considered multiple approaches when designing the system. Separating the reference data as an independent subsystem like other subsystems was one of the options considered, but this could lead to performance issues. The team took the decision to follow an exception approach for handling reference data as compared to other transactions. Considering the nature of the query patterns discussed earlier, the approach was to use the reference data as a shared library.

In this case, the subsystems were allowed to access the reference data directly using pass-by-reference semantic data instead of going through the EJB interfaces. This also meant that irrespective of the subsystems, hibernate entities could use the reference data as a part of their entity relationships:

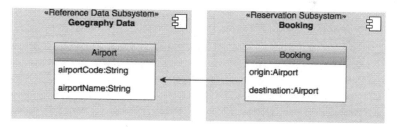

As depicted in the preceding diagram, the **Booking** entity in the reservation subsystem is allowed to use the reference data entities, in this case **Airport**, as part of their relationships.

Single database

Though enough segregation was enforced at the middle tier, all functions pointed to a single database, even to the same database schema. The single schema approach opened a plethora of issues.

Native queries

The Hibernate framework provides a good abstraction over the underlying databases. It generates efficient SQL statements, in most of the cases targeting the database using specific dialects. However, sometimes, writing native JDBC SQLs offers better performance and resource efficiency. In some cases, using native database functions gives an even better performance.

The single database approach worked well at the beginning. But over a period of time, it opened up a loophole for the developers by connecting database tables owned by different subsystems. Native JDBC SQL was a good vehicle for doing this.

The following diagram shows an example of connecting two tables owned by two subsystems using a native JDBC SQL:

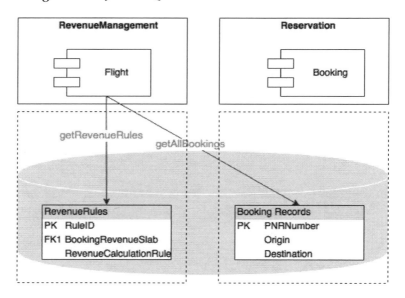

As shown in the preceding diagram, the Accounting component requires all booking records for a day, for a given city, from the Booking component to process the day-end billing. The subsystem-based design enforces Accounting to make a service call to Booking to get all booking records for a given city. Assume this results in N booking records. Now, for each booking record, Accounting has to execute a database call to find the applicable rules based on the fare code attached to each booking record. This could result in $N+1$ JDBC calls, which is inefficient. Workarounds, such as batch queries or parallel and batch executions, are available, but this would lead to increased coding efforts and higher complexity. The developers tackled this issue with a native JDBC query as an easy-to-implement shortcut. Essentially, this approach could reduce the number of calls from $N+1$ to a single database call, with minimal coding efforts.

This habit continued with many JDBC native queries connecting tables across multiple components and subsystems. This resulted not only in tightly coupled components, but also led to undocumented, hard-to-detect code.

Stored procedures

Another issue that surfaced as a result of the use of a single database was the use of complex stored procedures. Some of the complex data-centric logic written at the middle layer was not performing well, causing slow response, memory issues, and thread-blocking issues.

In order to address this problem, the developers took the decision to move some of the complex business logic from the middle tier to the database tier by implementing the logic directly within the stored procedures. This decision resulted in better performance of some of the transactions, and removed some of the stability issues. More and more procedures were added over a period of time. However, this eventually broke the application's modularity.

Domain boundaries

Though the domain boundaries were well established, all the components were packaged as a single EAR file. Since all the components were set to run on a single container, there was no stopping the developers referencing objects across these boundaries. Over a period of time, the project teams changed, delivery pressure increased, and the complexity grew tremendously. The developers started looking for quick solutions rather than the right ones. Slowly, but steadily, the modular nature of the application went away.

As depicted in the following diagram, hibernate relationships were created across subsystem boundaries:

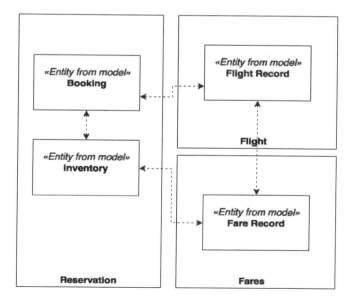

Microservices to the rescue

There are not many improvement opportunities left to support the growing demand of BrownField Airline's business. BrownField Airline was looking to re-platform the system with an evolutionary approach rather than a revolutionary model.

Microservices is an ideal choice in these situations—for transforming a legacy monolithic application with minimal disruption to the business:

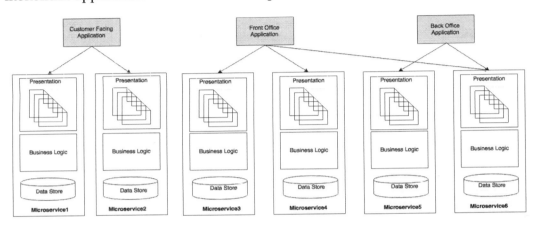

As shown in the preceding diagram, the objective is to move to a microservices-based architecture aligned to the business capabilities. Each microservice will hold the data store, the business logic, and the presentation layer.

The approach taken by BrownField Airline is to build a number of web portal applications targeting specific user communities such as customer facing, front office, and back office. The advantage of this approach lies in the flexibility for modeling, and also in the possibility to treat different communities differently. For example, the policies, architecture, and testing approaches for the Internet facing layer are different from the intranet-facing web application. Internet-facing applications may take advantage of **CDNs (Content Delivery Networks)** to move pages as close to the customer as possible, whereas intranet applications could serve pages directly from the data center.

The business case

When building business cases for migration, one of the commonly asked questions is "how does the microservices architecture avoid resurfacing of the same issues in another five years' time?"

Microservices offers a full list of benefits, which you learned in *Chapter 1, Demystifying Microservices*, but it is important to list a few here that are critical in this situation:

- **Service dependencies**: While migrating from monolithic applications to microservices, the dependencies are better known, and therefore the architects and developers are much better placed to avoid breaking dependencies and to future-proof dependency issues. Lessons from the monolithic application helps architects and developers to design a better system.

- **Physical boundaries**: Microservices enforce physical boundaries in all areas including the data store, the business logic, and the presentation layer. Access across subsystems or microservices are truly restricted due to their physical isolation. Beyond the physical boundaries, they could even run on different technologies.

- **Selective scaling**: Selective scale out is possible in microservices architecture. This provides a much more cost-effective scaling mechanism compared to the Y-scale approach used in the monolithic scenario.

- **Technology obsolescence**: Technology migrations could be applied at a microservices level rather than at the overall application level. Therefore, it does not require a humongous investment.

Plan the evolution

It is not simple to break an application that has millions of lines of code, especially if the code has complex dependencies. How do we break it? More importantly, where do we start, and how do we approach this problem?

Evolutionary approach

The best way to address this problem is to establish a transition plan, and gradually migrate the functions as microservices. At every step, a microservice will be created outside of the monolithic application, and traffic will be diverted to the new service as shown in the following diagram:

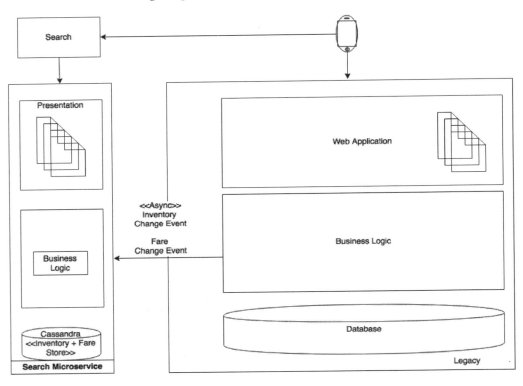

In order to run this migration successfully, a number of key questions need to be answered from the transition point of view:

- Identification of microservices' boundaries
- Prioritizing microservices for migration
- Handling data synchronization during the transition phase
- Handling user interface integration, working with old and new user interfaces

- Handling of reference data in the new system
- Testing strategy to ensure the business capabilities are intact and correctly reproduced
- Identification of any prerequisites for microservice development such as microservices capabilities, frameworks, processes, and so on

Identification of microservices boundaries

The first and foremost activity is to identify the microservices' boundaries. This is the most interesting part of the problem, and the most difficult part as well. If identification of the boundaries is not done properly, the migration could lead to more complex manageability issues.

Like in SOA, a service decomposition is the best way to identify services. However, it is important to note that decomposition stops at a business capability or bounded context. In SOA, service decomposition goes further into an atomic, granular service level.

A top-down approach is typically used for domain decomposition. The bottom-up approach is also useful in the case of breaking an existing system, as it can utilize a lot of practical knowledge, functions, and behaviors of the existing monolithic application.

The previous decomposition step will give a potential list of microservices. It is important to note that this isn't the final list of microservices, but it serves as a good starting point. We will run through a number of filtering mechanisms to get to a final list. The first cut of functional decomposition will, in this case, be similar to the diagram shown under the functional view introduced earlier in this chapter.

Analyze dependencies

The next step is to analyze the dependencies between the initial set of candidate microservices that we created in the previous section. At the end of this activity, a dependency graph will be produced.

 A team of architects, business analysts, developers, release management and support staff is required for this exercise.

One way to produce a dependency graph is to list out all the components of the legacy system and overlay dependencies. This could be done by combining one or more of the approaches listed as follows:

- Analyzing the manual code and regenerating dependencies.

- Using the experience of the development team to regenerate dependencies.

- Using a Maven dependency graph. There are a number of tools we could use to regenerate the dependency graph, such as PomExplorer, PomParser, and so on.

- Using performance engineering tools such as AppDynamics to identify the call stack and roll up dependencies.

Let us assume that we reproduce the functions and their dependencies as shown in the following diagram:

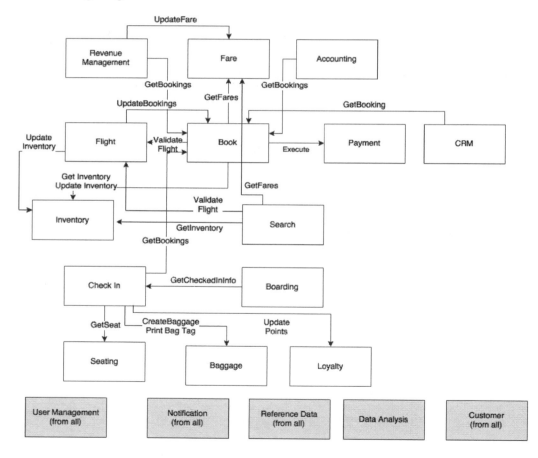

There are many dependencies going back and forth between different modules. The bottom layer shows cross-cutting capabilities that are used across multiple modules. At this point, the modules are more like spaghetti than autonomous units.

The next step is to analyze these dependencies, and come up with a better, simplified dependency map.

Events as opposed to query

Dependencies could be query-based or event-based. Event-based is better for scalable systems. Sometimes, it is possible to convert query-based communications to event-based ones. In many cases, these dependencies exist because either the business organizations are managed like that, or by virtue of the way the old system handled the business scenario.

From the previous diagram, we can extract the Revenue Management and the Fares services:

Revenue Management is a module used for calculating optimal fare values, based on the booking demand forecast. In case of a fare change between an origin and a destination, Update Fare on the Fare module is called by Revenue Management to update the respective fares in the Fare module.

An alternate way of thinking is that the Fare module is subscribed to Revenue Management for any changes in fares, and Revenue Management publishes whenever there is a fare change. This reactive programming approach gives an added flexibility by which the Fares and the Revenue Management modules could stay independent, and connect them through a reliable messaging system. This same pattern could be applied in many other scenarios from Check-In to the Loyalty and Boarding modules.

Next, examine the scenario of CRM and Booking:

This scenario is slightly different from the previously explained scenario. The CRM module is used to manage passenger complaints. When CRM receives a complaint, it retrieves the corresponding passenger's Booking data. In reality, the number of complaints are negligibly small when compared to the number of bookings. If we blindly apply the previous pattern where CRM subscribes to all bookings, we will find that it is not cost effective:

Examine another scenario between the Check-in and Booking modules. Instead of Check-in calling the Get Bookings service on Booking, can Check-in listen to booking events? This is possible, but the challenge here is that a booking can happen 360 days in advance, whereas Check-in generally starts only 24 hours before the fight departure. Duplicating all bookings and booking changes in the Check-in module 360 days in advance would not be a wise decision as Check-in does not require this data until 24 hours before the flight departure.

An alternate option is that when check-in opens for a flight (24 hours before departure), Check-in calls a service on the Booking module to get a snapshot of the bookings for a given flight. Once this is done, Check-in could subscribe for booking events specifically for that flight. In this case, a combination of query-based as well as event-based approaches is used. By doing so, we reduce the unnecessary events and storage apart from reducing the number of queries between these two services.

In short, there is no single policy that rules all scenarios. Each scenario requires logical thinking, and then the most appropriate pattern is applied.

Events as opposed to synchronous updates

Apart from the query model, a dependency could be an update transaction as well. Consider the scenario between Revenue Management and Booking:

In order to do a forecast and analysis of the current demand, Revenue Management requires all bookings across all flights. The current approach, as depicted in the dependency graph, is that Revenue Management has a schedule job that calls Get Booking on Booking to get all incremental bookings (new and changed) since the last synchronization.

An alternative approach is to send new bookings and the changes in bookings as soon as they take place in the Booking module as an asynchronous push. The same pattern could be applied in many other scenarios such as from Booking to Accounting, from Flight to Inventory, and also from Flight to Booking. In this approach, the source service publishes all state-change events to a topic. All interested parties could subscribe to this event stream and store locally. This approach removes many hard wirings, and keeps the systems loosely coupled.

The dependency is depicted in the next diagram:

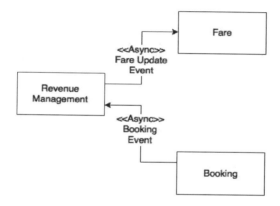

In this case depicted in the preceding diagram, we changed both dependencies and converted them to asynchronous events.

One last case to analyze is the Update Inventory call from the Booking module to the Inventory module:

When a booking is completed, the inventory status is updated by depleting the inventory stored in the Inventory service. For example, when there are 10 economy class seats available, at the end of the booking, we have to reduce it to 9. In the current system, booking and updating inventory are executed within the same transaction boundaries. This is to handle a scenario in which there is only one seat left, and multiple customers are trying to book. In the new design, if we apply the same event-driven pattern, sending the inventory update as an event to Inventory may leave the system in an inconsistent state. This needs further analysis, which we will address later in this chapter.

Challenge requirements

In many cases, the targeted state could be achieved by taking another look at the requirements:

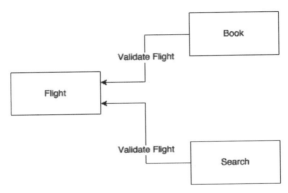

There are two Validate Flight calls, one from Booking and another one from the Search module. The Validate Flight call is to validate the input flight data coming from different channels. The end objective is to avoid incorrect data stored or serviced. When a customer does a flight search, say "BF100", the system validates this flight to see the following things:

- Whether this is a valid flight?
- Whether the flight exists on that particular date?
- Are there any booking restrictions set on this flight?

An alternate way of solving this is to adjust the inventory of the flight based on these given conditions. For example, if there is a restriction on the flight, update the inventory as zero. In this case, the intelligence will remain with Flight, and it keeps updating the inventory. As far as Search and Booking are concerned, both just look up the inventory instead of validating flights for every request. This approach is more efficient as compared to the original approach.

Next we will review the Payment use case. Payment is typically a disconnected function due to the nature of security constraints such as PCIDSS-like standards. The most obvious way to capture a payment is to redirect a browser to a payment page hosted in the Payment service. Since card handling applications come under the purview of PCIDSS, it is wise to remove any direct dependencies from the Payment service. Therefore, we can remove the Booking-to-Payment direct dependency, and opt for a UI-level integration.

Challenge service boundaries

In this section, we will review some of the service boundaries based on the requirements and dependency graph, considering Check-in and its dependencies to Seating and Baggage.

The Seating function runs a few algorithms based on the current state of the seat allocation in the airplane, and finds out the best way to position the next passenger so that the weight and balance requirements can be met. This is based on a number of predefined business rules. However, other than Check-in, no other module is interested in the Seating function. From a business capability perspective, Seating is just a function of Check-in, not a business capability by itself. Therefore, it is better to embed this logic inside Check-in itself.

The same is applicable to Baggage as well. BrownField has a separate baggage handling system. The Baggage function in the PSS context is to print the baggage tag as well as store the baggage data against the Check-in records. There is no business capability associated with this particular functionality. Therefore, it is ideal to move this function to Check-in itself.

The Book, Search, and Inventory functions, after redesigning, are shown in the following diagram:

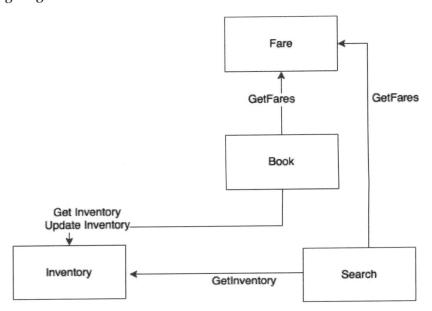

Similarly, Inventory and Search are more supporting functions of the Booking module. They are not aligned with any of the business capabilities as such. Similar to the previous judgement, it is ideal to move both the Search and Inventory functions to Booking. Assume, for the time being, that Search, Inventory, and Booking are moved to a single microservice named Reservation.

As per the statistics of BrownField, search transactions are 10 times more frequent than the booking transactions. Moreover, search is not a revenue-generating transaction when compared to booking. Due to these reasons, we need different scalability models for search and booking. Booking should not get impacted if there is a sudden surge of transactions in search. From the business point of view, dropping a search transaction in favor of saving a valid booking transaction is more acceptable.

This is an example of a polyglot requirement, which overrules the business capability alignment. In this case, it makes more sense to have Search as a service separate from the Booking service. Let us assume that we remove Search. Only Inventory and Booking remain under Reservation. Now Search has to hit back to Reservation to perform inventory searches. This could impact the booking transactions:

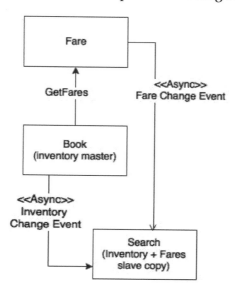

A better approach is to keep Inventory along with the Booking module, and keep a read-only copy of the inventory under Search, while continuously synchronizing the inventory data over a reliable messaging system. Since both Inventory and Booking are collocated, this will also solve the need to have two-phase commits. Since both of them are local, they could work well with local transactions.

Let us now challenge the Fare module design. When a customer searches for a flight between A and B for a given date, we would like to show the flights and fares together. That means that our read-only copy of inventory can also combine both fares as well as inventory. Search will then subscribe to Fare for any fare change events. The intelligence still stays with the Fare service, but it keeps sending fare updates to the cached fare data under Search.

Final dependency graph

There are still a few synchronized calls, which, for the time being, we will keep as they are.

By applying all these changes, the final dependency diagram will look like the following one:

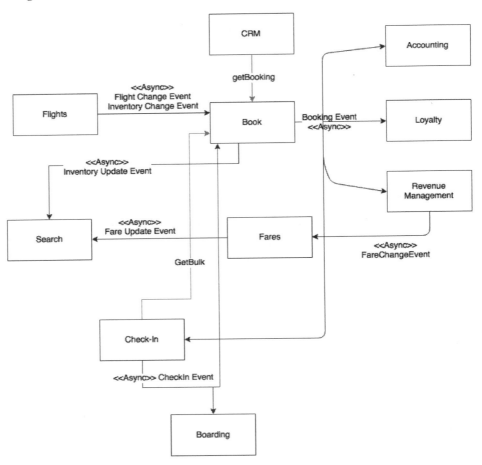

Now we can safely consider each box in the preceding diagram as a microservice. We have nailed down many dependencies, and modeled many of them as asynchronous as well. The overall system is more or less designed in the reactive style. There are still some synchronized calls shown in the diagram with bold lines, such as Get Bulk from Check-In, Get Booking from CRM, and Get Fare from Booking. These synchronous calls are essentially required as per the trade-off analysis.

Prioritizing microservices for migration

We have identified a first-cut version of our microservices-based architecture. As the next step, we will analyze the priorities, and identify the order of migration. This could be done by considering multiple factors explained as follows:

- **Dependency**: One of the parameters for deciding the priority is the dependency graph. From the service dependency graph, services with less dependency or no dependency at all are easy to migrate, whereas complex dependencies are way harder. Services with complex dependencies will also need dependent modules to be migrated along with them.

  Accounting, Loyalty, CRM, and Boarding have less dependencies as compared to Booking and Check-in. Modules with high dependencies will also have higher risks in their migration.

- **Transaction volume**: Another parameter that can be applied is analyzing the transaction volumes. Migrating services with the highest transaction volumes will relieve the load on the existing system. This will have more value from an IT support and maintenance perspective. However, the downside of this approach is the higher risk factor.

  As stated earlier, Search requests are ten times higher in volume as compared to Booking requests. Requests for Check-in are the third-highest in volume transaction after Search and Booking.

- **Resource utilization**: Resource utilization is measured based on the current utilizations such as CPU, memory, connection pools, thread pools, and so on. Migrating resource intensive services out of the legacy system provides relief to other services. This helps the remaining modules to function better.

  Flight, Revenue Management, and Accounting are resource-intensive services, as they involve data-intensive transactions such as forecasting, billing, flight schedule changes, and so on.

- **Complexity**: Complexity is perhaps measured in terms of the business logic associated with a service such as function points, lines of code, number of tables, number of services, and others. Less complex modules are easy to migrate as compared to the more complex ones.

  Booking is extremely complex as compared to the Boarding, Search, and Check-in services.

- **Business criticality**: The business criticality could be either based on revenue or customer experience. Highly critical modules deliver higher business value.

  Booking is the most revenue-generating service from the business stand point, whereas Check-in is business critical as it could lead to flight departure delays, which could lead to revenue loss as well as customer dissatisfaction.

- **Velocity of changes**: Velocity of change indicates the number of change requests targeting a function in a short time frame. This translates to speed and agility of delivery. Services with high velocity of change requests are better candidates for migration as compared to stable modules.

  Statistics show that Search, Booking, and Fares go through frequent changes, whereas Check-in is the most stable function.

- **Innovation**: Services that are part of a disruptive innovative process need to get priority over back office functions that are based on more established business processes. Innovations in legacy systems are harder to achieve as compared to applying innovations in the microservices world.

  Most of the innovations are around Search, Booking, Fares, Revenue Management, and Check-in as compared to back office Accounting.

Based on BrownField's analysis, Search has the highest priority, as it requires innovation, has high velocity of changes, is less business critical, and gives better relief for both business and IT. The Search service has minimal dependency with no requirements to synchronize data back to the legacy system.

Data synchronization during migration

During the transition phase, the legacy system and the new microservices will run in parallel. Therefore, it is important to keep the data synchronized between the two systems.

The simplest option is to synchronize the data between the two systems at the database level by using any data synchronization tool. This approach works well when both the old and the new systems are built on the same data store technologies. The complexity will be higher if the data store technologies are different. The second problem with this approach is that we allow a backdoor entry, hence exposing the microservices' internal data store outside. This is against the principle of microservices.

Let us take this on a case-by-case basis before we can conclude with a generic solution. The following diagram shows the data migration and synchronization aspect once Search is taken out:

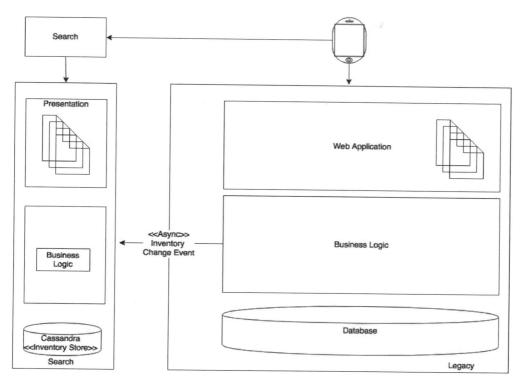

Let us assume that we use a NoSQL database for keeping inventory and fares under the Search service. In this particular case, all we need is the legacy system to supply data to the new service using asynchronous events. We will have to make some changes in the existing system to send the fare changes or any inventory changes as events. The Search service then accepts these events, and stores them locally into the local NoSQL store.

This is a bit more tedious in the case of the complex Booking service.

In this case, the new Booking microservice sends the inventory change events to the Search service. In addition to this, the legacy application also has to send the fare change events to Search. Booking will then store the new Booking service in its My SQL data store.

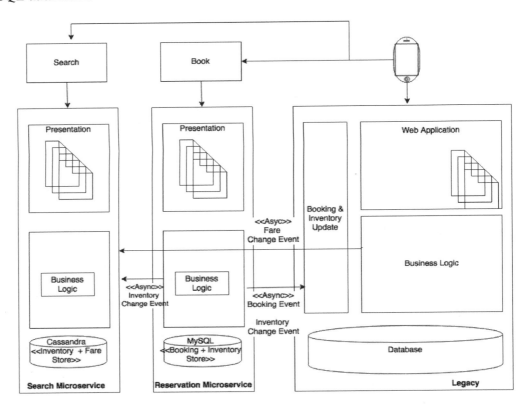

The most complex piece, the Booking service, has to send the booking events and the inventory events back to the legacy system. This is to ensure that the functions in the legacy system continue to work as before. The simplest approach is to write an update component which accepts the events and updates the old booking records table so that there are no changes required in the other legacy modules. We will continue this until none of the legacy components are referring the booking and inventory data. This will help us minimize changes in the legacy system, and therefore, reduce the risk of failures.

In short, a single approach may not be sufficient. A multi-pronged approach based on different patterns is required.

Managing reference data

One of the biggest challenges in migrating monolithic applications to microservices is managing reference data. A simple approach is to build the reference data as another microservice itself as shown in the following diagram:

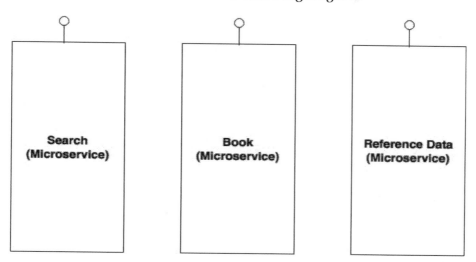

In this case, whoever needs reference data should access it through the microservice endpoints. This is a well-structured approach, but could lead to performance issues as encountered in the original legacy system.

An alternate approach is to have reference data as a microservice service for all the admin and CRUD functions. A near cache will then be created under each service to incrementally cache data from the master services. A thin reference data access proxy library will be embedded in each of these services. The reference data access proxy abstracts whether the data is coming from cache or from a remote service.

This is depicted in the next diagram. The master node in the given diagram is the actual reference data microservice:

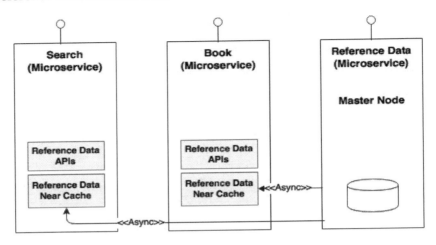

The challenge is to synchronize the data between the master and the slave. A subscription mechanism is required for those data caches that change frequently.

A better approach is to replace the local cache with an in-memory data grid, as shown in the following diagram:

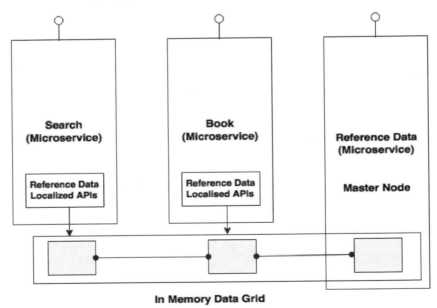

The reference data microservice will write to the data grid, whereas the proxy libraries embedded in other services will have read-only APIs. This eliminates the requirement to have subscription of data, and is much more efficient and consistent.

User interfaces and web applications

During the transition phase, we have to keep both the old and new user interfaces together. There are three general approaches usually taken in this scenario.

The first approach is to have the old and new user interfaces as separate user applications with no link between them, as depicted in the following diagram:

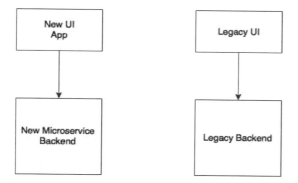

A user signs in to the new application as well as into the old application, much like two different applications, with no **single sign-on (SSO)** between them. This approach is simple, and there is no overhead. In most of the cases, this may not be acceptable to the business unless it is targeted at two different user communities.

The second approach is to use the legacy user interface as the primary application, and then transfer page controls to the new user interfaces when the user requests pages of the new application:

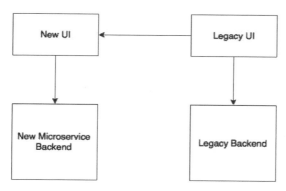

In this case, since the old and the new applications are web-based applications running in a web browser window, users will get a seamless experience. SSO has to be implemented between the old and the new user interfaces.

The third approach is to integrate the existing legacy user interface directly to the new microservices backend, as shown in the next diagram:

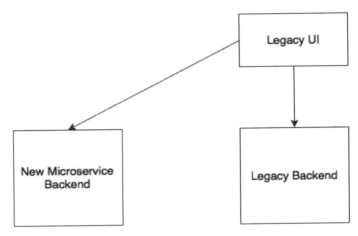

In this case, the new microservices are built as headless applications with no presentation layer. This could be challenging, as it may require many changes in the old user interface such as introducing service calls, data model conversions, and so on.

Another issue in the last two cases is how to handle the authentication of resources and services.

Session handling and security

Assume that the new services are written based on Spring Security with a token-based authorization strategy, whereas the old application uses a custom-built authentication with its local identity store.

The following diagram shows how to integrate between the old and the new services:

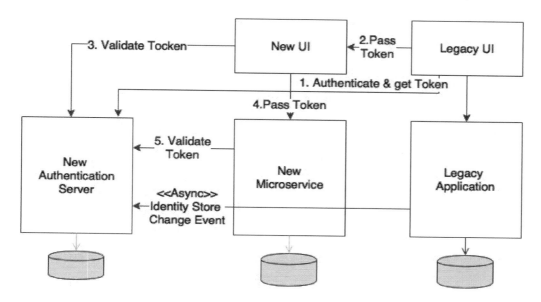

The simplest approach, as shown in the preceding diagram, is to build a new identity store with an authentication service as a new microservice using Spring Security. This will be used for all our future resource and service protections, for all microservices.

The existing user interface application authenticates itself against the new authentication service, and secures a token. This token will be passed to the new user interface or new microservice. In both cases, the user interface or microservice will make a call to the authentication service to validate the given token. If the token is valid, then the UI or microservice accepts the call.

The catch here is that the legacy identity store has to be synchronized with the new one.

Test strategy

One important question to answer from a testing point of view is how can we ensure that all functions work in the same way as before the migration?

Integration test cases should be written for the services that are getting migrated before the migration or refactoring. This ensures that once migrated, we get the same expected result, and the behavior of the system remains the same. An automated regression test pack has to be in place, and has to be executed every time we make a change in the new or old system.

In the following diagram, for each service we need one test against the EJB endpoint, and another one against the microservices endpoint:

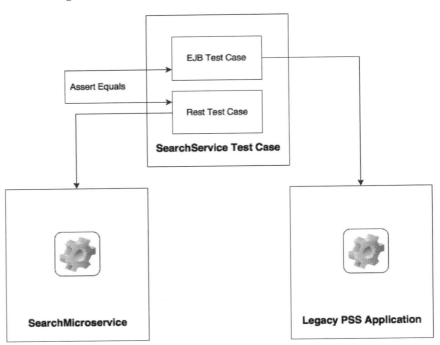

Building ecosystem capabilities

Before we embark on actual migration, we have to build all of the microservice's capabilities mentioned under the capability model, as documented in *Chapter 3, Applying Microservices Concepts*. These are the prerequisites for developing microservices-based systems.

In addition to these capabilities, certain application functions are also required to be built upfront such as reference data, security and SSO, and Customer and Notification. A data warehouse or a data lake is also required as a prerequisite. An effective approach is to build these capabilities in an incremental fashion, delaying development until it is really required.

Migrate modules only if required

In the previous chapters, we have examined approaches and steps for transforming from a monolithic application to microservices. It is important to understand that it is not necessary to migrate all modules to the new microservices architecture, unless it is really required. A major reason is that these migrations incur cost.

We will review a few such scenarios here. BrownField has already taken a decision to use an external revenue management system in place of the PSS revenue management function. BrownField is also in the process of centralizing their accounting functions, and therefore, need not migrate the accounting function from the legacy system. Migration of CRM does not add much value at this point to the business. Therefore, it is decided to keep the CRM in the legacy system itself. The business has plans to move to a SaaS-based CRM solution as part of their cloud strategy. Also note that stalling the migration halfway through could seriously impact the complexity of the system.

Target architecture

The architecture blueprint shown in the following diagram consolidates earlier discussions into an architectural view. Each block in the diagram represents a microservice. The shaded boxes are core microservices, and the others are supporting microservices. The diagram also shows the internal capabilities of each microservice. User management is moved under security in the target architecture:

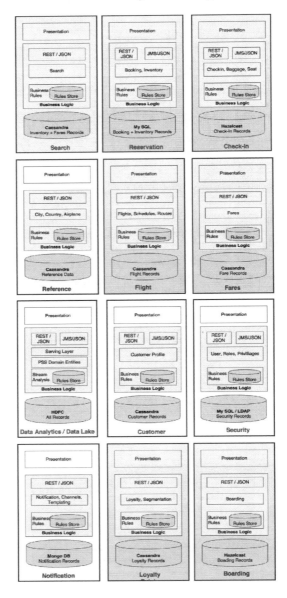

Each service has its own architecture, typically consisting of a presentation layer, one or more service endpoints, business logic, business rules, and database. As we can see, we use different selections of databases that are more suitable for each microservice. Each one is autonomous with minimal orchestration between the services. Most of the services interact with each other using the service endpoints.

Internal layering of microservices

In this section, we will further explore the internal structure of microservices. There is no standard to be followed for the internal architecture of a microservice. The rule of thumb is to abstract realizations behind simple service endpoints.

A typical structure would look like the one shown in the following diagram:

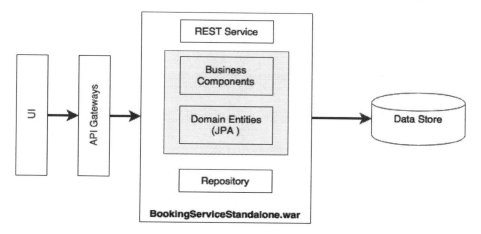

The UI accesses REST services through a service gateway. The API gateway may be one per microservice or one for many microservices—it depends on what we want to do with the API gateway. There could be one or more rest endpoints exposed by microservices. These endpoints, in turn, connect to one of the business components within the service. Business components then execute all the business functions with the help of domain entities. A repository component is used for interacting with the backend data store.

Orchestrating microservices

The logic of the booking orchestration and the execution of rules sits within the Booking service. The brain is still inside the Booking service in the form of one or more booking business components. Internally, business components orchestrate private APIs exposed by other business components or even external services:

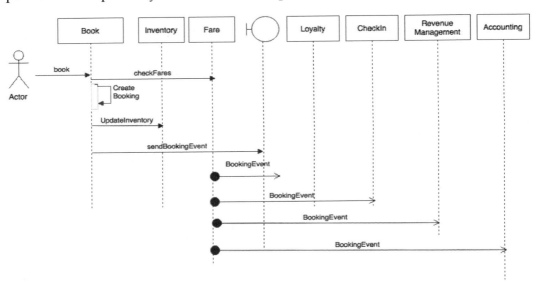

As shown in the preceding diagram, the booking service internally calls to update the inventory of its own component other than calling the Fare service.

Is there any orchestration engine required for this activity? It depends on the requirements. In complex scenarios, we may have to do a number of things in parallel. For example, creating a booking internally applies a number of booking rules, it validates the fare, and it validates the inventory before creating a booking. We may want to execute them in parallel. In such cases, we may use Java concurrency APIs or reactive Java libraries.

In extremely complex situations, we may opt for an integration framework such as Spring Integration or Apache Camel in embedded mode.

Integration with other systems

In the microservices world, we use an API gateway or a reliable message bus for integrating with other non-microservices.

Let us assume that there is another system in BrownField that needs booking data. Unfortunately, the system is not capable of subscribing to the booking events that the Booking microservice publishes. In such cases, an **Enterprise Application integration** (EAI) solution could be employed, which listens to our booking events, and then uses a native adaptor to update the database.

Managing shared libraries

Certain business logic is used in more than one microservice. Search and Reservation, in this case, use inventory rules. In such cases, these shared libraries will be duplicated in both the microservices.

Handling exceptions

Examine the booking scenario to understand the different exception handling approaches. In the following service sequence diagram, there are three lines marked with a cross mark. These are the potential areas where exceptions could occur:

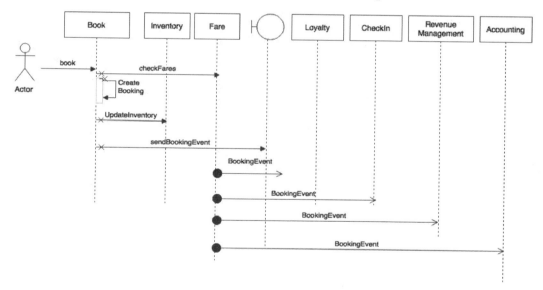

There is a synchronous communication between Booking and Fare. What if the Fare service is not available? If the Fare service is not available, throwing an error back to the user may cause revenue loss. An alternate thought is to trust the fare which comes as part of the incoming request. When we serve search, the search results will have the fare as well. When the user selects a flight and submits, the request will have the selected fare. In case the Fare service is not available, we trust the incoming request, and accept the Booking. We will use a circuit breaker and a fallback service which simply creates the booking with a special status, and queues the booking for manual action or a system retry.

What if creating the booking fails? If creating a booking fails unexpectedly, a better option is to throw a message back to the user. We could try alternative options, but that could increase the overall complexity of the system. The same is applicable for inventory updates.

In the case of creating a booking and updating the inventory, we avoid a situation where a booking is created, and an inventory update somehow fails. As the inventory is critical, it is better to have both, create booking and update inventory, to be in a local transaction. This is possible as both components are under the same subsystem.

If we consider the Check-in scenario, Check-in sends an event to Boarding and Booking as shown in the next diagram:

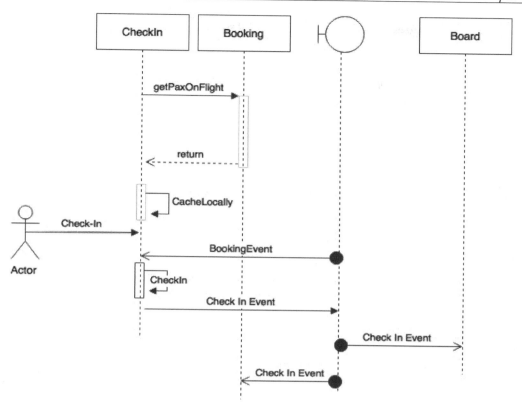

Consider a scenario where the Check-in services fail immediately after the Check-in Complete event is sent out. The other consumers processed this event, but the actual check-in is rolled back. This is because we are not using a two-phase commit. In this case, we need a mechanism for reverting that event. This could be done by catching the exception, and sending another Check-in Cancelled event.

In this case, note that to minimize the use of compensating transactions, sending the Check-in event is moved towards the end of the Check-in transaction. This reduces the chance of failure after sending out the event.

On the other hand, what if the check-in is successful, but sending the event failed? We could think of two approaches. The first approach would be to invoke a fallback service to store it locally, and then use another sweep-and-scan program to send the event at a later time. It could even retry multiple times. This could add more complexity and may not be efficient in all cases. An alternate approach is to throw the exception back to the user so that the user can retry. However, this might not always be good from a customer engagement standpoint. On the other hand, the earlier option is better for the system's health. A trade-off analysis is required to find out the best solution for the given situation.

Target implementation view

The next diagram represents the implementation view of the BrownField PSS microservices system:

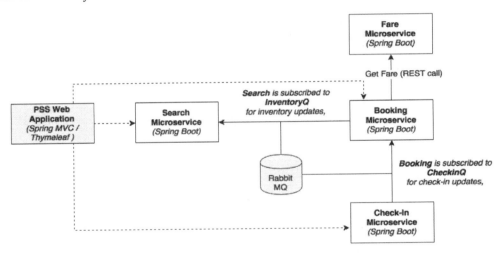

As shown in the preceding diagram, we are implementing four microservices as an example: Search, Fare, Booking, and Check-in. In order to test the application, there is a website application developed using Spring MVC with Thymeleaf templates. The asynchronous messaging is implemented with the help of RabbitMQ. In this sample implementation, the default H2 database is used as the in-memory store for demonstration purposes.

The code in this section demonstrates all the capabilities highlighted in the *Reviewing the microservices capability model* section of this chapter.

Implementation projects

The basic implementation of the BrownField Airline's PSS microservices system has five core projects as summarized in the following table. The table also shows the port range used for these projects to ensure consistency throughout the book:

Microservice	Projects	Port Range
Book microservice	`chapter4.book`	8060-8069
Check-in microservice	`chapter4.checkin`	8070-8079
Fare microservice	`chapter4.fares`	8080-8089
Search microservice	`chapter4.search`	8090-8099
Website	`chapter4.website`	8001

The website is the UI application for testing the PSS microservices.

All microservice projects in this example follow the same pattern for package structure as shown in the following screenshot:

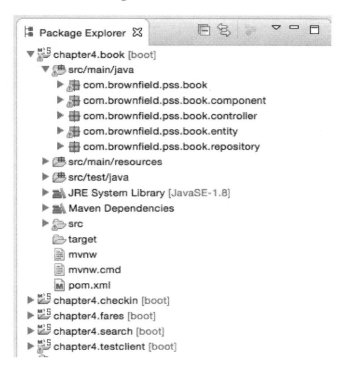

The different packages and their purposes are explained as follows:

- The root folder (`com.brownfield.pss.book`) contains the default Spring Boot application.

- The `component` package hosts all the service components where the business logic is implemented.

- The `controller` package hosts the REST endpoints and the messaging endpoints. Controller classes internally utilize the component classes for execution.

- The `entity` package contains the JPA entity classes for mapping to the database tables.

- Repository classes are packaged inside the `repository` package, and are based on Spring Data JPA.

Running and testing the project

Follow the steps listed next to build and test the microservices developed in this chapter:

1. Build each of the projects using Maven. Ensure that the `test` flag is switched off. The test programs assume other dependent services are up and running. It fails if the dependent services are not available. In our example, Booking and Fare have direct dependencies. We will learn how to circumvent this dependency in *Chapter 7, Logging and Monitoring Microservices*:

   ```
   mvn -Dmaven.test.skip=true install
   ```

2. Run the RabbitMQ server:

   ```
   rabbitmq_server-3.5.6/sbin$ ./rabbitmq-server
   ```

3. Run the following commands in separate terminal windows:

   ```
   java -jar target/fares-1.0.jar
   java -jar target/search-1.0.jar
   java -jar target/checkin-1.0.jar
   java -jar target/book-1.0.jar
   java -jar target/website-1.0.jar
   ```

4. The website project has a `CommandLineRunner`, which executes all the test cases at startup. Once all the services are successfully started, open `http://localhost:8001` in a browser.

5. The browser asks for basic security credentials. Use `guest` or `guest123` as the credentials. This example only shows the website security with a basic authentication mechanism. As explained in *Chapter 2, Building Microservices with Spring Boot*, service-level security can be achieved using OAuth2.

6. Entering the correct security credentials displays the following screen. This is the home screen of our BrownField PSS application:

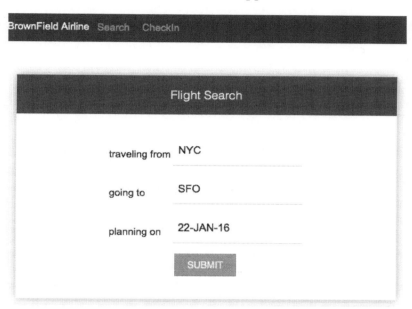

7. The **SUBMIT** button invokes the Search microservice to fetch the available flights that meet the conditions mentioned on the screen. A few flights are pre-populated at the startup of the Search microservice. Edit the Search microservice code to feed in additional flights, if required.

8. The output screen with a list of flights is shown in the next screenshot. The **Book** link will take us to the booking screen for the selected flight:

9. The following screenshot shows the booking screen. The user can enter the passenger details, and create a booking by clicking on the **CONFIRM** button. This invokes the Booking microservice, and internally, the Fare service as well. It also sends a message back to the Search microservice:

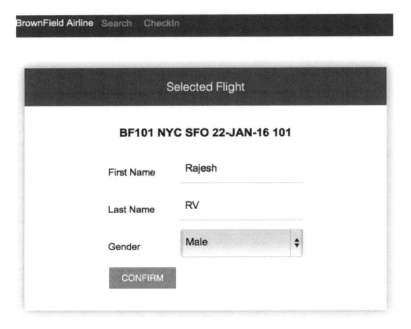

10. If booking is successful, the next confirmation screen is displayed with a booking reference number:

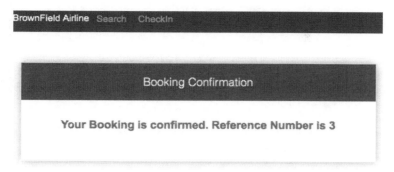

11. Let us test the Check-in microservice. This can be done by clicking on **CheckIn** in the menu at the top of the screen. Use the booking reference number obtained in the previous step to test Check-in. This is shown in the following screenshot:

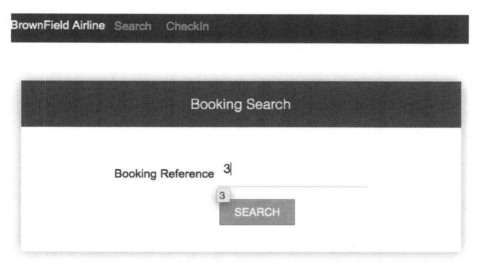

12. Clicking on the **SEARCH** button in the previous screen invokes the Booking microservice, and retrieves the booking information. Click on the **CheckIn** link to perform the check-in. This invokes the Check-in microservice:

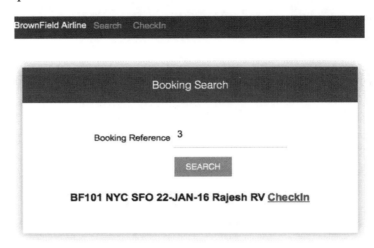

13. If check-in is successful, it displays the confirmation message, as shown in the next screenshot, with a confirmation number. This is done by calling the Check-in service internally. The Check-in service sends a message to Booking to update the check-in status:

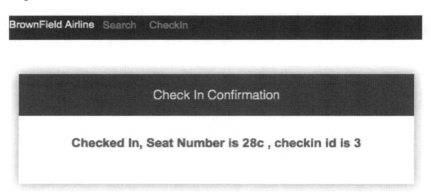

Summary

In this chapter, we implemented and tested the BrownField PSS microservice with basic Spring Boot capabilities. We learned how to approach a real use case with a microservices architecture.

We examined the various stages of a real-world evolution towards microservices from a monolithic application. We also evaluated the pros and cons of multiple approaches, and the obstacles encountered when migrating a monolithic application. Finally, we explained the end-to-end microservices design for the use case that we examined. Design and implementation of a fully-fledged microservice implementation was also validated.

In the next chapter, we will see how the Spring Cloud project helps us to transform the developed BrownField PSS microservices to an Internet-scale deployment.

5
Scaling Microservices with Spring Cloud

In order to manage Internet-scale microservices, one requires more capabilities than what are offered by the Spring Boot framework. The Spring Cloud project has a suite of purpose-built components to achieve these additional capabilities effortlessly.

This chapter will provide a deep insight into the various components of the Spring Cloud project such as Eureka, Zuul, Ribbon, and Spring Config by positioning them against the microservices capability model discussed in *Chapter 3, Applying Microservices Concepts*. It will demonstrate how the Spring Cloud components help to scale the BrownField Airline's PSS microservices system, developed in the previous chapter.

By the end of this chapter, you will learn about the following:

- The Spring Config server for externalizing configuration
- The Eureka server for service registration and discovery
- The relevance of Zuul as a service proxy and gateway
- The implementation of automatic microservice registration and service discovery
- Spring Cloud messaging for asynchronous microservice composition

Reviewing microservices capabilities

The examples in this chapter explore the following microservices capabilities from the microservices capability model discussed in *Chapter 3, Applying Microservices Concepts*:

- **Software Defined Load Balancer**
- **Service Registry**
- **Configuration Service**
- **Reliable Cloud Messaging**
- **API Gateways**

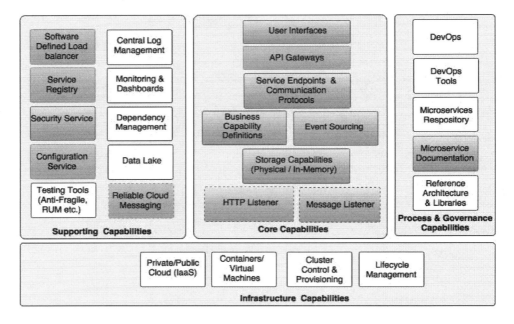

Reviewing BrownField's PSS implementation

In *Chapter 4, Microservices Evolution – A Case Study*, we designed and developed a microservice-based PSS system for BrownField Airlines using the Spring framework and Spring Boot. The implementation is satisfactory from the development point of view, and it serves the purpose for low volume transactions. However, this is not good enough for deploying large, enterprise-scale deployments with hundreds or even thousands of microservices.

In *Chapter 4, Microservices Evolution – A Case Study*, we developed four microservices: Search, Booking, Fares, and Check-in. We also developed a website to test the microservices.

We have accomplished the following items in our microservice implementation so far:

- Each microservice exposes a set of REST/JSON endpoints for accessing business capabilities

- Each microservice implements certain business functions using the Spring framework.

- Each microservice stores its own persistent data using H2, an in-memory database

- Microservices are built with Spring Boot, which has an embedded Tomcat server as the HTTP listener

- RabbitMQ is used as an external messaging service. Search, Booking, and Check-in interact with each other through asynchronous messaging

- Swagger is integrated with all microservices for documenting the REST APIs.

- An OAuth2-based security mechanism is developed to protect the microservices

What is Spring Cloud?

The Spring Cloud project is an umbrella project from the Spring team that implements a set of common patterns required by distributed systems, as a set of easy-to-use Java Spring libraries. Despite its name, Spring Cloud by itself is not a cloud solution. Rather, it provides a number of capabilities that are essential when developing applications targeting cloud deployments that adhere to the Twelve-Factor application principles. By using Spring Cloud, developers just need to focus on building business capabilities using Spring Boot, and leverage the distributed, fault-tolerant, and self-healing capabilities available out of the box from Spring Cloud.

The Spring Cloud solutions are agnostic to the deployment environment, and can be developed and deployed in a desktop PC or in an elastic cloud. The cloud-ready solutions that are developed using Spring Cloud are also agnostic and portable across many cloud providers such as Cloud Foundry, AWS, Heroku, and so on. When not using Spring Cloud, developers will end up using services natively provided by the cloud vendors, resulting in deep coupling with the PaaS providers. An alternate option for developers is to write quite a lot of boilerplate code to build these services. Spring Cloud also provides simple, easy-to-use Spring-friendly APIs, which abstract the cloud provider's service APIs such as those APIs coming with AWS Notification Service.

Built on Spring's "convention over configuration" approach, Spring Cloud defaults all configurations, and helps the developers get off to a quick start. Spring Cloud also hides the complexities, and provides simple declarative configurations to build systems. The smaller footprints of the Spring Cloud components make it developer friendly, and also make it easy to develop cloud-native applications.

Spring Cloud offers many choices of solutions for developers based on their requirements. For example, the service registry can be implemented using popular options such as Eureka, ZooKeeper, or Consul. The components of Spring Cloud are fairly decoupled, hence, developers get the flexibility to pick and choose what is required.

What is the difference between Spring Cloud and Cloud Foundry?

Spring Cloud is a developer kit for developing Internet-scale Spring Boot applications, whereas Cloud Foundry is an open-source Platform as a Service for building, deploying, and scaling applications.

Spring Cloud releases

The Spring Cloud project is an overarching Spring project that includes a combination of different components. The versions of these components are defined in the `spring-cloud-starter-parent` BOM.

In this book, we are relying on the `Brixton.RELEASE` version of the Spring Cloud:

```
<dependency>
  <groupId>org.springframework.cloud</groupId>
  <artifactId>spring-cloud-dependencies</artifactId>
  <version>Brixton.RELEASE</version>
  <type>pom</type>
  <scope>import</scope>
</dependency>
```

The `spring-cloud-starter-parent` defines different versions of its subcomponents as follows:

```
<spring-cloud-aws.version>1.1.0.RELEASE</spring-cloud-aws.version>
<spring-cloud-bus.version>1.1.0.RELEASE</spring-cloud-bus.version>
<spring-cloud-cloudfoundry.version>1.0.0.RELEASE</spring-cloud-
cloudfoundry.version>
<spring-cloud-commons.version>1.1.0.RELEASE</spring-cloud-commons.
version>
<spring-cloud-config.version>1.1.0.RELEASE</spring-cloud-config.
version>
<spring-cloud-netflix.version>1.1.0.RELEASE</spring-cloud-netflix.
version>
```

```
<spring-cloud-security.version>1.1.0.RELEASE</spring-cloud-security.
version>
<spring-cloud-cluster.version>1.0.0.RELEASE</spring-cloud-cluster.
version>
<spring-cloud-consul.version>1.0.0.RELEASE</spring-cloud-consul.
version>
<spring-cloud-sleuth.version>1.0.0.RELEASE</spring-cloud-sleuth.
version>
<spring-cloud-stream.version>1.0.0.RELEASE</spring-cloud-stream.
version>
<spring-cloud-zookeeper.version>1.0.0.RELEASE </spring-cloud-
zookeeper.version>
```

The names of the Spring Cloud releases are in an alphabetic sequence, starting with A, following the names of the London Tube stations. **Angel** was the first release, and **Brixton** is the second release.

Components of Spring Cloud

Each Spring Cloud component specifically addresses certain distributed system capabilities. The grayed-out boxes at the bottom of the following diagram show the capabilities, and the boxes placed on top of these capabilities showcase the Spring Cloud subprojects addressing these capabilities:

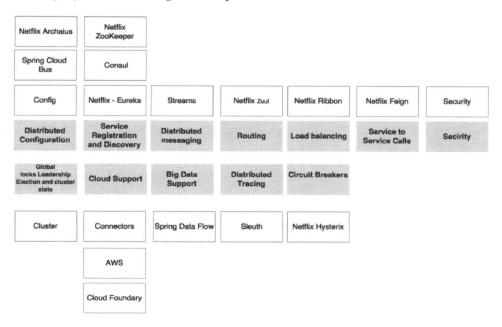

The Spring Cloud capabilities are explained as follows:

- **Distributed configuration**: Configuration properties are hard to manage when there are many microservice instances running under different profiles such as development, test, production, and so on. It is, therefore, important to manage them centrally, in a controlled way. The distributed configuration management module is to externalize and centralize microservice configuration parameters. Spring Cloud Config is an externalized configuration server with Git or SVN as the backing repository. Spring Cloud Bus provides support for propagating configuration changes to multiple subscribers, generally a microservice instance. Alternately, ZooKeeper or HashiCorp's Consul can also be used for distributed configuration management.

- **Routing**: Routing is an API gateway component, primarily used similar to a reverse proxy that forwards requests from consumers to service providers. The gateway component can also perform software-based routing and filtering. Zuul is a lightweight API gateway solution that offers fine-grained controls to developers for traffic shaping and request/response transformations.

- **Load balancing**: The load balancer capability requires a software-defined load balancer module which can route requests to available servers using a variety of load balancing algorithms. Ribbon is a Spring Cloud subproject which supports this capability. Ribbon can work as a standalone component, or integrate and work seamlessly with Zuul for traffic routing.

- **Service registration and discovery**: The service registration and discovery module enables services to programmatically register with a repository when a service is available and ready to accept traffic. The microservices advertise their existence, and make them discoverable. The consumers can then look up the registry to get a view of the service availability and the endpoint locations. The registry, in many cases, is more or less a dump. But the components around the registry make the ecosystem intelligent. There are many subprojects existing under Spring Cloud which support registry and discovery capability. Eureka, ZooKeeper, and Consul are three subprojects implementing the registry capability.

- **Service-to-service calls**: The Spring Cloud Feign subproject under Spring Cloud offers a declarative approach for making RESTful service-to-service calls in a synchronous way. The declarative approach allows applications to work with **POJO (Plain Old Java Object)** interfaces instead of low-level HTTP client APIs. Feign internally uses reactive libraries for communication.

- **Circuit breaker**: The circuit breaker subproject implements the circuit breaker pattern. The circuit breaker breaks the circuit when it encounters failures in the primary service by diverting traffic to another temporary fallback service. It also automatically reconnects back to the primary service when the service is back to normal. It finally provides a monitoring dashboard for monitoring the service state changes. The Spring Cloud Hystrix project and Hystrix Dashboard implement the circuit breaker and the dashboard respectively.

- **Global locks, leadership election and cluster state**: This capability is required for cluster management and coordination when dealing with large deployments. It also offers global locks for various purposes such as sequence generation. The Spring Cloud Cluster project implements these capabilities using Redis, ZooKeeper, and Consul.

- **Security**: Security capability is required for building security for cloud-native distributed systems using externalized authorization providers such as OAuth2. The Spring Cloud Security project implements this capability using customizable authorization and resource servers. It also offers SSO capabilities, which are essential when dealing with many microservices.

- **Big data support**: The big data support capability is a capability that is required for data services and data flows in connection with big data solutions. The Spring Cloud Streams and the Spring Cloud Data Flow projects implement these capabilities. The Spring Cloud Data Flow is the re-engineered version of Spring XD.

- **Distributed tracing**: The distributed tracing capability helps to thread and correlate transitions that are spanned across multiple microservice instances. Spring Cloud Sleuth implements this by providing an abstraction on top of various distributed tracing mechanisms such as Zipkin and HTrace with the support of a 64-bit ID.

- **Distributed messaging**: Spring Cloud Stream provides declarative messaging integration on top of reliable messaging solutions such as Kafka, Redis, and RabbitMQ.

- **Cloud support**: Spring Cloud also provides a set of capabilities that offers various connectors, integration mechanisms, and abstraction on top of different cloud providers such as the Cloud Foundry and AWS.

Spring Cloud and Netflix OSS

Many of the Spring Cloud components which are critical for microservices' deployment came from the **Netflix Open Source Software** (**Netflix OSS**) center. Netflix is one of the pioneers and early adaptors in the microservices space. In order to manage large scale microservices, engineers at Netflix came up with a number of homegrown tools and techniques for managing their microservices. These are fundamentally crafted to fill some of the software gaps recognized in the AWS platform for managing Netflix services. Later, Netflix open-sourced these components, and made them available under the Netflix OSS platform for public use. These components are extensively used in production systems, and are battle-tested with large scale microservice deployments at Netflix.

Spring Cloud offers higher levels of abstraction for these Netflix OSS components, making it more Spring developer friendly. It also provides a declarative mechanism, well-integrated and aligned with Spring Boot and the Spring framework.

Setting up the environment for BrownField PSS

In this chapter, we will amend the BrownField PSS microservices developed in *Chapter 4*, *Microservices Evolution – A Case Study*, using Spring Cloud capabilities. We will also examine how to make these services enterprise grade using Spring Cloud components.

Subsequent sections of this chapter will explore how to scale the microservices developed in the previous chapter for cloud scale deployments, using some out-of-the-box capabilities provided by the Spring Cloud project. The rest of this chapter will explore Spring Cloud capabilities such as configuration using the Spring Config server, Ribbon-based service load balancing, service discovery using Eureka, Zuul for API gateway, and finally, Spring Cloud messaging for message-based service interactions. We will demonstrate the capabilities by modifying the BrownField PSS microservices developed in *Chapter 4*, *Microservices Evolution – A Case Study*.

In order to prepare the environment for this chapter, import and rename (chapter4.* to chapter5.*) projects into a new STS workspace.

 The full source code of this chapter is available under the Chapter 5 projects in the code files.

Spring Cloud Config

The Spring Cloud Config server is an externalized configuration server in which applications and services can deposit, access, and manage all runtime configuration properties. The Spring Config server also supports version control of the configuration properties.

In the earlier examples with Spring Boot, all configuration parameters were read from a property file packaged inside the project, either `application.properties` or `application.yaml`. This approach is good, since all properties are moved out of code to a property file. However, when microservices are moved from one environment to another, these properties need to undergo changes, which require an application re-build. This is violation of one of the Twelve-Factor application principles, which advocate one-time build and moving of the binaries across environments.

A better approach is to use the concept of profiles. Profiles, as discussed in *Chapter 2, Building Microservices with Spring Boot*, is used for partitioning different properties for different environments. The profile-specific configuration will be named `application-{profile}.properties`. For example, `application-development.properties` represents a property file targeted for the development environment.

However, the disadvantage of this approach is that the configurations are statically packaged along with the application. Any changes in the configuration properties require the application to be rebuilt.

There are alternate ways to externalize the configuration properties from the application deployment package. Configurable properties can also be read from an external source in a number of ways:

- From an external JNDI server using JNDI namespace (`java:comp/env`)
- Using the Java system properties (`System.getProperties()`) or using the `-D` command line option
- Using the `PropertySource` configuration:
  ```
  @PropertySource("file:${CONF_DIR}/application.properties")
    public class ApplicationConfig {
  }
  ```
- Using a command-line parameter pointing a file to an external location:
  ```
  java -jar myproject.jar --spring.config.location=
  ```

JNDI operations are expensive, lack flexibility, have difficulties in replication, and are not version controlled. `System.properties` is not flexible enough for large-scale deployments. The last two options rely on a local or a shared filesystem mounted on the server.

For large scale deployments, a simple yet powerful centralized configuration management solution is required:

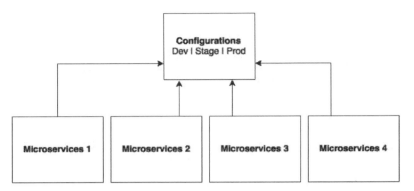

As shown in the preceding diagram, all microservices point to a central server to get the required configuration parameters. The microservices then locally cache these parameters to improve performance. The Config server propagates the configuration state changes to all subscribed microservices so that the local cache's state can be updated with the latest changes. The Config server also uses profiles to resolve values specific to an environment.

As shown in the following screenshot, there are multiple options available under the Spring Cloud project for building the configuration server. **Config Server**, **Zookeeper Configuration**, and **Consul Configuration** are available as options. However, this chapter will only focus on the Spring Config server implementation:

Cloud Config

☐ Config Client
  spring-cloud-config Client

☐ Config Server
  Central management for configuration via a git or svn backend

☐ Zookeeper Configuration
  Configuration management with Zookeeper and spring-cloud-zookeeper-config

☐ Consul Configuration
  Configuration management with Hashicorp Consul

The Spring Config server stores properties in a version-controlled repository such as Git or SVN. The Git repository can be local or remote. A highly available remote Git server is preferred for large scale distributed microservice deployments.

The Spring Cloud Config server architecture is shown in the following diagram:

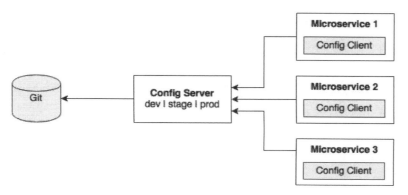

As shown in the preceding diagram, the Config client embedded in the Spring Boot microservices does a configuration lookup from a central configuration server using a simple declarative mechanism, and stores properties into the Spring environment. The configuration properties can be application-level configurations such as trade limit per day, or infrastructure-related configurations such as server URLs, credentials, and so on.

Unlike Spring Boot, Spring Cloud uses a bootstrap context, which is a parent context of the main application. Bootstrap context is responsible for loading configuration properties from the Config server. The bootstrap context looks for bootstrap.yaml or bootstrap.properties for loading initial configuration properties. To make this work in a Spring Boot application, rename the application.* file to bootstrap.*.

What's next?

The next few sections demonstrate how to use the Config server in a real-world scenario. In order to do this, we will modify our search microservice (`chapter5.search`) to use the Config server. The following diagram depicts the scenario:

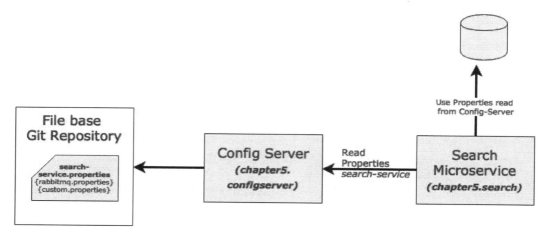

In this example, the Search service will read the Config server at startup by passing the service name. In this case, the service name of the search service will be `search-service`. The properties configured for the `search-service` include the RabbitMQ properties as well as a custom property.

 The full source code of this section is available under the `chapter5.configserver` project in the code files.

Setting up the Config server

The following steps need to be followed to create a new Config server using STS:

1. Create a new **Spring Starter Project**, and select **Config Server** and **Actuator** as shown in the following diagram:

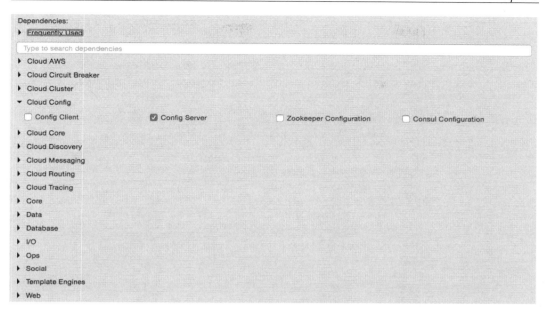

2. Set up a Git repository. This can be done by pointing to a remote Git configuration repository like the one at `https://github.com/spring-cloud-samples/config-repo`. This URL is an indicative one, a Git repository used by the Spring Cloud examples. We will have to use our own Git repository instead.

3. Alternately, a local filesystem-based Git repository can be used. In a real production scenario, an external Git is recommended. The Config server in this chapter will use a local filesystem-based Git repository for demonstration purposes.

4. Enter the commands listed next to set up a local Git repository:

```
$ cd $HOME
$ mkdir config-repo
$ cd config-repo
$ git init .
$ echo message : helloworld > application.properties
$ git add -A .
$ git commit -m "Added sample application.properties"
```

This code snippet creates a new Git repository on the local filesystem. A property file named `application.properties` with a `message` property and value `helloworld` is also created.

The file `application.properties` is created for demonstration purposes. We will change this in the subsequent sections.

5. The next step is to change the configuration in the Config server to use the Git repository created in the previous step. In order to do this, rename the file `application.properties` to `bootstrap.properties`:

6. Edit the contents of the new `bootstrap.properties` file to match the following:

```
server.port=8888
spring.cloud.config.server.git.uri: file://${user.home}/config-
repo
```

Port `8888` is the default port for the Config server. Even without configuring `server.port`, the Config server should bind to `8888`. In the Windows environment, an extra `/` is required in the file URL.

7. Optionally, rename the default package of the auto-generated `Application.java` from `com.example` to `com.brownfield.configserver`. Add `@EnableConfigServer` in `Application.java`:

```
@EnableConfigServer
@SpringBootApplication
public class ConfigserverApplication {
```

8. Run the Config server by right-clicking on the project, and running it as a Spring Boot app.

9. Visit `http://localhost:8888/env` to see whether the server is running. If everything is fine, this will list all environment configurations. Note that `/env` is an actuator endpoint.

10. Check `http://localhost:8888/application/default/master` to see the properties specific to `application.properties`, which were added in the earlier step. The browser will display the properties configured in `application.properties`. The browser should display contents similar to the following:

```
{"name":"application","profiles":["default"],"label":"master","ver
sion":"6046fd2ff4fa09d3843767660d963866ffcc7d28","propertySources"
:[{"name":"file:///Users/rvlabs /config-repo /application.properti
es","source":{"message":"helloworld"}}]}
```

Understanding the Config server URL

In the previous section, we used `http://localhost:8888/application/default/master` to explore the properties. How do we interpret this URL?

The first element in the URL is the application name. In the given example, the application name should be `application`. The application name is a logical name given to the application, using the `spring.application.name` property in `bootstrap.properties` of the Spring Boot application. Each application must have a unique name. The Config server will use the name to resolve and pick up appropriate properties from the Config server repository. The application name is also sometimes referred to as service ID. If there is an application with the name `myapp`, then there should be a `myapp.properties` in the configuration repository to store all the properties related to that application.

The second part of the URL represents the profile. There can be more than one profile configured within the repository for an application. The profiles can be used in various scenarios. The two common scenarios are segregating different environments such as `Dev`, `Test`, `Stage`, `Prod`, and the like, or segregating server configurations such as `Primary`, `Secondary`, and so on. The first one represents different environments of an application, whereas the second one represents different servers where an application is deployed.

The profile names are logical names that will be used for matching the file name in the repository. The default profile is named `default`. To configure properties for different environments, we have to configure different files as given in the following example. In this example, the first file is for the development environment whereas the second is for the production environment:

```
application-development.properties
application-production.properties
```

These are accessible using the following URLs respectively:

- `http://localhost:8888/application/development`
- `http://localhost:8888/application/production`

The last part of the URL is the label, and is named `master` by default. The label is an optional Git label that can be used, if required.

In short, the URL is based on the following pattern: `http://localhost:8888/{name}/{profile}/{label}`.

The configuration can also be accessed by ignoring the profile. In the preceding example, all the following three URLs point to the same configuration:

- `http://localhost:8888/application/default`
- `http://localhost:8888/application/master`
- `http://localhost:8888/application/default/master`

There is an option to have different Git repositories for different profiles. This makes sense for production systems, since the access to different repositories could be different.

Accessing the Config Server from clients

In the previous section, a Config server is set up and accessed using a web browser. In this section, the Search microservice will be modified to use the Config server. The Search microservice will act as a Config client.

Follow these steps to use the Config server instead of reading properties from the `application.properties` file:

1. Add the Spring Cloud Config dependency and the actuator (if the actuator is not already in place) to the `pom.xml` file. The actuator is mandatory for refreshing the configuration properties:

   ```
   <dependency>
     <groupId>org.springframework.cloud</groupId>
     <artifactId>spring-cloud-starter-config</artifactId>
   </dependency>
   ```

2. Since we are modifying the Spring Boot Search microservice from the earlier chapter, we will have to add the following to include the Spring Cloud dependencies. This is not required if the project is created from scratch:

   ```
   <dependencyManagement>
     <dependencies>
       <dependency>
   ```

```
        <groupId>org.springframework.cloud</groupId>
        <artifactId>spring-cloud-dependencies</artifactId>
        <version>Brixton.RELEASE</version>
        <type>pom</type>
        <scope>import</scope>
      </dependency>
    </dependencies>
  </dependencyManagement>
```

3. The next screenshot shows the Cloud starter library selection screen. If the application is built from the ground up, select the libraries as shown in the following screenshot:

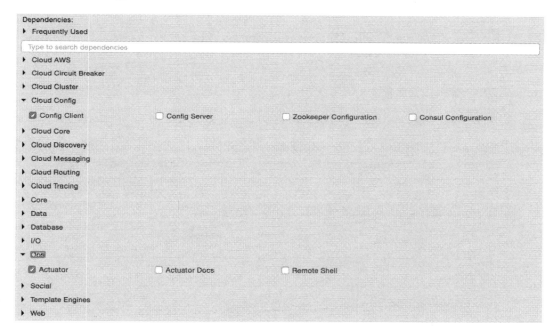

4. Rename `application.properties` to `bootstrap.properties`, and add an application name and a configuration server URL. The configuration server URL is not mandatory if the Config server is running on the default port (`8888`) on the local host:

The new `bootstrap.properties` file will look as follows:

```
spring.application.name=search-service
spring.cloud.config.uri=http://localhost:8888

server.port=8090
```

```
spring.rabbitmq.host=localhost
spring.rabbitmq.port=5672
spring.rabbitmq.username=guest
spring.rabbitmq.password=guest
```

`search-service` is a logical name given to the Search microservice. This will be treated as service ID. The Config server will look for `search-service.` `properties` in the repository to resolve the properties.

5. Create a new configuration file for `search-service`. Create a new `search-service.properties` under the `config-repo` folder where the Git repository is created. Note that `search-service` is the service ID given to the Search microservice in the `bootstrap.properties` file. Move service-specific properties from `bootstrap.properties` to the new `search-service.` `properties` file. The following properties will be removed from `bootstrap.` `properties`, and added to `search-service.properties`:

```
spring.rabbitmq.host=localhost
spring.rabbitmq.port=5672
spring.rabbitmq.username=guest
spring.rabbitmq.password=guest
```

6. In order to demonstrate the centralized configuration of properties and propagation of changes, add a new application-specific property to the property file. We will add `originairports.shutdown` to temporarily take out an airport from the search. Users will not get any flights when searching for an airport mentioned in the shutdown list:

```
originairports.shutdown=SEA
```

In this example, we will not return any flights when searching with SEA as origin.

7. Commit this new file into the Git repository by executing the following commands:

```
git add -A .
git commit -m "adding new configuration"
```

8. The final `search-service.properties` file should look as follows:

```
spring.rabbitmq.host=localhost
spring.rabbitmq.port=5672
spring.rabbitmq.username=guest
spring.rabbitmq.password=guest
originairports.shutdown:SEA
```

9. The `chapter5.search` project's `bootstrap.properties` should look like the following:

```
spring.application.name=search-service
server.port=8090
spring.cloud.config.uri=http://localhost:8888
```

10. Modify the Search microservice code to use the configured parameter, `originairports.shutdown`. A `RefreshScope` annotation has to be added at the class level to allow properties to be refreshed when there is a change. In this case, we are adding a refresh scope to the `SearchRestController` class:

```
@RefreshScope
```

11. Add the following instance variable as a place holder for the new property that is just added in the Config server. The property names in the `search-service.properties` file must match:

```
@Value("${originairports.shutdown}")
private String originAirportShutdownList;
```

12. Change the application code to use this property. This is done by modifying the `search` method as follows:

```
@RequestMapping(value="/get", method =
  RequestMethod.POST)
List<Flight> search(@RequestBody SearchQuery query){
  logger.info("Input : "+ query);
  if(Arrays.asList(originAirportShutdownList.split(","))
  .contains(query.getOrigin())){
  logger.info("The origin airport is in shutdown state");
  return new ArrayList<Flight>();
}
return searchComponent.search(query);
}
```

The `search` method is modified to read the parameter `originAirportShutdownList` and see whether the requested origin is in the shutdown list. If there is a match, then instead of proceeding with the actual search, the search method will return an empty flight list.

13. Start the Config server. Then start the Search microservice. Make sure that the RabbitMQ server is running.

14. Modify the `chapter5.website` project to match the `bootstrap.properties` content as follows to utilize the Config server:

```
spring.application.name=test-client
server.port=8001
spring.cloud.config.uri=http://localhost:8888
```

15. Change the `run` method of `CommandLineRunner` in `Application.java` to query SEA as the origin airport:

```
SearchQuery = new SearchQuery("SEA","SFO","22-JAN-16");
```

16. Run the `chapter5.website` project. The `CommandLineRunner` will now return an empty flight list. The following message will be printed in the server:

```
The origin airport is in shutdown state
```

Handling configuration changes

This section will demonstrate how to propagate configuration properties when there is a change:

1. Change the property in the `search-service.properties` file to the following:

```
originairports.shutdown:NYC
```

Commit the change in the Git repository. Refresh the Config server URL (`http://localhost:8888/search-service/default`) for this service and see whether the property change is reflected. If everything is fine, we will see the property change. The preceding request will force the Config server to read the property file again from the repository.

2. Rerun the website project again, and observe the `CommandLineRunner` execution. Note that in this case, we are not restarting the Search microservice nor the Config server. The service returns an empty flight list as earlier, and still complains as follows:

```
The origin airport is in shutdown state
```

This means the change is not reflected in the Search service, and the service is still working with an old copy of the configuration properties.

3. In order to force reloading of the configuration properties, call the `/refresh` endpoint of the Search microservice. This is actually the actuator's refresh endpoint. The following command will send an empty POST to the `/refresh` endpoint:

```
curl -d {} localhost:8090/refresh
```

4. Rerun the website project, and observe the `CommandLineRunner` execution. This should return the list of flights that we have requested from SEA. Note that the website project may fail if the Booking service is not up and running.

The `/refresh` endpoint will refresh the locally cached configuration properties, and reload fresh values from the Config server.

Spring Cloud Bus for propagating configuration changes

With the preceding approach, configuration parameters can be changed without restarting the microservices. This is good when there are only one or two instances of the services running. What happens if there are many instances? For example, if there are five instances, then we have to hit /refresh against each service instance. This is definitely a cumbersome activity:

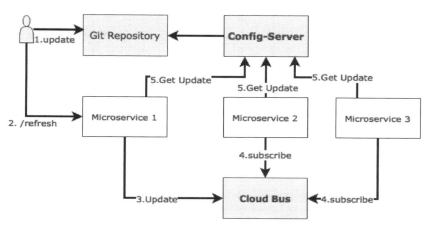

The Spring Cloud Bus provides a mechanism to refresh configurations across multiple instances without knowing how many instances there are, or their locations. This is particularly handy when there are many service instances of a microservice running or when there are many microservices of different types running. This is done by connecting all service instances through a single message broker. Each instance subscribes for change events, and refreshes its local configuration when required. This refresh is triggered by making a call to any one instance by hitting the /bus/refresh endpoint, which then propagates the changes through the cloud bus and the common message broker.

In this example, RabbitMQ is used as the AMQP message broker. Implement this by following the steps documented as follows:

1. Add a new dependency in the chapter5.search project's pom.xml file to introduce the Cloud Bus dependency:

```
<dependency>
    <groupId>org.springframework.cloud</groupId>
    <artifactId>spring-cloud-starter-bus-amqp</artifactId>
</dependency>
```

2. The Search microservice also needs connectivity to the RabbitMQ, but this is already provided in `search-service.properties`.

3. Rebuild and restart the Search microservice. In this case, we will run two instances of the Search microservice from a command line, as follows:

```
java -jar -Dserver.port=8090  search-1.0.jar
java -jar -Dserver.port=8091  search-1.0.jar
```

The two instances of the Search service will be now running, one on port `8090` and another one on `8091`.

4. Rerun the website project. This is just to make sure that everything is working. The Search service should return one flight at this point.

5. Now, update `search-service.properties` with the following value, and commit to Git:

```
originairports.shutdown:SEA
```

6. Run the following command to `/bus/refresh`. Note that we are running a new bus endpoint against one of the instances, `8090` in this case:

```
curl -d {} localhost:8090/bus/refresh
```

7. Immediately, we will see the following message for both instances:

```
Received remote refresh request. Keys refreshed [originairports.
shutdown]
```

The bus endpoint sends a message to the message broker internally, which is eventually consumed by all instances, reloading their property files. Changes can also be applied to a specific application by specifying the application name like so:

```
/bus/refresh?destination=search-service:**
```

We can also refresh specific properties by setting the property name as a parameter.

Setting up high availability for the Config server

The previous sections explored how to set up the Config server, allowing real-time refresh of configuration properties. However, the Config server is a single point of failure in this architecture.

There are three single points of failure in the default architecture that was established in the previous section. One of them is the availability of the Config server itself, the second one is the Git repository, and the third one is the RabbitMQ server.

The following diagram shows a high availability architecture for the Config server:

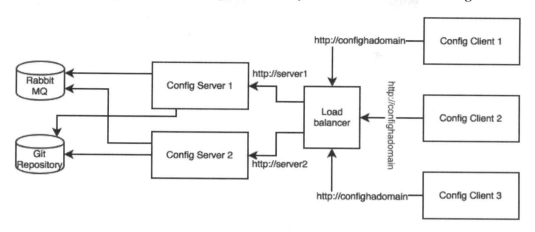

The architecture mechanisms and rationale are explained as follows:

The Config server requires high availability, since the services won't be able to bootstrap if the Config server is not available. Hence, redundant Config servers are required for high availability. However, the applications can continue to run if the Config server is unavailable after the services are bootstrapped. In this case, services will run with the last known configuration state. Hence, the Config server availability is not at the same critical level as the microservices availability.

In order to make the Config server highly available, we need multiple instances of the Config servers. Since the Config server is a stateless HTTP service, multiple instances of configuration servers can be run in parallel. Based on the load on the configuration server, a number of instances have to be adjusted. The `bootstrap. properties` file is not capable of handling more than one server address. Hence, multiple configuration servers should be configured to run behind a load balancer or behind a local DNS with failover and fallback capabilities. The load balancer or DNS server URL will be configured in the microservices' `bootstrap.properties` file. This is with the assumption that the DNS or the load balancer is highly available and capable of handling failovers.

In a production scenario, it is not recommended to use a local file-based Git repository. The configuration server should be typically backed with a highly available Git service. This is possible by either using an external highly available Git service or a highly available internal Git service. SVN can also be considered.

Having said that, an already bootstrapped Config server is always capable of working with a local copy of the configuration. Hence, we need a highly available Git only when the Config server needs to be scaled. Therefore, this too is not as critical as the microservices availability or the Config server availability.

 The GitLab example for setting up high availability is available at `https://about.gitlab.com/high-availability/`.

RabbitMQ also has to be configured for high availability. The high availability for RabbitMQ is needed only to push configuration changes dynamically to all instances. Since this is more of an offline controlled activity, it does not really require the same high availability as required by the components.

RabbitMQ high availability can be achieved by either using a cloud service or a locally configured highly available RabbitMQ service.

 Setting up high availability for Rabbit MQ is documented at `https://www.rabbitmq.com/ha.html`.

Monitoring the Config server health

The Config server is nothing but a Spring Boot application, and is, by default, configured with an actuator. Hence, all actuator endpoints are applicable for the Config server. The health of the server can be monitored using the following actuator URL: `http://localhost:8888/health`.

Config server for configuration files

We may run into scenarios where we need a complete configuration file such as `logback.xml` to be externalized. The Config server provides a mechanism to configure and store such files. This is achievable by using the URL format as follows: `/{name}/{profile}/{label}/{path}`.

The name, profile, and label have the same meanings as explained earlier. The path indicates the file name such as `logback.xml`.

Completing changes to use the Config server

In order to build this capability to complete BrownField Airline's PSS, we have to make use of the configuration server for all services. All microservices in the examples given in `chapter5.*` need to make similar changes to look to the Config server for getting the configuration parameters.

The following are a few key change considerations:

- The Fare service URL in the booking component will also be externalized:

```
private static final String FareURL = "/fares";

@Value("${fares-service.url}")
private String fareServiceUrl;

Fare = restTemplate.getForObject(fareServiceUrl+FareURL +"/
get?flightNumber="+record.getFlightNumber()+"&flightDate="+record.
getFlightDate(),Fare.class);
```

As shown in the preceding code snippet, the Fare service URL is fetched through a new property: `fares-service.url`.

- We are not externalizing the queue names used in the Search, Booking, and Check-in services at the moment. Later in this chapter, these will be changed to use Spring Cloud Streams.

Feign as a declarative REST client

In the Booking microservice, there is a synchronous call to Fare. `RestTemplate` is used for making the synchronous call. When using `RestTemplate`, the URL parameter is constructed programmatically, and data is sent across to the other service. In more complex scenarios, we will have to get to the details of the HTTP APIs provided by `RestTemplate` or even to APIs at a much lower level.

Feign is a Spring Cloud Netflix library for providing a higher level of abstraction over REST-based service calls. Spring Cloud Feign works on a declarative principle. When using Feign, we write declarative REST service interfaces at the client, and use those interfaces to program the client. The developer need not worry about the implementation of this interface. This will be dynamically provisioned by Spring at runtime. With this declarative approach, developers need not get into the details of the HTTP level APIs provided by `RestTemplate`.

The following code snippet is the existing code in the Booking microservice for calling the Fare service:

```
Fare fare = restTemplate.getForObject(FareURL +"/
get?flightNumber="+record.getFlightNumber()+"&flightDate="+record.
getFlightDate(),Fare.class);
```

In order to use Feign, first we need to change the `pom.xml` file to include the Feign dependency as follows:

```
<dependency>
   <groupId>org.springframework.cloud</groupId>
   <artifactId>spring-cloud-starter-feign</artifactId>
</dependency>
```

For a new Spring Starter project, **Feign** can be selected from the starter library selection screen, or from `http://start.spring.io/`. This is available under **Cloud Routing** as shown in the following screenshot:

Cloud Routing

☐ Zuul
   Intelligent and programmable routing with spring-cloud-netflix Zuul

☐ Ribbon
   Client side load balancing with spring-cloud-netflix and Ribbon

☐ Feign
   Declarative REST clients with spring-cloud-netflix Feign

The next step is to create a new `FareServiceProxy` interface. This will act as a proxy interface of the actual Fare service:

```
@FeignClient(name="fares-proxy", url="localhost:8080/fares")
public interface FareServiceProxy {
  @RequestMapping(value = "/get", method=RequestMethod.GET)
  Fare getFare(@RequestParam(value="flightNumber") String
    flightNumber, @RequestParam(value="flightDate") String
    flightDate);
}
```

The `FareServiceProxy` interface has a `@FeignClient` annotation. This annotation tells Spring to create a REST client based on the interface provided. The value could be a service ID or a logical name. The `url` indicates the actual URL where the target service is running. Either name or value is mandatory. In this case, since we have `url`, the `name` attribute is irrelevant.

Use this service proxy to call the Fare service. In the Booking microservice, we have to tell Spring that Feign clients exist in the Spring Boot application, which are to be scanned and discovered. This will be done by adding `@EnableFeignClients` at the class level of `BookingComponent`. Optionally, we can also give the package names to scan.

Change `BookingComponent`, and make changes to the calling part. This is as simple as calling another Java interface:

```
Fare = fareServiceProxy.getFare(record.getFlightNumber(), record.
getFlightDate());
```

Rerun the Booking microservice to see the effect.

The URL of the Fare service in the `FareServiceProxy` interface is hardcoded: `url="localhost:8080/fares"`.

For the time being, we will keep it like this, but we are going to change this later in this chapter.

Ribbon for load balancing

In the previous setup, we were always running with a single instance of the microservice. The URL is hardcoded both in client as well as in the service-to-service calls. In the real world, this is not a recommended approach, since there could be more than one service instance. If there are multiple instances, then ideally, we should use a load balancer or a local DNS server to abstract the actual instance locations, and configure an alias name or the load balancer address in the clients. The load balancer then receives the alias name, and resolves it with one of the available instances. With this approach, we can configure as many instances behind a load balancer. It also helps us to handle server failures transparent to the client.

This is achievable with Spring Cloud Netflix Ribbon. Ribbon is a client-side load balancer which can do round-robin load balancing across a set of servers. There could be other load balancing algorithms possible with the Ribbon library. Spring Cloud offers a declarative way to configure and use the Ribbon client.

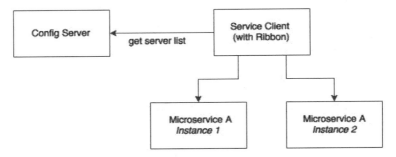

As shown in the preceding diagram, the Ribbon client looks for the Config server to get the list of available microservice instances, and, by default, applies a round-robin load balancing algorithm.

In order to use the Ribbon client, we will have to add the following dependency to the pom.xml file:

```
<dependency>
    <groupId>org.springframework.cloud</groupId>
    <artifactId>spring-cloud-starter-ribbon</artifactId>
</dependency>
```

In case of development from ground up, this can be selected from the Spring Starter libraries, or from http://start.spring.io/. Ribbon is available under **Cloud Routing**:

Cloud Routing

☐ **Zuul**

Intelligent and programmable routing with spring-cloud-netflix Zuul

☐ **Ribbon**

Client side load balancing with spring-cloud-netflix and Ribbon

☐ **Feign**

Declarative REST clients with spring-cloud-netflix Feign

Update the Booking microservice configuration file, `booking-service.properties`, to include a new property to keep the list of the Fare microservices:

```
fares-proxy.ribbon.listOfServers=localhost:8080,localhost:8081
```

Going back and editing the `FareServiceProxy` class created in the previous section to use the Ribbon client, we note that the value of the `@RequestMapping` annotations is changed from `/get` to `/fares/get` so that we can move the host name and port to the configuration easily:

```
@FeignClient(name="fares-proxy")
@RibbonClient(name="fares")
public interface FareServiceProxy {
  @RequestMapping(value = "fares/get", method=RequestMethod.GET)
```

We can now run two instances of the Fares microservices. Start one of them on `8080`, and the other one on `8081`:

```
java -jar -Dserver.port=8080 fares-1.0.jar
java -jar -Dserver.port=8081 fares-1.0.jar
```

Run the Booking microservice. When the Booking microservice is bootstrapped, the `CommandLineRunner` automatically inserts one booking record. This will go to the first server.

When running the website project, it calls the Booking service. This request will go to the second server.

On the Booking service, we see the following trace, which says there are two servers enlisted:

```
DynamicServerListLoadBalancer:{NFLoadBalancer:name=fares-proxy,current

list of Servers=[localhost:8080, localhost:8081],Load balancer stats=Zone
stats: {unknown=[Zone:unknown;  Instance count:2;  Active connections
count: 0;  Circuit breaker tripped count: 0;  Active connections per
server: 0.0;]
},
```

Eureka for registration and discovery

So far, we have achieved externalizing configuration parameters as well as load balancing across many service instances.

Ribbon-based load balancing is sufficient for most of the microservices requirements. However, this approach falls short in a couple of scenarios:

- If there is a large number of microservices, and if we want to optimize infrastructure utilization, we will have to dynamically change the number of service instances and the associated servers. It is not easy to predict and preconfigure the server URLs in a configuration file.

- When targeting cloud deployments for highly scalable microservices, static registration and discovery is not a good solution considering the elastic nature of the cloud environment.

- In the cloud deployment scenarios, IP addresses are not predictable, and will be difficult to statically configure in a file. We will have to update the configuration file every time there is a change in address.

The Ribbon approach partially addresses this issue. With Ribbon, we can dynamically change the service instances, but whenever we add new service instances or shut down instances, we will have to manually update the Config server. Though the configuration changes will be automatically propagated to all required instances, the manual configuration changes will not work with large scale deployments. When managing large deployments, automation, wherever possible, is paramount.

To fix this gap, the microservices should self-manage their life cycle by dynamically registering service availability, and provision automated discovery for consumers.

Understanding dynamic service registration and discovery

Dynamic registration is primarily from the service provider's point of view. With dynamic registration, when a new service is started, it automatically enlists its availability in a central service registry. Similarly, when a service goes out of service, it is automatically delisted from the service registry. The registry always keeps up-to-date information of the services available, as well as their metadata.

Dynamic discovery is applicable from the service consumer's point of view. Dynamic discovery is where clients look for the service registry to get the current state of the services topology, and then invoke the services accordingly. In this approach, instead of statically configuring the service URLs, the URLs are picked up from the service registry.

The clients may keep a local cache of the registry data for faster access. Some registry implementations allow clients to keep a watch on the items they are interested in. In this approach, the state changes in the registry server will be propagated to the interested parties to avoid using stale data.

There are a number of options available for dynamic service registration and discovery. Netflix Eureka, ZooKeeper, and Consul are available as part of Spring Cloud, as shown in the `http://start.spring.io/` screenshot given next. Etcd is another service registry available outside of Spring Cloud to achieve dynamic service registration and discovery. In this chapter, we will focus on the Eureka implementation:

Cloud Discovery

☐ Eureka Discovery

Service discovery using spring-cloud-netflix and Eureka

☐ Eureka Server

spring-cloud-netflix Eureka Server

☐ Zookeeper Discovery

Service discovery with Zookeeper and spring-cloud-zookeeper-discovery

☐ Cloud Foundry Discovery

Service discovery with Cloud Foundry

☐ Consul Discovery

Service discovery with Hashicorp Consul

Understanding Eureka

Spring Cloud Eureka also comes from Netflix OSS. The Spring Cloud project provides a Spring-friendly declarative approach for integrating Eureka with Spring-based applications. Eureka is primarily used for self-registration, dynamic discovery, and load balancing. Eureka uses Ribbon for load balancing internally:

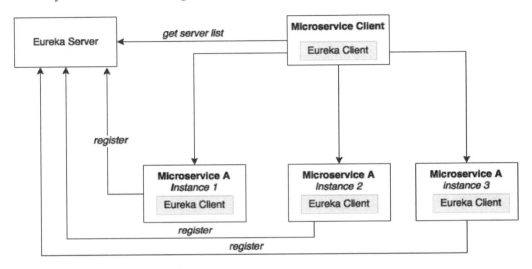

As shown in the preceding diagram, Eureka consists of a server component and a client-side component. The server component is the registry in which all microservices register their availability. The registration typically includes service identity and its URLs. The microservices use the Eureka client for registering their availability. The consuming components will also use the Eureka client for discovering the service instances.

When a microservice is bootstrapped, it reaches out to the Eureka server, and advertises its existence with the binding information. Once registered, the service endpoint sends ping requests to the registry every 30 seconds to renew its lease. If a service endpoint cannot renew its lease in a few attempts, that service endpoint will be taken out of the service registry. The registry information will be replicated to all Eureka clients so that the clients have to go to the remote Eureka server for each and every request. Eureka clients fetch the registry information from the server, and cache it locally. After that, the clients use that information to find other services. This information is updated periodically (every 30 seconds) by getting the delta updates between the last fetch cycle and the current one.

When a client wants to contact a microservice endpoint, the Eureka client provides a list of currently available services based on the requested service ID. The Eureka server is zone aware. Zone information can also be supplied when registering a service. When a client requests for a services instance, the Eureka service tries to find the service running in the same zone. The Ribbon client then load balances across these available service instances supplied by the Eureka client. The communication between the Eureka client and the server is done using REST and JSON.

Setting up the Eureka server

In this section, we will run through the steps required for setting up the Eureka server.

> The full source code of this section is available under the
> `chapter5.eurekaserver` project in the code files. Note that the
> Eureka server registration and refresh cycles take up to 30 seconds.
> Hence, when running services and clients, wait for 40-50 seconds.

1. Start a new Spring Starter project, and select **Config Client**, **Eureka Server**, and **Actuator**:

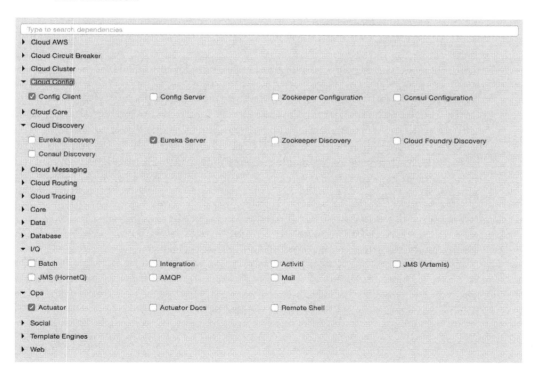

The project structure of the Eureka server is shown in the following image:

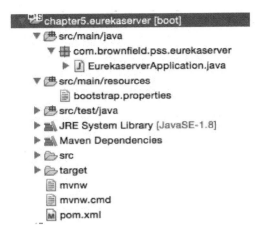

Note that the main application is named `EurekaserverApplication.java`.

2. Rename `application.properties` to `bootstrap.properties` since this is using the Config server. As we did earlier, configure the details of the Config server in the `bootsratp.properties` file so that it can locate the Config server instance. The `bootstrap.properties` file will look as follows:

```
spring.application.name=eureka-server1
server.port:8761
spring.cloud.config.uri=http://localhost:8888
```

The Eureka server can be set up in a standalone mode or in a clustered mode. We will start with the standalone mode. By default, the Eureka server itself is another Eureka client. This is particularly useful when there are multiple Eureka servers running for high availability. The client component is responsible for synchronizing state from the other Eureka servers. The Eureka client is taken to its peers by configuring the `eureka.client.serviceUrl.defaultZone` property.

In the standalone mode, we point `eureka.client.serviceUrl.defaultZone` back to the same standalone instance. Later we will see how we can run Eureka servers in a clustered mode.

3. Create a `eureka-server1.properties` file, and update it in the Git repository. `eureka-server1` is the name of the application given in the application's `bootstrap.properties` file in the previous step. As shown in the following code, `serviceUrl` points back to the same server. Once the following properties are added, commit the file to the Git repository:

```
spring.application.name=eureka-server1
eureka.client.serviceUrl.defaultZone:http://localhost:8761/eureka/
eureka.client.registerWithEureka:false
eureka.client.fetchRegistry:false
```

4. Change the default `Application.java`. In this example, the package is also renamed as `com.brownfield.pss.eurekaserver`, and the class name changed to `EurekaserverApplication`. In `EurekaserverApplication`, add `@EnableEurekaServer`:

```
@EnableEurekaServer
@SpringBootApplication
public class EurekaserverApplication {
```

5. We are now ready to start the Eureka server. Ensure that the Config server is also started. Right-click on the application and then choose **Run As | Spring Boot App**. Once the application is started, open `http://localhost:8761` in a browser to see the Eureka console.

6. In the console, note that there is no instance registered under **Instances currently registered with Eureka**. Since no services have been started with the Eureka client enabled, the list is empty at this point.

7. Making a few changes to our microservice will enable dynamic registration and discovery using the Eureka service. To do this, first we have to add the Eureka dependencies to the `pom.xml` file. If the services are being built up fresh using the Spring Starter project, then select **Config Client, Actuator, Web** as well as **Eureka discovery** client as follows:

- ▶ Cloud AWS
- ▶ Cloud Circuit Breaker
- ▶ Cloud Cluster
- ▼ Cloud Config
  - ☑ Config Client
  - ☐ Config Server
  - ☐ Zookeeper Configuration
  - ☐ Consul Configuration
- ▶ Cloud Core
- ▼ Cloud Discovery
  - ☑ Eureka Discovery
  - ☐ Eureka Server
  - ☐ Zookeeper Discovery
  - ☐ Cloud Foundry Discovery
  - ☐ Consul Discovery
- ▶ Cloud Messaging
- ▶ Cloud Routing
- ▶ Cloud Tracing
- ▶ Core
- ▶ Data
- ▶ Database
- ▶ I/O
- ▼ Ops
  - ☑ Actuator
  - ☐ Actuator Docs
  - ☐ Remote Shell
- ▶ Social
- ▶ Template Engines
- ▼ Web
  - ☑ Web
  - ☐ Websocket
  - ☐ WS
  - ☐ Jersey (JAX-RS)
  - ☐ Ratpack
  - ☐ Vaadin
  - ☐ Rest Repositories
  - ☐ HATEOAS
  - ☐ Rest Repositories HAL Browser
  - ☐ Mobile
  - ☐ REST Docs

8. Since we are modifying our microservices, add the following additional dependency to all microservices in their `pom.xml` files:

```
<dependency>
  <groupId>org.springframework.cloud</groupId>
  <artifactId>spring-cloud-starter-eureka</artifactId>
</dependency>
```

9. The following property has to be added to all microservices in their respective configuration files under `config-repo`. This will help the microservices to connect to the Eureka server. Commit to Git once updates are completed:

```
eureka.client.serviceUrl.defaultZone: http://localhost:8761/
eureka/
```

10. Add `@EnableDiscoveryClient` to all microservices in their respective Spring Boot main classes. This asks Spring Boot to register these services at start up to advertise their availability.

11. Start all servers except Booking. Since we are using the Ribbon client on the Booking service, the behavior could be different when we add the Eureka client in the class path. We will fix this soon.

12. Going to the Eureka URL (`http://localhost:8761`), you can see that all three instances are up and running:

Instances currently registered with Eureka

Application	AMIs	Availability Zones	Status
CHECKIN-SERVICE	n/a (1)	(1)	**UP** (1) - 192.168.0.102:checkin-service:8070
FARES-SERVICE	n/a (1)	(1)	**UP** (1) - 192.168.0.102:fares-service:8080
SEARCH-SERVICE	n/a (1)	(1)	**UP** (1) - 192.168.0.102:search-service:8090

Time to fix the issue with Booking. We will remove our earlier Ribbon client, and use Eureka instead. Eureka internally uses Ribbon for load balancing. Hence, the load balancing behavior will not change.

13. Remove the following dependency:

```
<dependency>
    <groupId>org.springframework.cloud</groupId>
    <artifactId>spring-cloud-starter-ribbon</artifactId>
</dependency>
```

14. Also remove the `@RibbonClient(name="fares")` annotation from the `FareServiceProxy` class.

15. Update `@FeignClient(name="fares-service")` to match the actual Fare microservices' service ID. In this case, `fare-service` is the service ID configured in the Fare microservices' `bootstrap.properties`. This is the name that the Eureka discovery client sends to the Eureka server. The service ID will be used as a key for the services registered in the Eureka server.

16. Also remove the list of servers from the `booking-service.properties` file. With Eureka, we are going to dynamically discover this list from the Eureka server:

```
fares-proxy.ribbon.listOfServers=localhost:8080, localhost:8081
```

17. Start the Booking service. You will see that `CommandLineRunner` successfully created a booking, which involves calling the Fare services using the Eureka discovery mechanism. Go back to the URL to see all the registered services:

Instances currently registered with Eureka

Application	AMIs	Availability Zones	Status
BOOK-SERVICE	n/a (1)	(1)	UP (1) - 192.168.0.102:book-service:8060
CHECKIN-SERVICE	n/a (1)	(1)	UP (1) - 192.168.0.102:checkin-service:8070
FARES-SERVICE	n/a (1)	(1)	UP (1) - 192.168.0.102:fares-service:8080
SEARCH-SERVICE	n/a (1)	(1)	UP (1) - 192.168.0.102:search-service:8090

18. Change the website project's `bootstrap.properties` file to make use of Eureka rather than connecting directly to the service instances. We will not use the Feign client in this case. Instead, for demonstration purposes, we will use the load balanced `RestTemplate`. Commit these changes to the Git repository:

```
spring.application.name=test-client
eureka.client.serviceUrl.defaultZone: http://localhost:8761/
eureka/
```

19. Add `@EnableDiscoveryClient` to the `Application` class to make the client Eureka-aware.

20. Edit both `Application.java` as well as `BrownFieldSiteController.java`. Add three `RestTemplate` instances. This time, we annotate them with `@Loadbalanced` to ensure that we use the load balancing features using Eureka and Ribbon. `RestTemplate` cannot be automatically injected. Hence, we have to provide a configuration entry as follows:

```
@Configuration
class AppConfiguration {
    @LoadBalanced
    @Bean
    RestTemplate restTemplate() {
        return new RestTemplate();
    }
}
@Autowired
RestTemplate searchClient;

@Autowired
RestTemplate bookingClient;

@Autowired
RestTemplate checkInClient;
```

21. We use these `RestTemplate` instances to call the microservices. Replace the hardcoded URLs with service IDs that are registered in the Eureka server. In the following code, we use the service names `search-service`, `book-service`, and `checkin-service` instead of explicit host names and ports:

```
Flight[] flights = searchClient.postForObject("http://search-service/search/get", searchQuery, Flight[].class);

long bookingId = bookingClient.postForObject("http://book-service/booking/create", booking, long.class);

long checkinId = checkInClient.postForObject("http://checkin-service/checkin/create", checkIn, long.class);
```

22. We are now ready to run the client. Run the website project. If everything is fine, the website project's `CommandLineRunner` will successfully perform search, booking, and check-in. The same can also be tested using the browser by pointing the browser to `http://localhost:8001`.

High availability for Eureka

In the previous example, there was only one Eureka server in standalone mode. This is not good enough for a real production system.

The Eureka client connects to the server, fetches registry information, and stores it locally in a cache. The client always works with this local cache. The Eureka client checks the server periodically for any state changes. In the case of a state change, it downloads the changes from the server, and updates the cache. If the Eureka server is not reachable, then the Eureka clients can still work with the last-known state of the servers based on the data available in the client cache. However, this could lead to stale state issues quickly.

This section will explore the high availability for the Eureka server. The high availability architecture is shown in the following diagram:

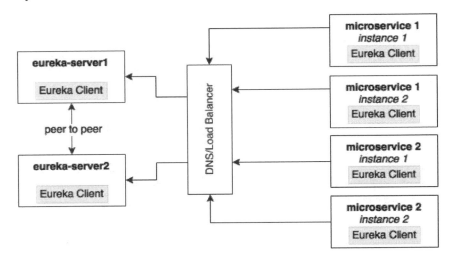

The Eureka server is built with a peer-to-peer data synchronization mechanism. The runtime state information is not stored in a database, but managed using an in-memory cache. The high availability implementation favors availability and partition tolerance in the CAP theorem, leaving out consistency. Since the Eureka server instances are synchronized with each other using an asynchronous mechanism, the states may not always match between server instances. The peer-to-peer synchronization is done by pointing serviceUrls to each other. If there is more than one Eureka server, each one has to be connected to at least one of the peer servers. Since the state is replicated across all peers, Eureka clients can connect to any one of the available Eureka servers.

The best way to achieve high availability for Eureka is to cluster multiple Eureka servers, and run them behind a load balancer or a local DNS. The clients always connect to the server using the DNS/load balancer. At runtime, the load balancer takes care of selecting the appropriate servers. This load balancer address will be provided to the Eureka clients.

This section will showcase how to run two Eureka servers in a cluster for high availability. For this, define two property files: eureka-server1 and eureka-server2. These are peer servers; if one fails, the other one will take over. Each of these servers will also act as a client for the other so that they can sync their states. Two property files are defined in the following snippet. Upload and commit these properties to the Git repository.

The client URLs point to each other, forming a peer network as shown in the following configuration:

eureka-server1.properties
```
eureka.client.serviceUrl.defaultZone:http://localhost:8762/eureka/
eureka.client.registerWithEureka:false
eureka.client.fetchRegistry:false
```

eureka-server2.properties
```
eureka.client.serviceUrl.defaultZone:http://localhost:8761/eureka/
eureka.client.registerWithEureka:false
eureka.client.fetchRegistry:false
```

Update the `bootstrap.properties` file of Eureka, and change the application name to `eureka`. Since we are using two profiles, based on the active profile supplied at startup, the Config server will look for either `eureka-server1` or `eureka-server2`:

```
spring.application.name=eureka
spring.cloud.config.uri=http://localhost:8888
```

Start two instances of the Eureka servers, `server1` on `8761` and `server2` on `8762`:

```
java -jar –Dserver.port=8761 -Dspring.profiles.active=server1 demo-0.0.1-
SNAPSHOT.jar
```

```
java -jar –Dserver.port=8762 -Dspring.profiles.active=server2 demo-0.0.1-
SNAPSHOT.jar
```

All our services still point to the first server, `server1`. Open both the browser windows: `http://localhost:8761` and `http://localhost:8762`.

Start all microservices. The one which opened `8761` will immediately reflect the changes, whereas the other one will take 30 seconds for reflecting the states. Since both the servers are in a cluster, the state is synchronized between these two servers. If we keep these servers behind a load balancer/DNS, then the client will always connect to one of the available servers.

After completing this exercise, switch back to the standalone mode for the remaining exercises.

Zuul proxy as the API gateway

In most microservice implementations, internal microservice endpoints are not exposed outside. They are kept as private services. A set of public services will be exposed to the clients using an API gateway. There are many reasons to do this:

- Only a selected set of microservices are required by the clients.
- If there are client-specific policies to be applied, it is easy to apply them in a single place rather than in multiple places. An example of such a scenario is the cross-origin access policy.
- It is hard to implement client-specific transformations at the service endpoint.
- If there is data aggregation required, especially to avoid multiple client calls in a bandwidth-restricted environment, then a gateway is required in the middle.

Zuul is a simple gateway service or edge service that suits these situations well. Zuul also comes from the Netflix family of microservice products. Unlike many enterprise API gateway products, Zuul provides complete control for the developers to configure or program based on specific requirements:

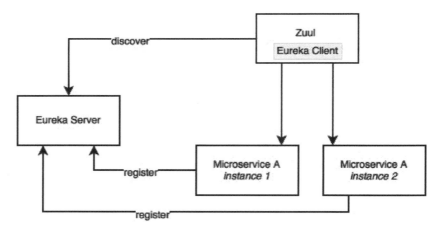

The Zuul proxy internally uses the Eureka server for service discovery, and Ribbon for load balancing between service instances.

The Zuul proxy is also capable of routing, monitoring, managing resiliency, security, and so on. In simple terms, we can consider Zuul a reverse proxy service. With Zuul, we can even change the behaviors of the underlying services by overriding them at the API layer.

Setting up Zuul

Unlike the Eureka server and the Config server, in typical deployments, Zuul is specific to a microservice. However, there are deployments in which one API gateway covers many microservices. In this case, we are going to add Zuul for each of our microservices: Search, Booking, Fare, and Check-in:

 The full source code of this section is available under the `chapter5.*-apigateway` project in the code files.

1. Convert the microservices one by one. Start with Search API Gateway. Create a new Spring Starter project, and select **Zuul**, **Config Client**, **Actuator**, and **Eureka Discovery**:

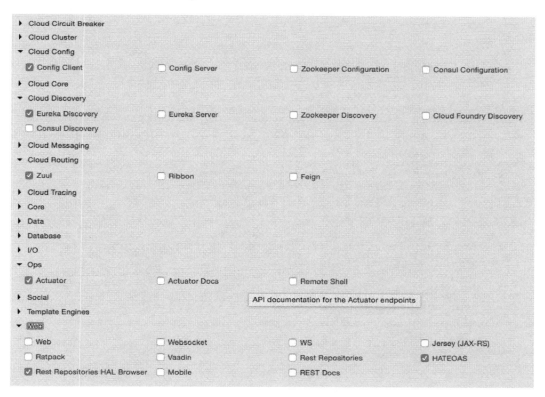

The project structure for `search-apigateway` is shown in the following diagram:

2. The next step is to integrate the API gateway with Eureka and the Config server. Create a `search-apigateway.property` file with the contents given next, and commit to the Git repository.

   This configuration also sets a rule on how to forward traffic. In this case, any request coming on the `/api` endpoint of the API gateway should be sent to `search-service`:

   ```
   spring.application.name=search-apigateway
   zuul.routes.search-apigateway.serviceId=search-service
   zuul.routes.search-apigateway.path=/api/**
   eureka.client.serviceUrl.defaultZone:http://localhost:8761/eureka/
   ```

   `search-service` is the service ID of the Search service, and it will be resolved using the Eureka server.

3. Update the `bootstrap.properties` file of `search-apigateway` as follows. There is nothing new in this configuration—a name to the service, the port, and the Config server URL:

   ```
   spring.application.name=search-apigateway
   server.port=8095
   spring.cloud.config.uri=http://localhost:8888
   ```

4. Edit `Application.java`. In this case, the package name and the class name are also changed to `com.brownfield.pss.search.apigateway` and `SearchApiGateway` respectively. Also add `@EnableZuulProxy` to tell Spring Boot that this is a Zuul proxy:

```
@EnableZuulProxy
@EnableDiscoveryClient
@SpringBootApplication
public class SearchApiGateway {
```

5. Run this as a Spring Boot app. Before that, ensure that the Config server, the Eureka server, and the Search microservice are running.

6. Change the website project's `CommandLineRunner` as well as `BrownFieldSiteController` to make use of the API gateway:

```
Flight[] flights = searchClient.postForObject("http://search-
apigateway/api/search/get", searchQuery, Flight[].class);
```

In this case, the Zuul proxy acts as a reverse proxy which proxies all microservice endpoints to consumers. In the preceding example, the Zuul proxy does not add much value, as we just pass through the incoming requests to the corresponding backend service.

Zuul is particularly useful when we have one or more requirements like the following:

- Enforcing authentication and other security policies at the gateway instead of doing that on every microservice endpoint. The gateway can handle security policies, token handling, and so on before passing the request to the relevant services behind. It can also do basic rejections based on some business policies such as blocking requests coming from certain black-listed users.

- Business insights and monitoring can be implemented at the gateway level. Collect real-time statistical data, and push it to an external system for analysis. This will be handy as we can do this at one place rather than applying it across many microservices.

- API gateways are useful in scenarios where dynamic routing is required based on fine-grained controls. For example, send requests to different service instances based on business specific values such as "origin country". Another example is all requests coming from a region to be sent to one group of service instances. Yet another example is all requests requesting for a particular product have to be routed to a group of service instances.

- Handling the load shredding and throttling requirements is another scenario where API gateways are useful. This is when we have to control load based on set thresholds such as number of requests in a day. For example, control requests coming from a low-value third party online channel.

- The Zuul gateway is useful for fine-grained load balancing scenarios. The Zuul, Eureka client, and Ribbon together provide fine-grained controls over the load balancing requirements. Since the Zuul implementation is nothing but another Spring Boot application, the developer has full control over the load balancing.

- The Zuul gateway is also useful in scenarios where data aggregation requirements are in place. If the consumer wants higher level coarse-grained services, then the gateway can internally aggregate data by calling more than one service on behalf of the client. This is particularly applicable when the clients are working in low bandwidth environments.

Zuul also provides a number of filters. These filters are classified as pre filters, routing filters, post filters, and error filters. As the names indicate, these are applied at different stages of the life cycle of a service call. Zuul also provides an option for developers to write custom filters. In order to write a custom filter, extend from the abstract `ZuulFilter`, and implement the following methods:

```
public class CustomZuulFilter extends ZuulFilter{
public Object run(){}
public boolean shouldFilter(){}
public int filterOrder(){}
public String filterType(){}
```

Once a custom filter is implemented, add that class to the main context. In our example case, add this to the `SearchApiGateway` class as follows:

```
@Bean
public CustomZuulFilter customFilter() {
    return new CustomZuulFilter();
}
```

As mentioned earlier, the Zuul proxy is a Spring Boot service. We can customize the gateway programmatically in the way we want. As shown in the following code, we can add custom endpoints to the gateway, which, in turn, can call the backend services:

```
@RestController
class SearchAPIGatewayController {

  @RequestMapping("/")
  String greet(HttpServletRequest req){
```

```
        return "<H1>Search Gateway Powered By Zuul</H1>";
    }
}
```

In the preceding case, it just adds a new endpoint, and returns a value from the gateway. We can further use `@Loadbalanced RestTemplate` to call a backend service. Since we have full control, we can do transformations, data aggregation, and so on. We can also use the Eureka APIs to get the server list, and implement completely independent load-balancing or traffic-shaping mechanisms instead of the out-of-the-box load balancing features provided by Ribbon.

High availability of Zuul

Zuul is just a stateless service with an HTTP endpoint, hence, we can have as many Zuul instances as we need. There is no affinity or stickiness required. However, the availability of Zuul is extremely critical as all traffic from the consumer to the provider flows through the Zuul proxy. However, the elastic scaling requirements are not as critical as the backend microservices where all the heavy lifting happens.

The high availability architecture of Zuul is determined by the scenario in which we are using Zuul. The typical usage scenarios are:

* When a client-side JavaScript MVC such as AngularJS accesses Zuul services from a remote browser.

* Another microservice or non-microservice accesses services via Zuul

In some cases, the client may not have the capabilities to use the Eureka client libraries, for example, a legacy application written on PL/SQL. In some cases, organization policies do not allow Internet clients to handle client-side load balancing. In the case of browser-based clients, there are third-party Eureka JavaScript libraries available.

It all boils down to whether the client is using Eureka client libraries or not. Based on this, there are two ways we can set up Zuul for high availability.

High availability of Zuul when the client is also a Eureka client

In this case, since the client is also another Eureka client, Zuul can be configured just like other microservices. Zuul registers itself to Eureka with a service ID. The clients then use Eureka and the service ID to resolve Zuul instances:

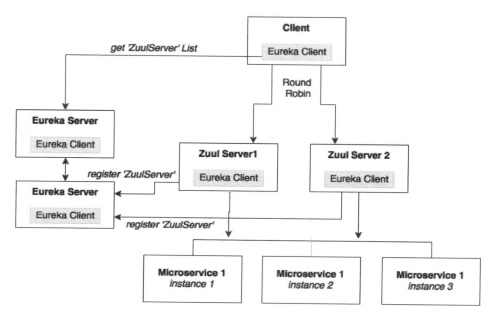

As shown in the preceding diagram, Zuul services register themselves with Eureka with a service ID, `search-apigateway` in our case. The Eureka client asks for the server list with the ID `search-apigateway`. The Eureka server returns the list of servers based on the current Zuul topology. The Eureka client, based on this list picks up one of the servers, and initiates the call.

As we saw earlier, the client uses the service ID to resolve the Zuul instance. In the following case, `search-apigateway` is the Zuul instance ID registered with Eureka:

```
Flight[] flights = searchClient.postForObject("http://search-
apigateway/api/search/get", searchQuery, Flight[].class);
```

High availability when the client is not a Eureka client

In this case, the client is not capable of handling load balancing by using the Eureka server. As shown in the following diagram, the client sends the request to a load balancer, which in turn identifies the right Zuul service instance. The Zuul instance, in this case, will be running behind a load balancer such as HAProxy or a hardware load balancer like NetScaler:

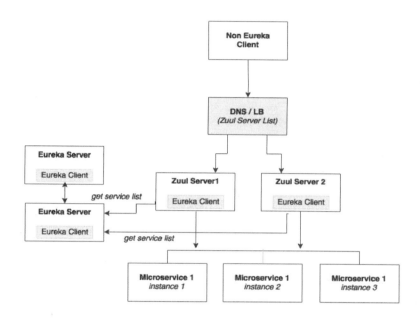

The microservices will still be load balanced by Zuul using the Eureka server.

Completing Zuul for all other services

In order to complete this exercise, add API gateway projects (name them as `*-apigateway`) for all our microservices. The following steps are required to achieve this task:

1. Create new property files per service, and check in to the Git repositories.

2. Change `application.properties` to `bootstrap.properties`, and add the required configurations.

3. Add `@EnableZuulProxy` to `Application.java` in each of the `*-apigateway` projects.

4. Add `@EnableDiscoveryClient` in all the `Application.java` files under each of the `*-apigateway` projects.

5. Optionally, change the package names and file names generated by default.

In the end, we will have the following API gateway projects:

- `chapter5.fares-apigateway`
- `chapter5.search-apigateway`
- `chapter5.checkin-apigateway`
- `chapter5.book-apigateway`

Streams for reactive microservices

Spring Cloud Stream provides an abstraction over the messaging infrastructure. The underlying messaging implementation can be RabbitMQ, Redis, or Kafka. Spring Cloud Stream provides a declarative approach for sending and receiving messages:

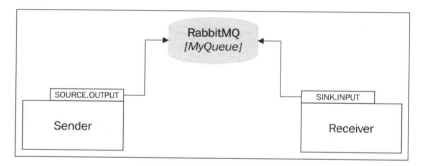

As shown in the preceding diagram, Cloud Stream works on the concept of a **source** and a **sink**. The source represents the sender perspective of the messaging, and sink represents the receiver perspective of the messaging.

In the example shown in the diagram, the sender defines a logical queue called `Source.OUTPUT` to which the sender sends messages. The receiver defines a logical queue called `Sink.INPUT` from which the receiver retrieves messages. The physical binding of OUTPUT to INPUT is managed through the configuration. In this case, both link to the same physical queue—`MyQueue` on RabbitMQ. So, while at one end, `Source.OUTPUT` points to `MyQueue`, on the other end, `Sink.INPUT` points to the same `MyQueue`.

Spring Cloud offers the flexibility to use multiple messaging providers in one application such as connecting an input stream from Kafka to a Redis output stream, without managing the complexities. Spring Cloud Stream is the basis for message-based integration. The Cloud Stream Modules subproject is another Spring Cloud library that provides many endpoint implementations.

As the next step, rebuild the inter-microservice messaging communication with the Cloud Streams. As shown in the next diagram, we will define a `SearchSink` connected to `InventoryQ` under the Search microservice. Booking will define a `BookingSource` for sending inventory change messages connected to `InventoryQ`. Similarly, Check-in defines a `CheckinSource` for sending the check-in messages. Booking defines a sink, `BookingSink`, for receiving messages, both bound to the `CheckinQ` queue on the RabbitMQ:

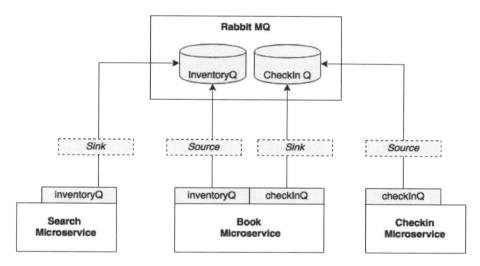

In this example, we will use RabbitMQ as the message broker:

1. Add the following Maven dependency to Booking, Search, and Check-in, as these are the three modules using messaging:

```
<dependency>
    <groupId>org.springframework.cloud</groupId>
    <artifactId>spring-cloud-starter-stream-rabbit
        </artifactId>
</dependency>
```

2. Add the following two properties to `booking-service.properties`. These properties bind the logical queue `inventoryQ` to physical `inventoryQ`, and the logical `checkinQ` to the physical `checkinQ`:

```
spring.cloud.stream.bindings.inventoryQ.destination=inventoryQ
spring.cloud.stream.bindings.checkInQ.destination=checkInQ
```

3. Add the following property to `search-service.properties`. This property binds the logical queue `inventoryQ` to the physical `inventoryQ`:

```
spring.cloud.stream.bindings.inventoryQ.destination=inventoryQ
```

4. Add the following property to `checkin-service.properties`. This property binds the logical queue `checkinQ` to the physical `checkinQ`:

```
spring.cloud.stream.bindings.checkInQ.destination=checkInQ
```

5. Commit all files to the Git repository.

6. The next step is to edit the code. The Search microservice consumes a message from the Booking microservice. In this case, Booking is the source and Search is the sink.

   Add `@EnableBinding` to the `Sender` class of the Booking service. This enables the Cloud Stream to work on autoconfigurations based on the message broker library available in the class path. In our case, it is RabbitMQ. The parameter `BookingSource` defines the logical channels to be used for this configuration:

```
@EnableBinding(BookingSource.class)
public class Sender {
```

7. In this case, `BookingSource` defines a message channel called `inventoryQ`, which is physically bound to RabbitMQ's `inventoryQ`, as configured in the configuration. `BookingSource` uses an annotation, `@Output`, to indicate that this is of the output type—a message that is outgoing from a module. This information will be used for autoconfiguration of the message channel:

```
interface BookingSource {
    public static String InventoryQ="inventoryQ";
    @Output("inventoryQ")
    public MessageChannel inventoryQ();
}
```

8. Instead of defining a custom class, we can also use the default `Source` class that comes with Spring Cloud Stream if the service has only one source and sink:

```
public interface Source {
  @Output("output")
```

```
MessageChannel output();
}
```

9. Define a message channel in the sender, based on `BookingSource`. The following code will inject an output message channel with the name `inventory`, which is already configured in `BookingSource`:

```
@Output (BookingSource.InventoryQ)
@Autowired
private MessageChannel;
```

10. Reimplement the `send` message method in `BookingSender`:

```
public void send(Object message){
  messageChannel.
    send(MessageBuilder.withPayload(message).
    build());
}
```

11. Now add the following to the `SearchReceiver` class the same way we did for the Booking service:

```
@EnableBinding(SearchSink.class)
public class Receiver {
```

12. In this case, the `SearchSink` interface will look like the following. This will define the logical sink queue it is connected with. The message channel in this case is defined as `@Input` to indicate that this message channel is to accept messages:

```
interface SearchSink {
    public static String INVENTORYQ="inventoryQ";
    @Input("inventoryQ")
    public MessageChannel inventoryQ();
}
```

13. Amend the Search service to accept this message:

```
@ServiceActivator(inputChannel = SearchSink.INVENTORYQ)
public void accept(Map<String,Object> fare){
        searchComponent.updateInventory((String)fare.
        get("FLIGHT_NUMBER"),(String)fare.
        get("FLIGHT_DATE"),(int)fare.
        get("NEW_INVENTORY"));
}
```

14. We will still need the RabbitMQ configurations that we have in our configuration files to connect to the message broker:

```
spring.rabbitmq.host=localhost
spring.rabbitmq.port=5672
spring.rabbitmq.username=guest
spring.rabbitmq.password=guest
server.port=8090
```

15. Run all services, and run the website project. If everything is fine, the website project successfully executes the Search, Booking, and Check-in functions. The same can also be tested using the browser by pointing to `http://localhost:8001`.

Summarizing the BrownField PSS architecture

The following diagram shows the overall architecture that we have created with the Config server, Eureka, Feign, Zuul, and Cloud Streams. The architecture also includes the high availability of all components. In this case, we assume that the client uses the Eureka client libraries:

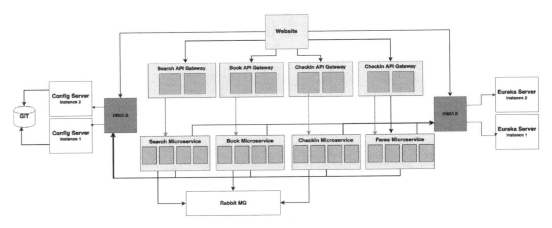

The summary of the projects and the port they are listening on is given in the following table:

Microservice	Projects	Port
Book microservice	chapter5.book	8060 to 8064
Check-in microservice	chapter5.checkin	8070 to 8074
Fare microservice	chapter5.fares	8080 to 8084
Search microservice	chapter5.search	8090 to 8094
Website client	chapter5.website	8001
Spring Cloud Config server	chapter5.configserver	8888/8889
Spring Cloud Eureka server	chapter5.eurekaserver	8761/8762
Book API gateway	chapter5.book-apigateway	8095 to 8099
Check-in API gateway	chapter5.checkin-apigateway	8075 to 8079
Fares API gateway	chapter5.fares-apigateway	8085 to 8089
Search API gateway	chapter5.search-apigateway	8065 to 8069

Follow these steps to do a final run:

1. Run RabbitMQ.

2. Build all projects using pom.xml at the root level:

   ```
   mvn –Dmaven.test.skip=true clean install
   ```

3. Run the following projects from their respective folders. Remember to wait for 40 to 50 seconds before starting the next service. This will ensure that the dependent services are registered and are available before we start a new service:

   ```
   java -jar target/fares-1.0.jar
   java -jar target/search-1.0.jar
   java -jar target/checkin-1.0.jar
   java -jar target/book-1.0.jar
   java –jar target/fares-apigateway-1.0.jar
   java –jar target/search-apigateway-1.0.jar
   java –jar target/checkin-apigateway-1.0.jar
   java –jar target/book-apigateway-1.0.jar
   java -jar target/website-1.0.jar
   ```

4. Open the browser window, and point to `http://localhost:8001`. Follow the steps mentioned in the *Running and testing the project* section in *Chapter 4, Microservices Evolution – A Case Study.*

Summary

In this chapter, you learned how to scale a Twelve-Factor Spring Boot microservice using the Spring Cloud project. What you learned was then applied to the BrownField Airline's PSS microservice that we developed in the previous chapter.

We then explored the Spring Config server for externalizing the microservices' configuration, and the way to deploy the Config server for high availability. We also discussed the declarative service calls using Feign, examined the use of Ribbon and Eureka for load balancing, dynamic service registration, and discovery. Implementation of an API gateway was examined by implementing Zuul. Finally, we concluded with a reactive style integration of microservices using Spring Cloud Stream.

BrownField Airline's PSS microservices are now deployable on the Internet scale. Other Spring Cloud components such as Hyterix, Sleuth, and so on will be covered in *Chapter 7, Logging and Monitoring Microservices.* The next chapter will demonstrate autoscaling features, extending the BrownField PSS implementation.

Autoscaling Microservices

6

Spring Cloud provides the support essential for the deployment of microservices at scale. In order to get the full power of a cloud-like environment, the microservices instances should also be capable of scaling out and shrinking automatically based on traffic patterns.

This chapter will detail out how to make microservices elastically grow and shrink by effectively using the actuator data collected from Spring Boot microservices to control the deployment topology by implementing a simple life cycle manager.

By the end of this chapter, you will learn about the following topics:

- The basic concept of autoscaling and different approaches for autoscaling
- The importance and capabilities of a life cycle manager in the context of microservices
- Examining the custom life cycle manager to achieve autoscaling
- Programmatically collecting statistics from the Spring Boot actuator and using it to control and shape incoming traffic

Reviewing the microservice capability model

This chapter will cover the **Application Lifecycle Management** capability in the microservices capability model discussed in *Chapter 3, Applying Microservices Concepts*, highlighted in the following diagram:

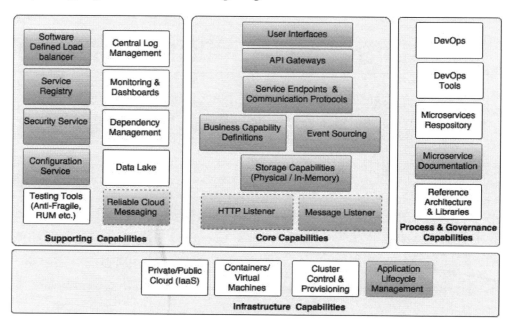

We will see a basic version of the life cycle manager in this chapter, which will be enhanced in later chapters.

Scaling microservices with Spring Cloud

In *Chapter 5, Scaling Microservices with Spring Cloud*, you learned how to scale Spring Boot microservices using Spring Cloud components. The two key concepts of Spring Cloud that we implemented are self-registration and self-discovery. These two capabilities enable automated microservices deployments. With self-registration, microservices can automatically advertise the service availability by registering service metadata to a central service registry as soon as the instances are ready to accept traffic. Once the microservices are registered, consumers can consume the newly registered services from the very next moment by discovering service instances using the registry service. Registry is at the heart of this automation.

This is quite different from the traditional clustering approach employed by the traditional JEE application servers. In the case of JEE application servers, the server instances' IP addresses are more or less statically configured in a load balancer. Therefore, the cluster approach is not the best solution for automatic scaling in Internet-scale deployments. Also, clusters impose other challenges, such as they have to have exactly the same version of binaries on all cluster nodes. It is also possible that the failure of one cluster node can poison other nodes due to the tight dependency between nodes.

The registry approach decouples the service instances. It also eliminates the need to manually maintain service addresses in the load balancer or configure virtual IPs:

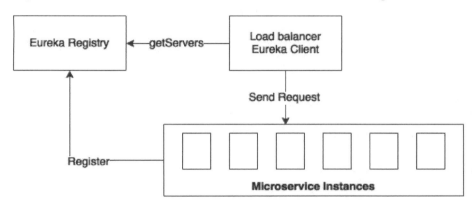

As shown in the diagram, there are three key components in our automated microservices deployment topology:

- **Eureka** is the central registry component for microservice registration and discovery. REST APIs are used by both consumers as well as providers to access the registry. The registry also holds the service metadata such as the service identity, host, port, health status, and so on.

- The **Eureka** client, together with the **Ribbon** client, provide client-side dynamic load balancing. Consumers use the Eureka client to look up the Eureka server to identify the available instances of a target service. The Ribbon client uses this server list to load-balance between the available microservice instances. In a similar way, if the service instance goes out of service, these instances will be taken out of the Eureka registry. The load balancer automatically reacts to these dynamic topology changes.

- The third component is the **microservices** instances developed using Spring Boot with the actuator endpoints enabled.

However, there is one gap in this approach. When there is need for an additional microservice instance, a manual task is required to kick off a new instance. In an ideal scenario, the starting and stopping of microservice instances also require automation.

For example, when there is a requirement to add another Search microservice instance to handle the increase in traffic volumes or a load burst scenario, the administrator has to manually bring up a new instance. Also, when the Search instance is idle for some time, it needs to be manually taken out of service to have optimal infrastructure usage. This is especially relevant when services run on a pay-as-per-usage cloud environment.

Understanding the concept of autoscaling

Autoscaling is an approach to automatically scaling out instances based on the resource usage to meet the SLAs by replicating the services to be scaled.

The system automatically detects an increase in traffic, spins up additional instances, and makes them available for traffic handling. Similarly, when the traffic volumes go down, the system automatically detects and reduces the number of instances by taking active instances back from the service:

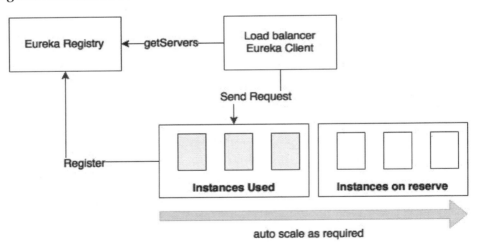

As shown in the preceding diagram, autoscaling is done, generally, using a set of reserve machines.

As many of the cloud subscriptions are based on a pay-as-you-go model, this is an essential capability when targeting cloud deployments. This approach is often called **elasticity**. It is also called **dynamic resource provisioning and deprovisioning**. Autoscaling is an effective approach specifically for microservices with varying traffic patterns. For example, an Accounting service would have high traffic during month ends and year ends. There is no point in permanently provisioning instances to handle these seasonal loads.

In the autoscaling approach, there is often a resource pool with a number of spare instances. Based on the demand, instances will be moved from the resource pool to the active state to meet the surplus demand. These instances are not pretagged for any particular microservices or prepackaged with any of the microservice binaries. In advanced deployments, the Spring Boot binaries are downloaded on demand from an artifact repository such as Nexus or Artifactory.

The benefits of autoscaling

There are many benefits in implementing the autoscaling mechanism. In traditional deployments, administrators reserve a set of servers against each application. With autoscaling, this preallocation is no longer required. This prefixed server allocation may result in underutilized servers. In this case, idle servers cannot be utilized even when neighboring services struggle for additional resources.

With hundreds of microservice instances, preallocating a fixed number of servers to each of the microservices is not cost effective. A better approach is to reserve a number of server instances for a group of microservices without preallocating or tagging them against a microservice. Instead, based on the demand, a group of services can share a set of available resources. By doing so, microservices can be dynamically moved across the available server instances by optimally using the resources:

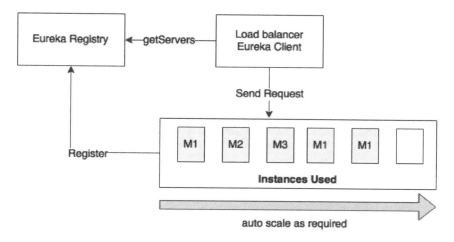

As shown in the preceding diagram, there are three instances of the **M1** microservice, one instance of **M2**, and one instance of **M3** up and running. There is another server kept unallocated. Based on the demand, the unallocated server can be used for any of the microservices: **M1**, **M2**, or **M3**. If **M1** has more service requests, then the unallocated instance will be used for **M1**. When the service usage goes down, the server instance will be freed up and moved back to the pool. Later, if the **M2** demand increases, the same server instance can be activated using **M2**.

Some of the key benefits of autoscaling are:

- **It has high availability and is fault tolerant**: As there are multiple service instances, even if one fails, another instance can take over and continue serving clients. This failover will be transparent to the consumers. If no other instance of this service is available, the autoscaling service will recognize this situation and bring up another server with the service instance. As the whole process of bringing up or bringing down instances is automatic, the overall availability of the services will be higher than the systems implemented without autoscaling. The systems without autoscaling require manual intervention to add or remove service instances, which will be hard to manage in large deployments.

  For example, assume that two of instances of the Booking service are running. If there is an increase in the traffic flow, in a normal scenario, the existing instance might become overloaded. In most of the scenarios, the entire set of services will be jammed, resulting in service unavailability. In the case of autoscaling, a new Booking service instance can be brought up quickly. This will balance the load and ensure service availability.

- **It increases scalability**: One of the key benefits of autoscaling is horizontal scalability. Autoscaling allows us to selectively scale up or scale down services automatically based on traffic patterns.

- **It has optimal usage and is cost saving**: In a pay-as-you-go subscription model, billing is based on actual resource utilization. With the autoscaling approach, instances will be started and shut down based on the demand. Hence, resources are optimally utilized, thereby saving cost.

- **It gives priority to certain services or group of services**: With autoscaling, it is possible to give priority to certain critical transactions over low-value transactions. This will be done by removing an instance from a low-value service and reallocating it to a high-value service. This will also eliminate situations where a low-priority transaction heavily utilizes resources when high-value transactions are cramped up for resources.

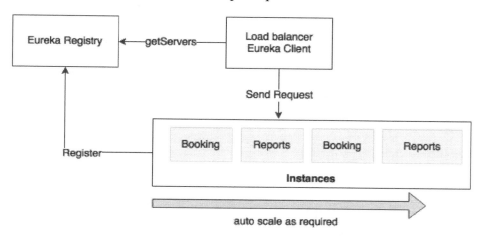

For instance, the **Booking** and **Reports** services run with two instances, as shown in the preceding diagram. Let's assume that the **Booking** service is a revenue generation service and therefore has a higher value than the **Reports** service. If there are more demands for the **Booking** service, then one can set policies to take one **Reports** service out of the service and release this server for the **Booking** service.

Different autoscaling models

Autoscaling can be applied at the application level or at the infrastructure level. In a nutshell, application scaling is scaling by replicating application binaries only, whereas infrastructure scaling is replicating the entire virtual machine, including application binaries.

Autoscaling an application

In this scenario, scaling is done by replicating the microservices, not the underlying infrastructure, such as virtual machines. The assumption is that there is a pool of VMs or physical infrastructures available to scale up microservices. These VMs have the basic image fused with any dependencies, such as JRE. It is also assumed that microservices are homogeneous in nature. This gives flexibility in reusing the same virtual or physical machines for different services:

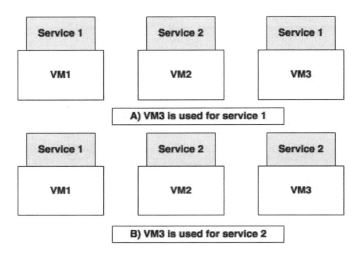

As shown in the preceding diagram, in scenario **A**, **VM3** is used for **Service 1**, whereas in scenario **B**, the same **VM3** is used for **Service 2**. In this case, we only swapped the application library and not the underlying infrastructure.

This approach gives faster instantiation as we are only handling the application binaries and not the underlying VMs. The switching is easier and faster as the binaries are smaller in size and there is no OS boot required either. However, the downside of this approach is that if certain microservices require OS-level tuning or use polyglot technologies, then dynamically swapping microservices will not be effective.

Autoscaling the infrastructure

In contrast to the previous approach, in this case, the infrastructure is also provisioned automatically. In most cases, this will create a new VM on the fly or destroy the VMs based on the demand:

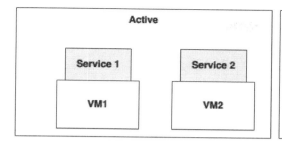 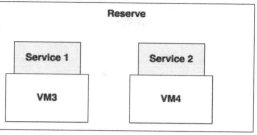

As shown in the preceding diagram, the reserve instances are created as VM images with predefined service instances. When there is demand for **Service 1**, **VM3** is moved to an active state. When there is a demand for **Service 2**, **VM4** is moved to the active state.

This approach is efficient if the applications depend upon the parameters and libraries at the infrastructure level, such as the operating system. Also, this approach is better for polyglot microservices. The downside is the heavy nature of VM images and the time required to spin up a new VM. Lightweight containers such as Dockers are preferred in such cases instead of traditional heavyweight virtual machines.

Autoscaling in the cloud

Elasticity or autoscaling is one of the fundamental features of most cloud providers. Cloud providers use infrastructure scaling patterns, as discussed in the previous section. These are typically based on a set of pooled machines.

For example, in AWS, these are based on introducing new EC2 instances with a predefined AMI. AWS supports autoscaling with the help of autoscaling groups. Each group is set with a minimum and maximum number of instances. AWS ensures that the instances are scaled on demand within these bounds. In case of predictable traffic patterns, provisioning can be configured based on timelines. AWS also provides ability for applications to customize autoscaling policies.

Microsoft Azure also supports autoscaling based on the utilization of resources such as the CPU, message queue length, and so on. IBM Bluemix supports autoscaling based on resources such as CPU usage.

Other PaaS platforms, such as CloudBees and OpenShift, also support autoscaling for Java applications. Pivotal Cloud Foundry supports autoscaling with the help of Pivotal Autoscale. Scaling policies are generally based on resource utilization, such as the CPU and memory thresholds.

There are components that run on top of the cloud and provide fine-grained controls to handle autoscaling. Netflix Fenzo, Eucalyptus, Boxfuse, and Mesosphere are some of the components in this category.

Autoscaling approaches

Autoscaling is handled by considering different parameters and thresholds. In this section, we will discuss the different approaches and policies that are typically applied to take decisions on when to scale up or down.

Scaling with resource constraints

This approach is based on real-time service metrics collected through monitoring mechanisms. Generally, the resource-scaling approach takes decisions based on the CPU, memory, or the disk of machines. This can also be done by looking at the statistics collected on the service instances themselves, such as heap memory usage.

A typical policy may be spinning up another instance when the CPU utilization of the machine goes beyond 60%. Similarly, if the heap size goes beyond a certain threshold, we can add a new instance. The same applies to downsizing the compute capacity when the resource utilization goes below a set threshold. This is done by gradually shutting down servers:

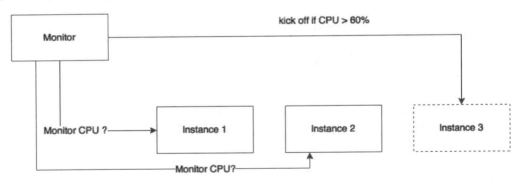

In typical production scenarios, the creation of additional services is not done on the first occurrence of a threshold breach. The most appropriate approach is to define a sliding window or a waiting period.

The following are some of the examples:

- An example of a **response sliding window** is if 60% of the response time of a particular transaction is consistently more than the set threshold value in a 60-second sampling window, increase service instances

- In a **CPU sliding window**, if the CPU utilization is consistently beyond 70% in a 5 minutes sliding window, then a new instance is created

- An example of the **exception sliding window** is if 80% of the transactions in a sliding window of 60 seconds or 10 consecutive executions result in a particular system exception, such as a connection timeout due to exhausting the thread pool, then a new service instance is created

In many cases, we will set a lower threshold than the actual expected thresholds. For example, instead of setting the CPU utilization threshold at 80%, set it at 60% so that the system gets enough time to spin up an instance before it stops responding. Similarly, when scaling down, we use a lower threshold than the actual. For example, we will use 40% CPU utilization to scale down instead of 60%. This allows us to have a cool-down period so that there will not be any resource struggle when shutting down instances.

Resource-based scaling is also applicable to service-level parameters such as the throughput of the service, latency, applications thread pool, connection pool, and so on. These can also be at the application level, such as the number of **sales orders** processing in a service instance, based on internal benchmarking.

Scaling during specific time periods

Time-based scaling is an approach to scaling services based on certain periods of the day, month, or year to handle seasonal or business peaks. For example, some services may experience a higher number of transactions during office hours and a considerably low number of transactions outside office hours. In this case, during the day, services autoscale to meet the demand and automatically downsize during the non-office hours:

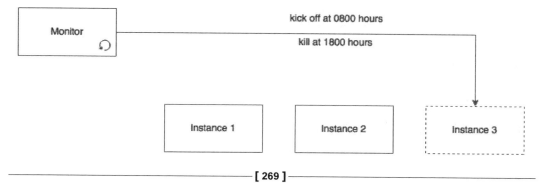

Many airports worldwide impose restrictions on night-time landing. As a result, the number of passengers checking in at the airports during the night time is less compared to the day time. Hence, it is cost effective to reduce the number of instances during the night time.

Scaling based on the message queue length

This is particularly useful when the microservices are based on asynchronous messaging. In this approach, new consumers are automatically added when the messages in the queue go beyond certain limits:

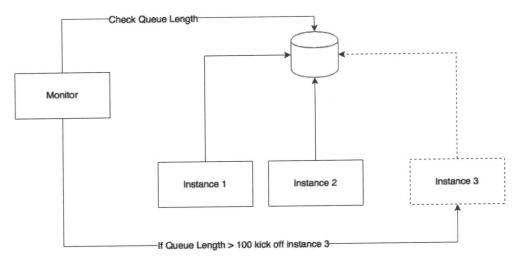

This approach is based on the competing consumer pattern. In this case, a pool of instances is used to consume messages. Based on the message threshold, new instances are added to consume additional messages.

Scaling based on business parameters

In this case, adding instances is based on certain business parameters—for example, spinning up a new instance just before handling **sales closing** transactions. As soon as the monitoring service receives a preconfigured business event (such as **sales closing minus 1 hour**), a new instance will be brought up in anticipation of large volumes of transactions. This will provide fine-grained control on scaling based on business rules:

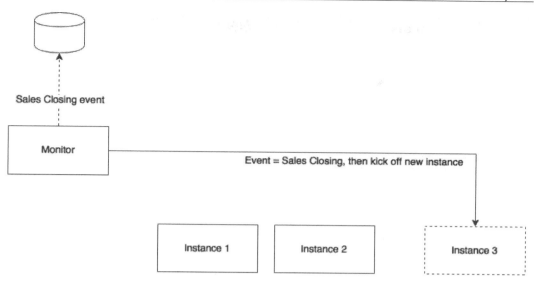

Predictive autoscaling

Predictive scaling is a new paradigm of autoscaling that is different from the traditional real-time metrics-based autoscaling. A prediction engine will take multiple inputs, such as historical information, current trends, and so on, to predict possible traffic patterns. Autoscaling is done based on these predictions. Predictive autoscaling helps avoid hardcoded rules and time windows. Instead, the system can automatically predict such time windows. In more sophisticated deployments, predictive analysis may use cognitive computing mechanisms to predict autoscaling.

In the cases of sudden traffic spikes, traditional autoscaling may not help. Before the autoscaling component can react to the situation, the spike would have hit and damaged the system. The predictive system can understand these scenarios and predict them before their actual occurrence. An example will be handling a flood of requests immediately after a planned outage.

Netflix Scryer is an example of such a system that can predict resource requirements in advance.

Autoscaling BrownField PSS microservices

In this section, we will examine how to enhance microservices developed in *Chapter 5*, *Scaling Microservices with Spring Cloud*, for autoscaling. We need a component to monitor certain performance metrics and trigger autoscaling. We will call this component the **life cycle manager**.

The service life cycle manager, or the application life cycle manager, is responsible for detecting scaling requirements and adjusting the number of instances accordingly. It is responsible for starting and shutting down instances dynamically.

In this section, we will take a look at a primitive autoscaling system to understand the basic concepts, which will be enhanced in later chapters.

The capabilities required for an autoscaling system

A typical autoscaling system has capabilities as shown in the following diagram:

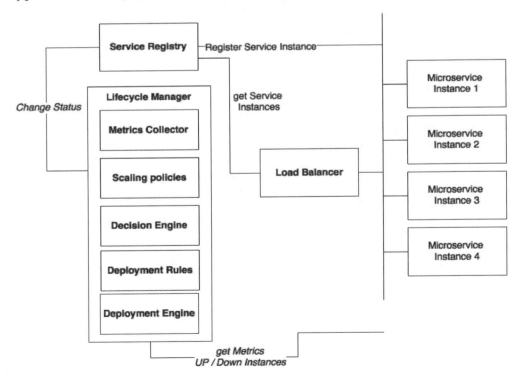

The components involved in the autoscaling ecosystem in the context of microservices are explained as follows:

- **Microservices**: These are sets of the up-and-running microservice instances that keep sending health and metrics information. Alternately, these services expose actuator endpoints for metrics collection. In the preceding diagram, these are represented as **Microservice 1** through **Microservice 4**.

- **Service Registry**: A service registry keeps track of all the services, their health states, their metadata, and their endpoint URI.

- **Load Balancer**: This is a client-side load balancer that looks up the service registry to get up-to-date information about the available service instances.

- **Lifecycle Manager**: The life cycle manger is responsible for autoscaling, which has the following subcomponents:

    - **Metrics Collector**: A metrics collection unit is responsible for collecting metrics from all service instances. The life cycle manager will aggregate the metrics. It may also keep a sliding time window. The metrics could be infrastructure-level metrics, such as CPU usage, or application-level metrics, such as transactions per minute.

    - **Scaling policies**: Scaling policies are nothing but sets of rules indicating when to scale up and scale down microservices—for example, 90% of CPU usage above 60% in a sliding window of 5 minutes.

    - **Decision Engine**: A decision engine is responsible for making decisions to scale up and scale down based on the aggregated metrics and scaling policies.

    - **Deployment Rules**: The deployment engine uses deployment rules to decide which parameters to consider when deploying services. For example, a service deployment constraint may say that the instance must be distributed across multiple availability regions or a 4 GB minimum of memory required for the service.

    - **Deployment Engine**: The deployment engine, based on the decisions of the decision engine, can start or stop microservice instances or update the registry by altering the health states of services. For example, it sets the health status as "out of service" to take out a service temporarily.

Implementing a custom life cycle manager using Spring Boot

The life cycle manager introduced in this section is a minimal implementation to understand autoscaling capabilities. In later chapters, we will enhance this implementation with containers and cluster management solutions. Ansible, Marathon, and Kubernetes are some of the tools useful in building this capability.

In this section, we will implement an application-level autoscaling component using Spring Boot for the services developed in *Chapter 5, Scaling Microservices with Spring Cloud*.

Understanding the deployment topology

The following diagram shows a sample deployment topology of BrownField PSS microservices:

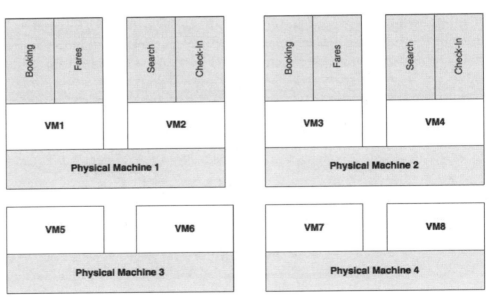

As shown in the diagram, there are four physical machines. Eight VMs are created from four physical machines. Each physical machine is capable of hosting two VMs, and each VM is capable of running two Spring Boot instances, assuming that all services have the same resource requirements.

Four VMs, **VM1** through **VM4**, are active and are used to handle traffic. **VM5** to **VM8** are kept as reserve VMs to handle scalability. **VM5** and **VM6** can be used for any of the microservices and can also be switched between microservices based on scaling demands. Redundant services use VMs created from different physical machines to improve fault tolerance.

Our objective is to scale out any services when there is increase in traffic flow using four VMs, **VM5** through **VM8**, and scale down when there is not enough load. The architecture of our solution is as follows.

Understanding the execution flow

Have a look at the following flowchart:

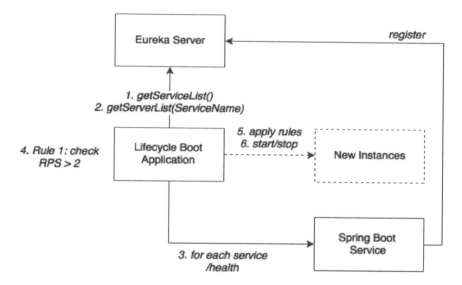

As shown in the preceding diagram, the following activities are important for us:

- The Spring Boot service represents microservices such as Search, Book, Fares, and Check-in. Services at startup automatically register endpoint details to the Eureka registry. These services are actuator-enabled, so the life cycle manager can collect metrics from the actuator endpoints.

- The life cycle manager service is nothing but another Spring Boot application. The life cycle manager has a metrics collector that runs a background job, periodically polls the Eureka server, and gets details of all the service instances. The metrics collector then invokes the actuator endpoints of each microservice registered in the Eureka registry to get the health and metrics information. In a real production scenario, a subscription approach for data collection is better.

- With the collected metrics information, the life cycle manager executes a list of policies and derives decisions on whether to scale up or scale down instances. These decisions are either to start a new service instance of a particular type on a particular VM or to shut down a particular instance.

- In the case of shutdown, it connects to the server using an actuator endpoint and calls the shutdown service to gracefully shut down an instance.

- In the case of starting a new instance, the deployment engine of the life cycle manager uses the scaling rules and decides where to start the new instance and what parameters are to be used when starting the instance. Then, it connects to the respective VMs using SSH. Once connected, it executes a preinstalled script (or passes this script as a part of the execution) by passing the required constraints as a parameter. This script fetches the application library from a central Nexus repository in which the production binaries are kept and initiates it as a Spring Boot application. The port number is parameterized by the life cycle manager. SSH needs to be enabled on the target machines.

In this example, we will use **TPM (Transactions Per Minute)** or **RPM (Requests Per Minute)** as sampler metrics for decision making. If the Search service has more than 10 TPM, then it will spin up a new Search service instance. Similarly, if the TPM is below 2, one of the instances will be shut down and released back to the pool.

When starting a new instance, the following policies will be applied:

- The number of service instances at any point should be a minimum of 1 and a maximum of 4. This also means that at least one service instance will always be up and running.

- A scaling group is defined in such a way that a new instance is created on a VM that is on a different physical machine. This will ensure that the services run across different physical machines.

These policies could be further enhanced. The life cycle manager ideally provides options to customize these rules through REST APIs or Groovy scripts.

A walkthrough of the life cycle manager code

We will take a look at how a simple life cycle manager is implemented. This section will be a walkthrough of the code to understand the different components of the life cycle manager.

 The full source code is available under the Chapter 6 project in the code files. The chapter5.configserver, chapter5.eurekaserver, chapter5.search, and chapter5.search-apigateway are copied and renamed as chapter6.*, respectively.

Perform the following steps to implement the custom life cycle manager:

1. Create a new Spring Boot application and name it chapter6.lifecyclemanager. The project structure is shown in the following diagram:

The flowchart for this example is as shown in the following diagram:

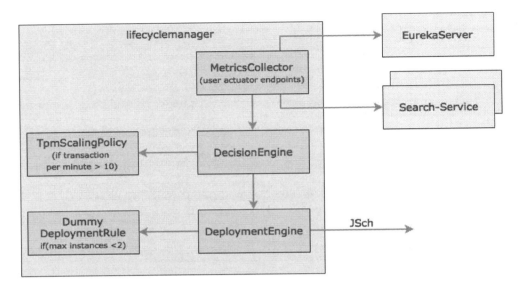

The components of this diagram are explained in details here.

2. Create a `MetricsCollector` class with the following method. At the startup of the Spring Boot application, this method will be invoked using `CommandLineRunner`, as follows:

```
public void start(){
   while(true){
      eurekaClient.getServices().forEach(service -> {          System.
out.println("discovered service "+ service);
         Map metrics = restTemplate.getForObject("http://"+service+"/
metrics",Map.class);
         decisionEngine.execute(service, metrics);
      });
   }
}
```

The preceding method looks for the services registered in the Eureka server and gets all the instances. In the real world, rather than polling, the instances should publish metrics to a common place, where metrics aggregation will happen.

3. The following `DecisionEngine` code accepts the metric and applies certain scaling policies to determine whether the service requires scaling up or not:

```
public boolean execute(String serviceId, Map metrics){
  if(scalingPolicies.getPolicy(serviceId).
    execute(serviceId, metrics)){
      return deploymentEngine.scaleUp(deploymentRules.
getDeploymentRules(serviceId), serviceId);
    }
    return false;
}
```

4. Based on the service ID, the policies that are related to the services will be picked up and applied. In this case, a minimal TPM scaling policy is implemented in `TpmScalingPolicy`, as follows:

```
public class TpmScalingPolicy implements ScalingPolicy {
  public boolean execute(String serviceId, Map metrics){
    if(metrics.containsKey("gauge.servo.tpm")){
      Double tpm = (Double) metrics.get("gauge.servo.tpm");
      System.out.println("gauge.servo.tpm " + tpm);
      return (tpm > 10);
    }
    return false;
  }
}
```

5. If the policy returns `true`, `DecisionEngine` then invokes `DeploymentEngine` to spin up another instance. `DeploymentEngine` makes use of `DeploymentRules` to decide how to execute scaling. The rules can enforce the number of min and max instances, in which region or machine the new instance has to be started, the resources required for the new instance, and so on. `DummyDeploymentRule` simply makes sure the max instance is not more than 2.

6. `DeploymentEngine`, in this case, uses the **JSch (Java Secure Channel)** library from JCraft to SSH to the destination server and start the service. This requires the following additional Maven dependency:

```
<dependency>
    <groupId>com.jcraft</groupId>
    <artifactId>jsch</artifactId>
    <version>0.1.53</version>
</dependency>
```

7. The current SSH implementation is kept simple enough as we will change this in future chapters. In this example, `DeploymentEngine` sends the following command over the SSH library on the target machine:

```
String command ="java -jar -Dserver.port=8091 ./work/codebox/
chapter6/chapter6.search/target/search-1.0.jar";
```

Integration with Nexus happens from the target machine using Linux scripts with Nexus CLI or using `curl`. In this example, we will not explore Nexus.

8. The next step is to change the Search microservice to expose a new gauge for TPM. We have to change all the microservices developed earlier to submit this additional metric.

We will only examine Search in this chapter, but in order to complete it, all the services have to be updated. In order to get the `gauge.servo.tpm` metrics, we have to add `TPMCounter` to all the microservices.

The following code counts the transactions over a sliding window of 1 minute:

```java
class TPMCounter {
  LongAdder count;
  Calendar expiry = null;
  TPMCounter(){
    reset();
  }
  void reset (){
    count = new LongAdder();
    expiry = Calendar.getInstance();
    expiry.add(Calendar.MINUTE, 1);
  }
  boolean isExpired(){
    return Calendar.getInstance().after(expiry);
  }
  void increment(){
    if(isExpired()){
      reset();
    }
    count.increment();
  }
}
```

9. The following code needs to be added to `SearchController` to set the `tpm` value:

```
class SearchRestController {
  TPMCounter tpm = new TPMCounter();
  @Autowired
  GaugeService gaugeService;
   //other code
```

10. The following code is from the get REST endpoint (the search method) of `SearchRestController`, which submits the `tpm` value as a gauge to the actuator endpoint:

```
tpm.increment();
gaugeService.submit("tpm", tpm.count.intValue());
```

Running the life cycle manager

Perform the following steps to run the life cycle manager developed in the previous section:

1. Edit `DeploymentEngine.java` and update the password to reflect the machine's password, as follows. This is required for the SSH connection:

```
session.setPassword("rajeshrv");
```

2. Build all the projects by running Maven from the root folder (`Chapter 6`) via the following command:

```
mvn -Dmaven.test.skip=true clean install
```

3. Then, run RabbitMQ, as follows:

```
./rabbitmq-server
```

4. Ensure that the Config server is pointing to the right configuration repository. We need to add a property file for the life cycle manager.

5. Run the following commands from the respective project folders:

```
java -jar target/config-server-0.0.1-SNAPSHOT.jar

java -jar target/eureka-server-0.0.1-SNAPSHOT.jar

java -jar target/lifecycle-manager-0.0.1-SNAPSHOT.jar

java -jar target/search-1.0.jar

java -jar target/search-apigateway-1.0.jar

java -jar target/website-1.0.jar
```

6. Once all the services are started, open a browser window and load `http://localhost:8001`.

7. Execute the flight search 11 times, one after the other, within a minute. This will trigger the decision engine to instantiate another instance of the Search microservice.

8. Open the Eureka console (`http://localhost:8761`) and watch for a second **SEARCH-SERVICE**. Once the server is started, the instances will appear as shown here:

Instances currently registered with Eureka

Application	AMIs	Availability Zones	Status
LIFECYCLE-MANAGER-SERVICE	n/a (1)	(1)	UP (1) - 192.168.0.106:lifecycle-manager-service:9090
SEARCH-APIGATEWAY	n/a (1)	(1)	UP (1) - 192.168.0.106:search-apigateway:8095
SEARCH-SERVICE	n/a (2)	(2)	UP (2) - 192.168.0.106:search-service:8091 , 192.168.0.106:search-service:8090
TEST-CLIENT	n/a (1)	(1)	UP (1) - 192.168.0.106:test-client:8001

Summary

In this chapter, you learned the importance of autoscaling when deploying large-scale microservices.

We also explored the concept of autoscaling and the different models of and approaches to autoscaling, such as the time-based, resource-based, queue length-based, and predictive ones. We then reviewed the role of a life cycle manager in the context of microservices and reviewed its capabilities. Finally, we ended this chapter by reviewing a sample implementation of a simple custom life cycle manager in the context of BrownField PSS microservices.

Autoscaling is an important supporting capability required when dealing with large-scale microservices. We will discuss a more mature implementation of the life cycle manager in *Chapter 9, Managing Dockerized Microservices with Mesos and Marathon*.

The next chapter will explore the logging and monitoring capabilities that are indispensable for successful microservice deployments.

7
Logging and Monitoring Microservices

One of the biggest challenges due to the very distributed nature of Internet-scale microservices deployment is the logging and monitoring of individual microservices. It is difficult to trace end-to-end transactions by correlating logs emitted by different microservices. As with monolithic applications, there is no single pane of glass to monitor microservices.

This chapter will cover the necessity and importance of logging and monitoring in microservice deployments. This chapter will further examine the challenges and solutions to address logging and monitoring with a number of potential architectures and technologies.

By the end of this chapter, you will learn about:

- The different options, tools, and technologies for log management
- The use of Spring Cloud Sleuth in tracing microservices
- The different tools for end-to-end monitoring of microservices
- The use of Spring Cloud Hystrix and Turbine for circuit monitoring
- The use of data lakes in enabling business data analysis

Reviewing the microservice capability model

In this chapter, we will explore the following microservice capabilities from the microservices capability model discussed in *Chapter 3, Applying Microservices Concepts*:

- **Central Log Management**
- **Monitoring and Dashboards**
- **Dependency Management** (part of Monitoring and Dashboards)
- **Data Lake**

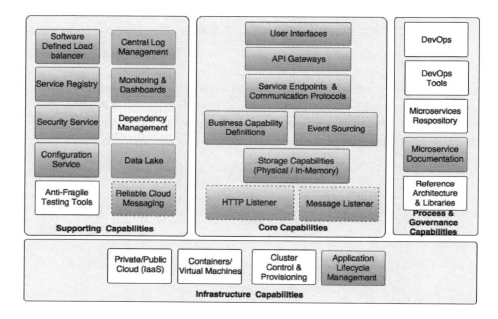

Understanding log management challenges

Logs are nothing but streams of events coming from a running process. For traditional JEE applications, a number of frameworks and libraries are available to log. Java Logging (JUL) is an option off the shelf from Java itself. Log4j, Logback, and SLF4J are some of the other popular logging frameworks available. These frameworks support both UDP as well as TCP protocols for logging. Applications send log entries to the console or to the filesystem. File recycling techniques are generally employed to avoid logs filling up all the disk space.

One of the best practices of log handling is to switch off most of the log entries in production due to the high cost of disk IOs. Not only do disk IOs slow down the application, but they can also severely impact scalability. Writing logs into the disk also requires high disk capacity. An out-of-disk-space scenario can bring down the application. Logging frameworks provide options to control logging at runtime to restrict what is to be printed and what not. Most of these frameworks provide fine-grained control over the logging controls. They also provide options to change these configurations at runtime.

On the other hand, logs may contain important information and have high value if properly analyzed. Therefore, restricting log entries essentially limits our ability to understand the application's behavior.

When moved from traditional to cloud deployment, applications are no longer locked to a particular, predefined machine. Virtual machines and containers are not hardwired with an application. The machines used for deployment can change from time to time. Moreover, containers such as Docker are ephemeral. This essentially means that one cannot rely on the persistent state of the disk. Logs written to the disk are lost once the container is stopped and restarted. Therefore, we cannot rely on the local machine's disk to write log files.

As we discussed in *Chapter 1, Demystifying Microservices,* one of the principles of the Twelve-Factor app is to avoid routing or storing log files by the application itself. In the context of microservices, they will run on isolated physical or virtual machines, resulting in fragmented log files. In this case, it is almost impossible to trace end-to-end transactions that span multiple microservices:

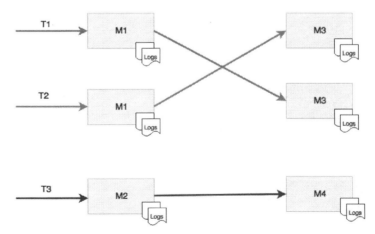

As shown in the diagram, each microservice emits logs to a local filesystem. In this case, microservice M1 calls M3. These services write their logs to their own local filesystems. This makes it harder to correlate and understand the end-to-end transaction flow. Also, as shown in the diagram, there are two instances of M1 and two instances of M2 running on two different machines. In this case, log aggregation at the service level is hard to achieve.

A centralized logging solution

In order to address the challenges stated earlier, traditional logging solutions require serious rethinking. The new logging solution, in addition to addressing the preceding challenges, is also expected to support the capabilities summarized here:

- The ability to collect all log messages and run analytics on top of the log messages
- The ability to correlate and track transactions end to end
- The ability to keep log information for longer time periods for trending and forecasting
- The ability to eliminate dependency on the local disk system
- The ability to aggregate log information coming from multiple sources such as network devices, operating system, microservices, and so on

The solution to these problems is to centrally store and analyze all log messages, irrespective of the source of log. The fundamental principle employed in the new logging solution is to detach log storage and processing from service execution environments. Big data solutions are better suited to storing and processing large numbers of log messages more effectively than storing and processing them in microservice execution environments.

In the centralized logging solution, log messages will be shipped from the execution environment to a central big data store. Log analysis and processing will be handled using big data solutions:

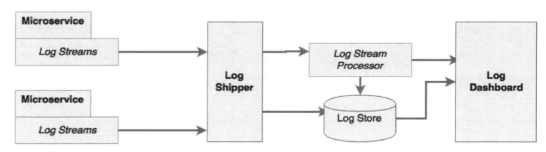

As shown in the preceding logical diagram, there are a number of components in the centralized logging solution, as follows:

- **Log streams**: These are streams of log messages coming out of source systems. The source system can be microservices, other applications, or even network devices. In typical Java-based systems, these are equivalent to streaming Log4j log messages.

- **Log shippers**: Log shippers are responsible for collecting the log messages coming from different sources or endpoints. The log shippers then send these messages to another set of endpoints, such as writing to a database, pushing to a dashboard, or sending it to stream-processing endpoint for further real-time processing.

- **Log store**: A log store is the place where all log messages are stored for real-time analysis, trending, and so on. Typically, a log store is a NoSQL database, such as HDFS, capable of handling large data volumes.

- **Log stream processor**: The log stream processor is capable of analyzing real-time log events for quick decision making. A stream processor takes actions such as sending information to a dashboard, sending alerts, and so on. In the case of self-healing systems, stream processors can even take actions to correct the problems.

- **Log dashboard**: A dashboard is a single pane of glass used to display log analysis results such as graphs and charts. These dashboards are meant for the operational and management staff.

The benefit of this centralized approach is that there is no local I/O or blocking disk writes. It also does not use the local machine's disk space. This architecture is fundamentally similar to the lambda architecture for big data processing.

 To read more on the Lambda architecture, go to `http://lambda-architecture.net.`

It is important to have in each log message a context, message, and correlation ID. The context typically has the timestamp, IP address, user information, process details (such as service, class, and functions), log type, classification, and so on. The message will be plain and simple free text information. The correlation ID is used to establish the link between service calls so that calls spanning microservices can be traced.

The selection of logging solutions

There are a number of options available to implement a centralized logging solution. These solutions use different approaches, architectures, and technologies. It is important to understand the capabilities required and select the right solution that meets the needs.

Cloud services

There are a number of cloud logging services available, such as the SaaS solution.

Loggly is one of the most popular cloud-based logging services. Spring Boot microservices can use Loggly's Log4j and Logback appenders to directly stream log messages into the Loggly service.

If the application or service is deployed in AWS, AWS CloudTrail can be integrated with Loggly for log analysis.

Papertrial, Logsene, Sumo Logic, Google Cloud Logging, and Logentries are examples of other cloud-based logging solutions.

The cloud logging services take away the overhead of managing complex infrastructures and large storage solutions by providing them as simple-to-integrate services. However, latency is one of the key factors to be considered when selecting cloud logging as a service.

Off-the-shelf solutions

There are many purpose-built tools to provide end-to-end log management capabilities that are installable locally in an on-premises data center or in the cloud.

Graylog is one of the popular open source log management solutions. Graylog uses Elasticsearch for log storage and MongoDB as a metadata store. Graylog also uses GELF libraries for Log4j log streaming.

Splunk is one of the popular commercial tools available for log management and analysis. Splunk uses the log file shipping approach, compared to log streaming used by other solutions to collect logs.

Best-of-breed integration

The last approach is to pick and choose best-of-breed components and build a custom logging solution.

Log shippers

There are log shippers that can be combined with other tools to build an end-to-end log management solution. The capabilities differ between different log shipping tools.

Logstash is a powerful data pipeline tool that can be used to collect and ship log files. Logstash acts as a broker that provides a mechanism to accept streaming data from different sources and sync them to different destinations. Log4j and Logback appenders can also be used to send log messages directly from Spring Boot microservices to Logstash. The other end of Logstash is connected to Elasticsearch, HDFS, or any other database.

Fluentd is another tool that is very similar to Logstash, as is Logspout, but the latter is more appropriate in a Docker container-based environment.

Log stream processors

Stream-processing technologies are optionally used to process log streams on the fly. For example, if a 404 error is continuously occurring as a response to a particular service call, it means there is something wrong with the service. Such situations have to be handled as soon as possible. Stream processors are pretty handy in such cases as they are capable of reacting to certain streams of events that a traditional reactive analysis can't.

A typical architecture used for stream processing is a combination of Flume and Kafka together with either Storm or Spark Streaming. Log4j has Flume appenders, which are useful to collect log messages. These messages are pushed into distributed Kafka message queues. The stream processors collect data from Kafka and process them on the fly before sending it to Elasticsearch and other log stores.

Spring Cloud Stream, Spring Cloud Stream Modules, and Spring Cloud Data Flow can also be used to build the log stream processing.

Log storage

Real-time log messages are typically stored in Elasticsearch. Elasticsearch allows clients to query based on text-based indexes. Apart from Elasticsearch, HDFS is also commonly used to store archived log messages. MongoDB or Cassandra is used to store summary data, such as monthly aggregated transaction counts. Offline log processing can be done using Hadoop's MapReduce programs.

Dashboards

The last piece required in the central logging solution is a dashboard. The most commonly used dashboard for log analysis is Kibana on top of an Elasticsearch data store. Graphite and Grafana are also used to display log analysis reports.

A custom logging implementation

The tools mentioned before can be leveraged to build a custom end-to-end logging solution. The most commonly used architecture for custom log management is a combination of Logstash, Elasticsearch, and Kibana, also known as the ELK stack.

> The full source code of this chapter is available under the `Chapter 7` project in the code files. Copy `chapter5.configserver`, `chapter5.eurekaserver`, `chapter5.search`, `chapter5.search-apigateway`, and `chapter5.website` into a new STS workspace and rename them `chapter7.*`.

The following diagram shows the log monitoring flow:

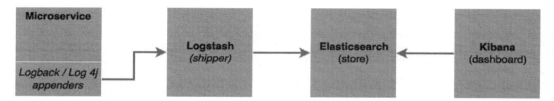

In this section, a simple implementation of a custom logging solution using the ELK stack will be examined.

Follow these steps to implement the ELK stack for logging:

1. Download and install Elasticsearch, Kibana, and Logstash from `https://www.elastic.co`.

2. Update the Search microservice (`chapter7.search`). Review and ensure that there are some log statements in the Search microservice. The log statements are nothing special but simple log statements using `slf4j`, as follows:

```
import org.slf4j.Logger;
import org.slf4j.LoggerFactory;
  //other code goes here
   private static final Logger logger = LoggerFactory.
     getLogger(SearchRestController.class);
//other code goes here
```

```
logger.info("Looking to load flights...");
for (Flight flight : flightRepository.
   findByOriginAndDestinationAndFlightDate
   ("NYC", "SFO", "22-JAN-16")) {
       logger.info(flight.toString());
}
```

3. Add the `logstash` dependency to integrate `logback` to Logstash in the Search service's `pom.xml` file, as follows:

```xml
<dependency>
   <groupId>net.logstash.logback</groupId>
   <artifactId>logstash-logback-encoder</artifactId>
   <version>4.6</version>
</dependency>
```

4. Also, downgrade the `logback` version to be compatible with Spring 1.3.5.RELEASE via the following line:

```
<logback.version>1.1.6</logback.version>
```

5. Override the default Logback configuration. This can be done by adding a new `logback.xml` file under `src/main/resources`, as follows:

```xml
<?xml version="1.0" encoding="UTF-8"?>
<configuration>
    <include resource="org/springframework/boot/logging/logback/
defaults.xml"/>
    <include resource="org/springframework/boot/logging/logback/
console-appender.xml" />
    <appender name="stash" class="net.logstash.logback.
      appender.LogstashTcpSocketAppender">
        <destination>localhost:4560</destination>
        <!-- encoder is required -->
        <encoder class="net.logstash.logback.encoder.
          LogstashEncoder" />
    </appender>
  <root level="INFO">
    <appender-ref ref="CONSOLE" />
    <appender-ref ref="stash" />
  </root>
</configuration>
```

The preceding configuration overrides the default Logback configuration by adding a new TCP socket `appender`, which streams all the log messages to a Logstash service, which is listening on port 4560. It is important to add an encoder, as mentioned in the previous configuration.

6. Create a configuration as shown in the following code and store it in a `logstash.conf` file. The location of this file is irrelevant as it will be passed as an argument when starting Logstash. This configuration will take input from the socket listening on `4560` and send the output to Elasticsearch running on `9200`. The `stdout` is optional and is set to debug:

```
input {
  tcp {
      port => 4560
      host => localhost
  }
}
output {
elasticsearch { hosts => ["localhost:9200"] }
  stdout { codec => rubydebug }
}
```

7. Run Logstash, Elasticsearch, and Kibana from their respective installation folders, as follows:

```
./bin/logstash -f logstash.conf
```

```
./bin/elasticsearch
```

```
./bin/kibana
```

8. Run the Search microservice. This will invoke the unit test cases and result in printing the log statements mentioned before.

9. Go to a browser and access Kibana, at `http://localhost:5601`.

10. Go to **Settings | Configure an index pattern**, as shown here:

Configure an index pattern

In order to use Kibana you must configure at least one index pattern. Index patterns are used to identify the Elasticsearch index to run search and analytics against. They are also used to configure fields.

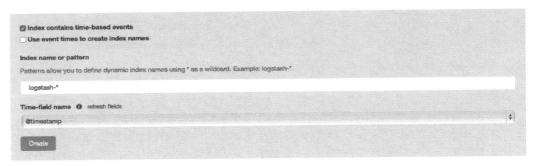

11. Go to the **Discover** menu to see the logs. If everything is successful, we will see the Kibana screenshot as follows. Note that the log messages are displayed in the Kibana screen.

Kibana provides out-of-the-box features to build summary charts and graphs using log messages:

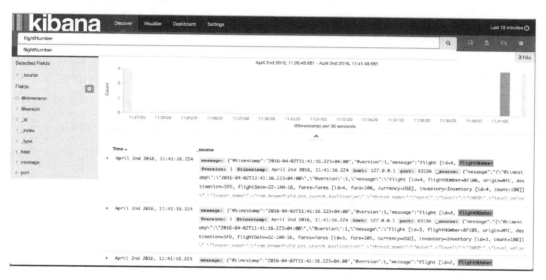

Distributed tracing with Spring Cloud Sleuth

The previous section addressed microservices' distributed and fragmented logging issue by centralizing the log data. With the central logging solution, we can have all the logs in a central storage. However, it is still almost impossible to trace end-to-end transactions. In order to do end-to-end tracking, transactions spanning microservices need to have a correlation ID.

Twitter's Zipkin, Cloudera's HTrace, and Google's Dapper systems are examples of distributed tracing systems. Spring Cloud provides a wrapper component on top of these using the Spring Cloud Sleuth library.

Distributed tracing works with the concepts of **span** and **trace**. The span is a unit of work; for example, calling a service is identified by a 64-bit span ID. A set of spans form a tree-like structure is called a trace. Using the trace ID, the call can be tracked end to end:

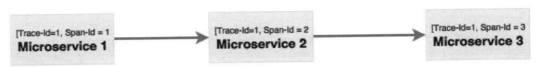

As shown in the diagram, **Microservice 1** calls **Microservice 2**, and **Microservice 2** calls **Microservice 3**. In this case, as shown in the diagram, the same trace ID is passed across all microservices, which can be used to track transactions end to end.

In order to demonstrate this, we will use the Search API Gateway and Search microservices. A new endpoint has to be added in Search API Gateway (`chapter7.search-apigateway`) that internally calls the Search service to return data. Without the trace ID, it is almost impossible to trace or link calls coming from the Website to Search API Gateway to Search microservice. In this case, it only involves two to three services, whereas in a complex environment, there could be many interdependent services.

Follow these steps to create the example using Sleuth:

1. Update Search and Search API Gateway. Before this, the Sleuth dependency needs to be added to the respective POM files, which can be done via the following code:

```
<dependency>
    <groupId>org.springframework.cloud</groupId>
    <artifactId>spring-cloud-starter-sleuth</artifactId>
</dependency>
```

2. In the case of building a new service, select **Sleuth** and **Web**, as shown here:

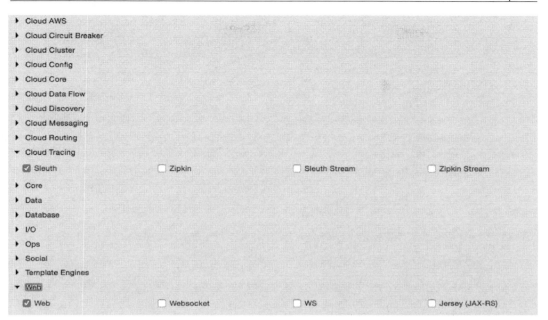

3. Add the Logstash dependency to the Search service as well as the Logback configuration, as in the previous example.

4. The next step is to add two more properties in the Logback configuration, as follows:

```
<property name="spring.application.name" value="search-service"/>
<property name="CONSOLE_LOG_PATTERN" value="%d{yyyy-MM-dd
HH:mm:ss.SSS} [${spring.application.name}] [trace=%X{X-Trace-Id:-
},span=%X{X-Span-Id:-}] [%15.15t] %-40.40logger{39}: %m%n"/>
```

The first property is the name of the application. The names given in this are the service IDs: `search-service` and `search-apigateway` in Search and Search API Gateway, respectively. The second property is an optional pattern used to print the console log messages with a trace ID and span ID. The preceding change needs to be applied to both the services.

5. Add the following piece of code to advise Sleuth when to start a new span ID in the Spring Boot Application class. In this case, `AlwaysSampler` is used to indicate that the span ID has to be created every time a call hits the service. This change needs to be applied in both the services:

```
@Bean
  public AlwaysSampler defaultSampler() {
    return new AlwaysSampler();
  }
```

6. Add a new endpoint to Search API Gateway, which will call the Search service as follows. This is to demonstrate the propagation of the trace ID across multiple microservices. This new method in the gateway returns the operating hub of the airport by calling the Search service, as follows:

```
@RequestMapping("/hubongw")
String getHub(HttpServletRequest req){
   logger.info("Search Request in API gateway for getting Hub,
forwarding to search-service ");
   String hub = restTemplate.getForObject("http://search-service/
search/hub", String.class);
   logger.info("Response for hub received,  Hub "+ hub);
   return hub;
}
```

7. Add another endpoint in the Search service, as follows:

```
@RequestMapping("/hub")
String getHub(){
   logger.info("Searching for Hub, received from search-
apigateway ");
   return "SFO";
}
```

8. Once added, run both the services. Hit the gateway's new hub on the gateway (/hubongw) endpoint using a browser (http://localhost:8095/ hubongw).

   As mentioned earlier, the Search API Gateway service is running on 8095 and the Search service is running on 8090.

9. Look at the console logs to see the trace ID and span IDs printed. The first print is from Search API Gateway, and the second one came from the Search service. Note that the trace IDs are the same in both the cases, as follows:

```
2016-04-02 17:24:37.624 [search-apigateway] [trace=8a7e278f-7b2b-
43e3-a45c-69d3ca66d663,span=8a7e278f-7b2b-43e3-a45c-69d3ca66d663]
[io-8095-exec-10] c.b.p.s.a.SearchAPIGatewayController    :
Response for hub received,  Hub DXB


2016-04-02 17:24:37.612 [search-service] [trace=8a7e278f-7b2b-
43e3-a45c-69d3ca66d663,span=fd309bba-5b4d-447f-a5e1-7faaab90cfb1]
[nio-8090-exec-1] c.b.p.search.component.SearchComponent   :
Searching for Hub, received from search-apigateway
```

10. Open the Kibana console and search for the trace ID using this trace ID printed in the console. In this case, it is `8a7e278f-7b2b-43e3-a45c-69d3ca66d663`. As shown in the following screenshot, with a trace ID, one can trace service calls that span multiple services:

Monitoring microservices

Microservices are truly distributed systems with a fluid deployment topology. Without sophisticated monitoring in place, operations teams may run into trouble managing large-scale microservices. Traditional monolithic application deployments are limited to a number of known services, instances, machines, and so on. This is easier to manage compared to the large number of microservices instances potentially running across different machines. To add more complication, these services dynamically change their topologies. A centralized logging capability only addresses part of the issue. It is important for operations teams to understand the runtime deployment topology and also the behavior of the systems. This demands more than a centralized logging can offer.

In general application, monitoring is more a collection of metrics, aggregation, and their validation against certain baseline values. If there is a service-level breach, then monitoring tools generate alerts and send them to administrators. With hundreds and thousands of interconnected microservices, traditional monitoring does not really offer true value. The one-size-fits-all approach to monitoring or monitoring everything with a single pane of glass is not easy to achieve in large-scale microservices.

One of the main objectives of microservice monitoring is to understand the behavior of the system from a user experience point of view. This will ensure that the end-to-end behavior is consistent and is in line with what is expected by the users.

Monitoring challenges

Similar to the fragmented logging issue, the key challenge in monitoring microservices is that there are many moving parts in a microservice ecosystem.

The typical issues are summarized here:

- The statistics and metrics are fragmented across many services, instances, and machines.

- Heterogeneous technologies may be used to implement microservices, which makes things even more complex. A single monitoring tool may not give all the required monitoring options.

- Microservices deployment topologies are dynamic, making it impossible to preconfigure servers, instances, and monitoring parameters.

Many of the traditional monitoring tools are good to monitor monolithic applications but fall short in monitoring large-scale, distributed, interlinked microservice systems. Many of the traditional monitoring systems are agent-based preinstall agents on the target machines or application instances. This poses two challenges:

- If the agents require deep integration with the services or operating systems, then this will be hard to manage in a dynamic environment

- If these tools impose overheads when monitoring or instrumenting the application, it may lead to performance issues

Many traditional tools need baseline metrics. Such systems work with preset rules, such as if the CPU utilization goes above 60% and remains at this level for 2 minutes, then an alert should be sent to the administrator. It is extremely hard to preconfigure these values in large, Internet-scale deployments.

New-generation monitoring applications learn the application's behavior by themselves and set automatic threshold values. This frees up administrators from doing this mundane task. Automated baselines are sometimes more accurate than human forecasts:

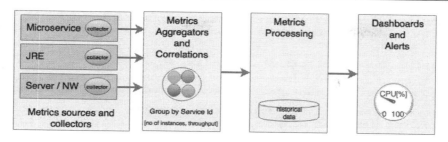

As shown in the diagram, the key areas of microservices monitoring are:

- **Metrics sources and data collectors**: Metrics collection at the source is done either by the server pushing metrics information to a central collector or by embedding lightweight agents to collect information. Data collectors collect monitoring metrics from different sources, such as network, physical machines, containers, software components, applications, and so on. The challenge is to collect this data using autodiscovery mechanisms instead of static configurations.

  This is done by either running agents on the source machines, streaming data from the sources, or polling at regular intervals.

- **Aggregation and correlation of metrics**: Aggregation capability is required for aggregating metrics collected from different sources, such as user transaction, service, infrastructure, network, and so on. Aggregation can be challenging as it requires some level of understanding of the application's behavior, such as service dependencies, service grouping, and so on. In many cases, these are automatically formulated based on the metadata provided by the sources.

  Generally, this is done by an intermediary that accept the metrics.

- **Processing metrics and actionable insights**: Once data is aggregated, the next step is to do the measurement. Measurements are typically done using set thresholds. In the new-generation monitoring systems, these thresholds are automatically discovered. Monitoring tools then analyze the data and provide actionable insights.

  These tools may use big data and stream analytics solutions.

- **Alerting, actions, and dashboards**: As soon as issues are detected, they have to be notified to the relevant people or systems. Unlike traditional systems, the microservices monitoring systems should be capable of taking actions on a real-time basis. Proactive monitoring is essential to achieving self-healing. Dashboards are used to display SLAs, KPIs, and so on.

  Dashboards and alerting tools are capable of handling these requirements.

Microservice monitoring is typically done with three approaches. A combination of these is really required for effective monitoring:

- **Application performance monitoring (APM)**: This is more of a traditional approach to system metrics collection, processing, alerting, and dashboard rendering. These are more from the system's point of view. Application topology discovery and visualization are new capabilities implemented by many of the APM tools. The capabilities vary between different APM providers.

- **Synthetic monitoring**: This is a technique that is used to monitor the system's behavior using end-to-end transactions with a number of test scenarios in a production or production-like environment. Data is collected to validate the system's behavior and potential hotspots. Synthetic monitoring helps understand the system dependencies as well.

- **Real user monitoring (RUM)** or **user experience monitoring**: This is typically a browser-based software that records real user statistics, such as response time, availability, and service levels. With microservices, with more frequent release cycle and dynamic topology, user experience monitoring is more important.

Monitoring tools

There are many tools available to monitor microservices. There are also overlaps between many of these tools. The selection of monitoring tools really depends upon the ecosystem that needs to be monitored. In most cases, more than one tool is required to monitor the overall microservice ecosystem.

The objective of this section is to familiarize ourselves with a number of common microservices-friendly monitoring tools:

- AppDynamics, Dynatrace, and New Relic are top commercial vendors in the APM space, as per Gartner Magic Quadrant 2015. These tools are microservice friendly and support microservice monitoring effectively in a single console. Ruxit, Datadog, and Dataloop are other commercial offerings that are purpose-built for distributed systems that are essentially microservices friendly. Multiple monitoring tools can feed data to Datadog using plugins.

- Cloud vendors come with their own monitoring tools, but in many cases, these monitoring tools alone may not be sufficient for large-scale microservice monitoring. For instance, AWS uses CloudWatch and Google Cloud Platform uses Cloud Monitoring to collect information from various sources.

- Some of the data collecting libraries, such as Zabbix, statd, collectd, jmxtrans, and so on operate at a lower level in collecting runtime statistics, metrics, gauges, and counters. Typically, this information is fed into data collectors and processors such as Riemann, Datadog, and Librato, or dashboards such as Graphite.

- Spring Boot Actuator is one of the good vehicles to collect microservices metrics, gauges, and counters, as we discussed in *Chapter 2, Building Microservices with Spring Boot*. Netflix Servo, a metric collector similar to Actuator, and the QBit and Dropwizard metrics also fall in the same category of metric collectors. All these metrics collectors need an aggregator and dashboard to facilitate full-sized monitoring.

- Monitoring through logging is popular but a less effective approach in microservices monitoring. In this approach, as discussed in the previous section, log messages are shipped from various sources, such as microservices, containers, networks, and so on to a central location. Then, we can use the logs files to trace transactions, identify hotspots, and so on. Loggly, ELK, Splunk, and Trace are candidates in this space.

- Sensu is a popular choice for microservice monitoring from the open source community. Weave Scope is another tool, primarily targeting containerized deployments. Spigo is one of the purpose-built microservices monitoring systems closely aligned with the Netflix stack.

- Pingdom, New Relic Synthetics, Runscope, Catchpoint, and so on provide options for synthetic transaction monitoring and user experience monitoring on live systems.

- Circonus is classified more as a DevOps monitoring tool but can also do microservices monitoring. Nagios is a popular open source monitoring tool but falls more into the traditional monitoring system.

- Prometheus provides a time series database and visualization GUI useful in building custom monitoring tools.

Monitoring microservice dependencies

When there are a large number of microservices with dependencies, it is important to have a monitoring tool that can show the dependencies among microservices. It is not a scalable approach to statically configure and manage these dependencies. There are many tools that are useful in monitoring microservice dependencies, as follows:

- Mentoring tools such as AppDynamics, Dynatrace, and New Relic can draw dependencies among microservices. End-to-end transaction monitoring can also trace transaction dependencies. Other monitoring tools, such as Spigo, are also useful for microservices dependency management.

- CMDB tools such as Device42 or purpose-built tools such as Accordance are useful in managing the dependency of microservices. **Veritas Risk Advisor (VRA)** is also useful for infrastructure discovery.

- A custom implementation with a Graph database, such as Neo4j, is also useful. In this case, a microservice has to preconfigure its direct and indirect dependencies. At the startup of the service, it publishes and cross-checks its dependencies with a Neo4j database.

Spring Cloud Hystrix for fault-tolerant microservices

This section will explore Spring Cloud Hystrix as a library for a fault-tolerant and latency-tolerant microservice implementation. Hystrix is based on the *fail fast* and *rapid recovery* principles. If there is an issue with a service, Hystrix helps isolate it. It helps to recover quickly by falling back to another preconfigured fallback service. Hystrix is another battle-tested library from Netflix. Hystrix is based on the circuit breaker pattern.

Read more about the circuit breaker pattern at `https://msdn.microsoft.com/en-us/library/dn589784.aspx`.

In this section, we will build a circuit breaker with Spring Cloud Hystrix. Perform the following steps to change the Search API Gateway service to integrate it with Hystrix:

1. Update the Search API Gateway service. Add the Hystrix dependency to the service. If developing from scratch, select the following libraries:

2. In the Spring Boot Application class, add `@EnableCircuitBreaker`. This command will tell Spring Cloud Hystrix to enable a circuit breaker for this application. It also exposes the `/hystrix.stream` endpoint for metrics collection.

3. Add a component class to the Search API Gateway service with a method; in this case, this is `getHub` annotated with `@HystrixCommand`. This tells Spring that this method is prone to failure. Spring Cloud libraries wrap these methods to handle fault tolerance and latency tolerance by enabling circuit breaker. The Hystrix command typically follows with a fallback method. In case of failure, Hystrix automatically enables the fallback method mentioned and diverts traffic to the fallback method. As shown in the following code, in this case, `getHub` will fall back to `getDefaultHub`:

```
@Component
class SearchAPIGatewayComponent {
    @LoadBalanced
    @Autowired
    RestTemplate restTemplate;
```

```
@HystrixCommand(fallbackMethod = "getDefaultHub")
public String getHub(){
   String hub = restTemplate.getForObject("http://search-service/
search/hub", String.class);
   return hub;
}
public String getDefaultHub(){
   return "Possibily SFO";
}
}
```

4. The getHub **method of** SearchAPIGatewayController **calls the** getHub
    method of SearchAPIGatewayComponent, **as follows:**

```
@RequestMapping("/hubongw")
String getHub(){
   logger.info("Search Request in API gateway for getting Hub,
forwarding to search-service ");
   return component.getHub();
}
```

5. The last part of this exercise is to build a Hystrix Dashboard. For this, build
    another Spring Boot application. Include Hystrix, Hystrix Dashboard, and
    Actuator when building this application.

6. In the Spring Boot Application class, add the @EnableHystrixDashboard
    annotation.

7. Start the Search service, Search API Gateway, and Hystrix Dashboard
    applications. Point the browser to the Hystrix Dashboard application's URL.
    In this example, the Hystrix Dashboard is started on port 9999. So, open the
    URL http://localhost:9999/hystrix.

8. A screen similar to the following screenshot will be displayed. In the Hystrix
    Dashboard, enter the URL of the service to be monitored.

    In this case, Search API Gateway is running on port 8095. Hence, the
    hystrix.stream URL will be http://localhost:8095/hytrix.stream,
    as shown:

Hystrix Dashboard

http://localhost:8095/hystrix.stream

Cluster via Turbine (default cluster): http://turbine-hostname:port/turbine.stream
Cluster via Turbine (custom cluster): http://turbine-hostname:port/turbine.stream?cluster=[clusterName]
Single Hystrix App: http://hystrix-app:port/hystrix.stream

Delay: 2000 ms   Title: SearchAPIGateway

Monitor Stream

9. The Hystrix Dashboard will be displayed as follows:

Hystrix Stream: SearchAPIGateway

HYSTRIX
DEFEND YOUR APP

Circuit   Sort: Error then Volume I Alphabetical I Volume I Error I Mean I Median I 90 I 99 I 99.5

Success I Short-Circuited I Timeout I Rejected I Failure I Error %

getHub

6 | 0 | 0.0 %
0 | 0
  | 0

Host: **0.6/s**

Cluster: **0.6/s**

Circuit Closed

Hosts	1	90th	16ms
Median	12ms	99th	19ms
Mean	12ms	99.5th	19ms

Thread Pools   Sort: Alphabetical I Volume I

SearchAPIGatewayComponent

Host: **0.6/s**

Cluster: **0.6/s**

Active	0	Max Active	1
Queued	0	Executions	6
Pool Size	10	Queue Size	5

Note that at least one transaction has to be executed to see the display. This can be done by hitting `http://localhost:8095/hubongw`.

10. Create a failure scenario by shutting down the Search service. Note that the fallback method will be called when hitting the URL `http://localhost:8095/hubongw`.

11. If there are continuous failures, then the circuit status will be changed to open. This can be done by hitting the preceding URL a number of times. In the open state, the original service will no longer be checked. The Hystrix Dashboard will show the status of the circuit as **Open**, as shown in the following screenshot. Once a circuit is opened, periodically, the system will check for the original service status for recovery. When the original service is back, the circuit breaker will fall back to the original service and the status will be set to **Closed**:

Hystrix Stream: SearchAPIGateway

Circuit   Sort: Error then Volume | Alphabetical | Volume | Error | Mean | Median | 90 | 99 | 99.5

Success | Short-Circuited | Timeout | Rejected | Failure | Error %

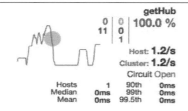

getHub

0   0   100.0 %
11 0
    1

Host: **1.2/s**
Cluster: **1.2/s**
Circuit Open

Hosts	1	90th	0ms
Median	0ms	99th	0ms
Mean	0ms	99.5th	0ms

Thread Pools   Sort: Alphabetical | Volume |

SearchAPIGatewayComponent

Host: **0.1/s**
Cluster: **0.1/s**

Active	0	Max Active	1
Queued	0	Executions	1
Pool Size	10	Queue Size	5

To know the meaning of each of these parameters, visit the Hystrix wiki at `https://github.com/Netflix/Hystrix/wiki/Dashboard`.

Aggregating Hystrix streams with Turbine

In the previous example, the /hystrix.stream endpoint of our microservice was given in the Hystrix Dashboard. The Hystrix Dashboard can only monitor one microservice at a time. If there are many microservices, then the Hystrix Dashboard pointing to the service has to be changed every time we switch the microservices to monitor. Looking into one instance at a time is tedious, especially when there are many instances of a microservice or multiple microservices.

We have to have a mechanism to aggregate data coming from multiple /hystrix. stream instances and consolidate it into a single dashboard view. Turbine does exactly the same thing. Turbine is another server that collects Hystrix streams from multiple instances and consolidates them into one /turbine.stream instance. Now, the Hystrix Dashboard can point to /turbine.stream to get the consolidated information:

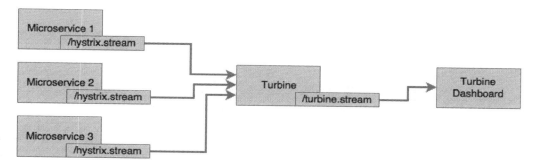

 Turbine currently works only with different hostnames. Each instance has to be run on separate hosts. If you are testing multiple services locally on the same host, then update the host file (/etc/hosts) to simulate multiple hosts. Once done, bootstrap.properties has to be configured as follows:

```
eureka.instance.hostname: localdomain2
```

This example showcases how to use Turbine to monitor circuit breakers across multiple instances and services. We will use the Search service and Search API Gateway in this example. Turbine internally uses Eureka to resolve service IDs that are configured for monitoring.

Perform the following steps to build and execute this example:

1. The Turbine server can be created as just another Spring Boot application using Spring Boot Starter. Select Turbine to include the Turbine libraries.

2. Once the application is created, add `@EnableTurbine` to the main Spring Boot Application class. In this example, both Turbine and Hystrix Dashboard are configured to be run on the same Spring Boot application. This is possible by adding the following annotations to the newly created Turbine application:

```
@EnableTurbine
@EnableHystrixDashboard
@SpringBootApplication
public class TurbineServerApplication {
```

3. Add the following configuration to the `.yaml` or property file to point to the instances that we are interested in monitoring:

```
spring:
  application:
    name : turbineserver
turbine:
  clusterNameExpression: new String('default')
  appConfig : search-service,search-apigateway
server:
  port: 9090
eureka:
  client:
    serviceUrl:
      defaultZone: http://localhost:8761/eureka/
```

4. The preceding configuration instructs the Turbine server to look up the Eureka server to resolve the `search-service` and `search-apigateway` services. The `search-service` and `search-apigateways` service IDs are used to register services with Eureka. Turbine uses these names to resolve the actual service host and port by checking with the Eureka server. It will then use this information to read `/hystrix.stream` from each of these instances. Turbine will then read all the individual Hystrix streams, aggregate all of them, and expose them under the Turbine server's `/turbine.stream` URL.

5. The cluster name expression is pointing to the default cluster as there is no explicit cluster configuration done in this example. If the clusters are manually configured, then the following configuration has to be used:

```
turbine:
  aggregator:
    clusterConfig: [comma separated clusternames]
```

6. Change the Search service's `SearchComponent` to add another circuit breaker, as follows:

```
@HystrixCommand(fallbackMethod = "searchFallback")
public List<Flight> search(SearchQuery query){
```

7. Also, add `@EnableCircuitBreaker` to the main Application class in the Search service.

8. Add the following configuration to `bootstrap.properties` of the Search service. This is required because all the services are running on the same host:

```
Eureka.instance.hostname: localdomain1
```

9. Similarly, add the following in `bootstrap.properties` of the Search API Gateway service. This is to make sure that both the services use different hostnames:

```
eureka.instance.hostname: localdomain2
```

10. In this example, we will run two instances of `search-apigateway`: one on `localdomain1:8095` and another one on `localdomain2:8096`. We will also run one instance of `search-service` on `localdomain1:8090`.

11. Run the microservices with command-line overrides to manage different host addresses, as follows:

```
java -jar -Dserver.port=8096 -Deureka.instance.
hostname=localdomain2 -Dserver.address=localdomain2 target/
chapter7.search-apigateway-1.0.jar
```

```
java -jar -Dserver.port=8095 -Deureka.instance.
hostname=localdomain1 -Dserver.address=localdomain1 target/
chapter7.search-apigateway-1.0.jar
```

```
java -jar -Dserver.port=8090 -Deureka.instance.
hostname=localdomain1 -Dserver.address=localdomain1 target/
chapter7.search-1.0.jar
```

12. Open Hystrix Dashboard by pointing the browser to `http://localhost:9090/hystrix`.

13. Instead of giving `/hystrix.stream`, this time, we will point to `/turbine.stream`. In this example, the Turbine stream is running on `9090`. Hence, the URL to be given in the Hystrix Dashboard is `http://localhost:9090/turbine.stream`.

14. Fire a few transactions by opening a browser window and hitting the following two URLs: `http://localhost:8095/hubongw` and `http://localhost:8096/hubongw`.

Once this is done, the dashboard page will show the **getHub** service.

15. Run `chapter7.website`. Execute the search transaction using the website `http://localhost:8001`.

   After executing the preceding search, the dashboard page will show **search-service** as well. This is shown in the following screenshot:

Hystrix Stream: http://localhost:9090/turbine.stream  HYSTRIX
DEFEND YOUR APP

Circuit   Sort: Error then Volume | Alphabetical | Volume | Error | Mean | Median | 90 | 99 | 99.5

Success | Short-Circuited | Timeout | Rejected | Failure | Error %

	search-service			getHub		
	0 0	0 0	0.0 %	0 0 0	0 0	0.0 %
	Host: **0.0/s**			Host: **0.0/s**		
	Cluster: **0.0/s**			Cluster: **0.0/s**		
	Circuit Closed			Circuit Closed		
Hosts	1	90th	30ms	Hosts 2	90th	0ms
Median	30ms	99th	30ms	Median 0ms	99th	0ms
Mean	30ms	99.5th	30ms	Mean 0ms	99.5th	0ms

Thread Pools   Sort: Alphabetical | Volume |

SearchAPIGatewayComponent

Host: **0.0/s**

Cluster: **0.0/s**

Active	0	Max Active	0
Queued	0	Executions	0
Pool Size	8	Queue Size	5

As we can see in the dashboard, **search-service** is coming from the Search microservice, and **getHub** is coming from Search API Gateway. As we have two instances of Search API Gateway, **getHub** is coming from two hosts, indicated by **Hosts 2**.

Data analysis using data lakes

Similarly to the scenario of fragmented logs and monitoring, fragmented data is another challenge in the microservice architecture. Fragmented data poses challenges in data analytics. This data may be used for simple business event monitoring, data auditing, or even deriving business intelligence out of the data.

A data lake or data hub is an ideal solution to handling such scenarios. An event-sourced architecture pattern is generally used to share the state and state changes as events with an external data store. When there is a state change, microservices publish the state change as events. Interested parties may subscribe to these events and process them based on their requirements. A central event store may also subscribe to these events and store them in a big data store for further analysis.

One of the commonly followed architectures for such data handling is shown in the following diagram:

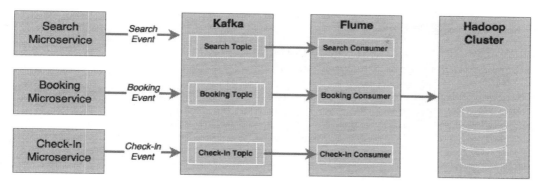

State change events generated from the microservice—in our case, the **Search**, **Booking**, and **Check-In** events—are pushed to a distributed high-performance messaging system, such as Kafka. A data ingestion service, such as Flume, can subscribe to these events and update them to an HDFS cluster. In some cases, these messages will be processed in real time by Spark Streaming. To handle heterogeneous sources of events, Flume can also be used between event sources and Kafka.

Spring Cloud Streams, Spring Cloud Streams modules, and Spring Data Flow are also useful as alternatives for high-velocity data ingestion.

Summary

In this chapter, you learned about the challenges around logging and monitoring when dealing with Internet-scale microservices.

We explored the various solutions for centralized logging. You also learned about how to implement a custom centralized logging using Elasticsearch, Logstash, and Kibana (ELK). In order to understand distributed tracing, we upgraded BrownField microservices using Spring Cloud Sleuth.

In the second half of this chapter, we went deeper into the capabilities required for microservices monitoring solutions and different approaches to monitoring. Subsequently, we examined a number of tools available for microservices monitoring.

The BrownField microservices are further enhanced with Spring Cloud Hystrix and Turbine to monitor latencies and failures in inter-service communications. The examples also demonstrated how to use the circuit breaker pattern to fall back to another service in case of failures.

Finally, we also touched upon the importance of data lakes and how to integrate a data lake architecture in a microservice context.

Microservice management is another important challenge we need to tackle when dealing with large-scale microservice deployments. The next chapter will explore how containers can help in simplifying microservice management.

8
Containerizing Microservices with Docker

In the context of microservices, containerized deployment is the icing on the cake. It helps microservices be more autonomous by self-containing the underlying infrastructure, thereby making the microservices cloud neutral.

This chapter will introduce the concepts and relevance of virtual machine images and the containerized deployment of microservices. Then, this chapter will further familiarize readers with building Docker images for the BrownField PSS microservices developed with Spring Boot and Spring Cloud. Finally, this chapter will also touch base on how to manage, maintain, and deploy Docker images in a production-like environment.

By the end of this chapter, you will learn about:

- The concept of containerization and its relevance in the context of microservices
- Building and deploying microservices as Docker images and containers
- Using AWS as an example of cloud-based Docker deployments

Reviewing the microservice capability model

In this chapter, we will explore the following microservice capabilities from the microservice capability model discussed in *Chapter 3, Applying Microservices Concepts*:

- Containers and virtual machines
- The private/public cloud
- The microservices repository

The model is shown in the following diagram:

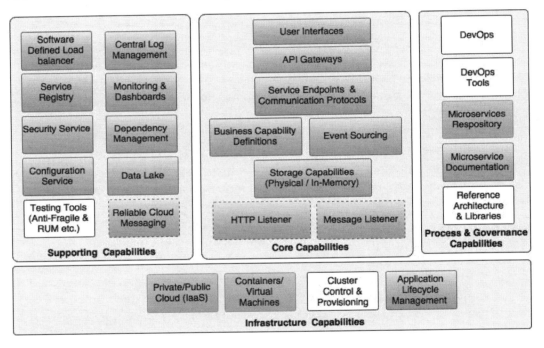

Understanding the gaps in BrownField PSS microservices

In *Chapter 5, Scaling Microservices with Spring Cloud*, BrownField PSS microservices were developed using Spring Boot and Spring Cloud. These microservices are deployed as versioned fat JAR files on bare metals, specifically on a local development machine.

In *Chapter 6, Autoscaling Microservices,* the autoscaling capability was added with the help of a custom life cycle manager. In *Chapter 7, Logging and Monitoring Microservices,* challenges around logging and monitoring were addressed using centralized logging and monitoring solutions.

There are still a few gaps in our BrownField PSS implementation. So far, the implementation has not used any cloud infrastructure. Dedicated machines, as in traditional monolithic application deployments, are not the best solution for deploying microservices. Automation such as automatic provisioning, the ability to scale on demand, self-service, and payment based on usage are essential capabilities required to manage large-scale microservice deployments efficiently. In general, a cloud infrastructure provides all these essential capabilities. Therefore, a private or public cloud with the capabilities mentioned earlier is better suited to deploying Internet-scale microservices.

Also, running one microservice instance per bare metal is not cost effective. Therefore, in most cases, enterprises end up deploying multiple microservices on a single bare metal server. Running multiple microservices on a single bare metal could lead to a "noisy neighbor" problem. There is no isolation between the microservice instances running on the same machine. As a result, services deployed on a single machine may eat up others' space, thus impacting their performance.

An alternate approach is to run the microservices on VMs. However, VMs are heavyweight in nature. Therefore, running many smaller VMs on a physical machine is not resource efficient. This generally results in resource wastage. In the case of sharing a VM to deploy multiple services, we would end up facing the same issues of sharing the bare metal, as explained earlier.

In the case of Java-based microservices, sharing a VM or bare metal to deploy multiple microservices also results in sharing JRE among microservices. This is because the fat JARs created in our BrownField PSS abstract only application code and its dependencies but not JREs. Any update on JRE installed on the machine will have an impact on all the microservices deployed on this machine. Similarly, if there are OS-level parameters, libraries, or tunings that are required for specific microservices, then it will be hard to manage them on a shared environment.

One microservice principle insists that it should be self-contained and autonomous by fully encapsulating its end-to-end runtime environment. In order to align with this principle, all components, such as the OS, JRE, and microservice binaries, have to be self-contained and isolated. The only option to achieve this is to follow the approach of deploying one microservice per VM. However, this will result in underutilized virtual machines, and in many cases, extra cost due to this can nullify benefits of microservices.

What are containers?

Containers are not revolutionary, ground-breaking concepts. They have been in action for quite a while. However, the world is witnessing the re-entry of containers, mainly due to the wide adoption of cloud computing. The shortcomings of traditional virtual machines in the cloud computing space also accelerated the use of containers. Container providers such as **Docker** simplified container technologies to a great extent, which also enabled a large adoption of container technologies in today's world. The recent popularity of DevOps and microservices also acted as a catalyst for the rebirth of container technologies.

So, what are containers? Containers provide private spaces on top of the operating system. This technique is also called operating system virtualization. In this approach, the kernel of the operating system provides isolated virtual spaces. Each of these virtual spaces is called a container or **virtual engine** (**VE**). Containers allow processes to run on an isolated environment on top of the host operating system. A representation of multiple containers running on the same host is shown as follows:

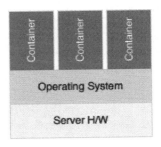

Containers are easy mechanisms to build, ship, and run compartmentalized software components. Generally, containers package all the binaries and libraries that are essential for running an application. Containers reserve their own filesystem, IP address, network interfaces, internal processes, namespaces, OS libraries, application binaries, dependencies, and other application configurations.

There are billions of containers used by organizations. Moreover, there are many large organizations heavily investing in container technologies. Docker is far ahead of the competition, supported by many large operating system vendors and cloud providers. **Lmctfy, SystemdNspawn, Rocket, Drawbridge, LXD, Kurma**, and **Calico** are some of the other containerization solutions. Open container specification is also under development.

The difference between VMs and containers

VMs such as **Hyper-V**, **VMWare**, and **Zen** were popular choices for data center virtualization a few years ago. Enterprises experienced a cost saving by implementing virtualization over the traditional bare metal usage. It has also helped many enterprises utilize their existing infrastructure in a much more optimized manner. As VMs support automation, many enterprises experienced that they had to make lesser management effort with virtual machines. Virtual machines also helped organizations get isolated environments for applications to run in.

Prima facie, both virtualization and containerization exhibit exactly the same characteristics. However, in a nutshell, containers and virtual machines are not the same. Therefore, it is unfair to make an apple-to-apple comparison between VMs and containers. Virtual machines and containers are two different techniques and address different problems of virtualization. This difference is evident from the following diagram:

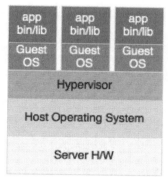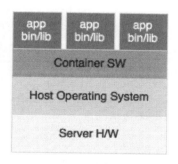

A) Virtual Machine Stack   B) Container Stack

Virtual machines operate at a much lower level compared to containers. VMs provide hardware virtualization, such as that of CPUs, motherboards, memory, and so on. A VM is an isolated unit with an embedded operating system, generally called a **Guest OS**. VMs replicate the whole operating system and run it within the VM with no dependency on the host operating system environment. As VMs embed the full operating system environment, these are heavyweight in nature. This is an advantage as well as a disadvantage. The advantage is that VMs offer complete isolation to the processes running on VMs. The disadvantage is that it limits the number of VMs one can spin up in a bare metal due to the resource requirements of VMs.

The size of a VM has a direct impact on the time to start and stop it. As starting a VM in turn boots the OS, the start time for VMs is generally high. VMs are more friendly with infrastructure teams as it requires a low level of infrastructure competency to manage VMs.

In the container world, containers do not emulate the entire hardware or operating system. Unlike VMs, containers share certain parts of the host kernel and operating system. There is no concept of guest OS in the case of containers. Containers provide an isolated execution environment directly on top of the host operating system. This is its advantage as well as disadvantage. The advantage is that it is lighter as well as faster. As containers on the same machine share the host operating system, the overall resource utilization of containers is fairly small. As a result, many smaller containers can be run on the same machine, as compared to heavyweight VMs. As containers on the same host share the host operating system, there are limitations as well. For example, it is not possible to set iptables firewall rules inside a container. Processes inside the container are completely independent from the processes on different containers running on the same host.

Unlike VMs, container images are publically available on community portals. This makes developers' lives much easier as they don't have to build the images from scratch; instead, they can now take a base image from certified sources and add additional layers of software components on top of the downloaded base image.

The lightweight nature of the containers is also opening up a plethora of opportunities, such as automated build, publishing, downloading, copying, and so on. The ability to download, build, ship, and run containers with a few commands or to use REST APIs makes containers more developer friendly. Building a new container does not take more than a few seconds. Containers are now part and parcel of continuous delivery pipelines as well.

In summary, containers have many advantages over VMs, but VMs have their own exclusive strengths. Many organizations use both containers and VMs, such as by running containers on top of VMs.

The benefits of containers

We have already considered the many benefits of containers over VMs. This section will explain the overall benefits of containers beyond the benefits of VMs:

- **Self-contained**: Containers package the essential application binaries and their dependencies together to make sure that there is no disparity between different environments such as development, testing, or production. This promotes the concept of Twelve-Factor applications and that of immutable containers. Spring Boot microservices bundle all the required application dependencies. Containers stretch this boundary further by embedding JRE and other operating system-level libraries, configurations, and so on, if there are any.

- **Lightweight**: Containers, in general, are smaller in size with a lighter footprint. The smallest container, Alpine, has a size of less than 5 MB. The simplest Spring Boot microservice packaged with an Alpine container with Java 8 would only come to around 170 MB in size. Though the size is still on the higher side, it is much less than the VM image size, which is generally in GBs. The smaller footprint of containers not only helps spin new containers quickly but also makes building, shipping, and storing easier.

- **Scalable**: As container images are smaller in size and there is no OS booting at startup, containers are generally faster to spin up and shut down. This makes containers the popular choice for cloud-friendly elastic applications.

- **Portable**: Containers provide portability across machines and cloud providers. Once the containers are built with all the dependencies, they can be ported across multiple machines or across multiple cloud providers without relying on the underlying machines. Containers are portable from desktops to different cloud environments.

- **Lower license cost**: Many software license terms are based on the physical core. As containers share the operating system and are not virtualized at the physical resources level, there is an advantage in terms of the license cost.

- **DevOps**: The lightweight footprint of containers makes it easy to automate builds and publish and download containers from remote repositories. This makes it easy to use in Agile and DevOps environments by integrating with automated delivery pipelines. Containers also support the concept of *build once* by creating immutable containers at build time and moving them across multiple environments. As containers are not deep into the infrastructure, multidisciplinary DevOps teams can manage containers as part of their day-to-day life.

- **Version controlled**: Containers support versions by default. This helps build versioned artifacts, just as with versioned archive files.

- **Reusable**: Container images are reusable artifacts. If an image is built by assembling a number of libraries for a purpose, it can be reused in similar situations.

- **Immutable containers**: In this concept, containers are created and disposed of after usage. They are never updated or patched. Immutable containers are used in many environments to avoid complexities in patching deployment units. Patching results in a lack of traceability and an inability to recreate environments consistently.

Microservices and containers

There is no direct relationship between microservices and containers. Microservices can run without containers, and containers can run monolithic applications. However, there is a sweet spot between microservices and containers.

Containers are good for monolithic applications, but the complexities and the size of the monolith application may kill some of the benefits of the containers. For example, spinning new containers quickly may not be easy with monolithic applications. In addition to this, monolithic applications generally have local environment dependencies, such as the local disk, stovepipe dependencies with other systems, and so on. Such applications are difficult to manage with container technologies. This is where microservices go hand in hand with containers.

The following diagram shows three polyglot microservices running on the same host machine and sharing the same operating system but abstracting the runtime environment:

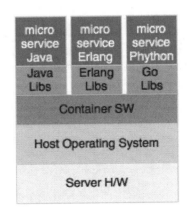

The real advantage of containers can be seen when managing many polyglot microservices—for instance, one microservice in Java and another one in Erlang or some other language. Containers help developers package microservices written in any language or technology in a platform- and technology-agnostic fashion and uniformly distribute them across multiple environments. Containers eliminate the need to have different deployment management tools to handle polyglot microservices. Containers not only abstract the execution environment but also how to access the services. Irrespective of the technologies used, containerized microservices expose REST APIs. Once the container is up and running, it binds to certain ports and exposes its APIs. As containers are self-contained and provide full stack isolation among services, in a single VM or bare metal, one can run multiple heterogeneous microservices and handle them in a uniform way.

Introduction to Docker

The previous sections talked about containers and their benefits. Containers have been in the business for years, but the popularity of Docker has given containers a new outlook. As a result, many container definitions and perspectives emerged from the Docker architecture. Docker is so popular that even containerization is referred to as **dockerization**.

Docker is a platform to build, ship, and run lightweight containers based on Linux kernels. Docker has default support for Linux platforms. It also has support for Mac and Windows using **Boot2Docker**, which runs on top of Virtual Box.

Amazon **EC2 Container Service (ECS)** has out-of-the-box support for Docker on AWS EC2 instances. Docker can be installed on bare metals and also on traditional virtual machines such as VMWare or Hyper-V.

The key components of Docker

A Docker installation has two key components: a **Docker daemon** and a **Docker client**. Both the Docker daemon and Docker client are distributed as a single binary.

The following diagram shows the key components of a Docker installation:

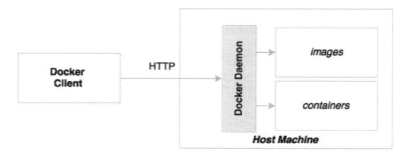

The Docker daemon

The Docker daemon is a server-side component that runs on the host machine responsible for building, running, and distributing Docker containers. The Docker daemon exposes APIs for the Docker client to interact with the daemon. These APIs are primarily REST-based endpoints. One can imagine that the Docker daemon as a controller service running on the host machine. Developers can programmatically use these APIs to build custom clients as well.

The Docker client

The Docker client is a remote command-line program that interacts with the Docker daemon through either a socket or REST APIs. The CLI can run on the same host as the daemon is running on or it can run on a completely different host and connect to the daemon remotely. Docker users use the CLI to build, ship, and run Docker containers.

Docker concepts

The Docker architecture is built around a few concepts: images, containers, the registry, and the Dockerfile.

Docker images

One of the key concepts of Docker is the image. A Docker image is the read-only copy of the operating system libraries, the application, and its libraries. Once an image is created, it is guaranteed to run on any Docker platform without alterations.

In Spring Boot microservices, a Docker image packages operating systems such as Ubuntu, Alpine, JRE, and the Spring Boot fat application JAR file. It also includes instructions to run the application and expose the services:

As shown in the diagram, Docker images are based on a layered architecture in which the base image is one of the flavors of Linux. Each layer, as shown in the preceding diagram, gets added to the base image layer with the previous image as the parent layer. Docker uses the concept of a union filesystem to combine all these layers into a single image, forming a single filesystem.

In typical cases, developers do not build Docker images from scratch. Images of an operating system, or other common libraries, such as Java 8 images, are publicly available from trusted sources. Developers can start building on top of these base images. The base image in Spring microservices can be JRE 8 rather than starting from a Linux distribution image such as Ubuntu.

Every time we rebuild the application, only the changed layer gets rebuilt, and the remaining layers are kept intact. All the intermediate layers are cached, and hence, if there is no change, Docker uses the previously cached layer and builds it on top. Multiple containers running on the same machine with the same type of base images would reuse the base image, thus reducing the size of the deployment. For instance, in a host, if there are multiple containers running with Ubuntu as the base image, they all reuse the same base image. This is applicable when publishing or downloading images as well:

As shown in the diagram, the first layer in the image is a boot filesystem called bootfs, which is similar to the Linux kernel and the boot loader. The boot filesystem acts as a virtual filesystem for all images.

On top of the boot filesystem, the operating system filesystem is placed, which is called rootfs. The root filesystem adds the typical operating system directory structure to the container. Unlike in the Linux systems, rootfs, in the case of Docker, is on a read-only mode.

On top of rootfs, other required images are placed as per the requirements. In our case, these are JRE and the Spring Boot microservice JARs. When a container is initiated, a writable filesystem is placed on top of all the other filesystems for the processes to run. Any changes made by the process to the underlying filesystem are not reflected in the actual container. Instead, these are written to the writable filesystem. This writable filesystem is volatile. Hence, the data is lost once the container is stopped. Due to this reason, Docker containers are ephemeral in nature.

The base operating system packaged inside Docker is generally a minimal copy of just the OS filesystem. In reality the process running on top may not use the entire OS services. In a Spring Boot microservice, in many cases, the container just initiates a CMD and JVM and then invokes the Spring Boot fat JAR.

Docker containers

Docker containers are the running instances of a Docker image. Containers use the kernel of the host operating system when running. Hence, they share the host kernel with other containers running on the same host. The Docker runtime ensures that the container processes are allocated with their own isolated process space using kernel features such as **cgroups** and the kernel **namespace** of the operating system. In addition to the resource fencing, containers get their own filesystem and network configurations as well.

The containers, when instantiated, can have specific resource allocations, such as the memory and CPU. Containers, when initiated from the same image, can have different resource allocations. The Docker container, by default, gets an isolated **subnet** and **gateway** to the network. The network has three modes.

The Docker registry

The Docker registry is a central place where Docker images are published and downloaded from. The URL `https://hub.docker.com` is the central registry provided by Docker. The Docker registry has public images that one can download and use as the base registry. Docker also has private images that are specific to the accounts created in the Docker registry. The Docker registry screenshot is shown as follows:

Docker also offers **Docker Trusted Registry**, which can be used to set up registries locally on premises.

Dockerfile

A Dockerfile is a build or scripting file that contains instructions to build a Docker image. There can be multiple steps documented in the Dockerfile, starting from getting a base image. A Dockerfile is a text file that is generally named Dockerfile. The `docker build` command looks up Dockerfile for instructions to build. One can compare a Dockerfile to a `pom.xml` file used in a Maven build.

Deploying microservices in Docker

This section will operationalize our learning by showcasing how to build containers for our BrownField PSS microservices.

 The full source code of this chapter is available under the `Chapter 8` project in the code files. Copy `chapter7.configserver`, `chapter7.eurekaserver`, `chapter7.search`, `chapter7.search-apigateway`, and `chapter7.website` into a new STS workspace and rename them `chapter8.*`.

Perform the following steps to build Docker containers for BrownField PSS microservices:

1. Install Docker from the official Docker site at `https://www.docker.com`.

    Follow the **Get Started** link for the download and installation instructions based on the operating system of choice. Once installed, use the following command to verify the installation:

    ```
    $docker -version
    Docker version 1.10.1, build 9e83765
    ```

2. In this section, we will take a look at how to dockerize the **Search** (`chapter8.search`) microservice, the **Search API Gateway** (`chapter8.search-apigateway`) microservice, and the **Website** (`chapter8.website`) Spring Boot application.

3. Before we make any changes, we need to edit `bootstrap.properties` to change the config server URL from localhost to the IP address as localhost is not resolvable from within the Docker containers. In the real world, this will point to a DNS or load balancer, as follows:

    ```
    spring.cloud.config.uri=http://192.168.0.105:8888
    ```

Replace the IP address with the IP address of your machine.

4. Similarly, edit `search-service.properties` on the Git repository and change localhost to the IP address. This is applicable for the Eureka URL as well as the RabbitMQ URL. Commit back to Git after updating. You can do this via the following code:

```
spring.application.name=search-service
spring.rabbitmq.host=192.168.0.105
spring.rabbitmq.port=5672
spring.rabbitmq.username=guest
spring.rabbitmq.password=guest
orginairports.shutdown:JFK
eureka.client.serviceUrl.defaultZone: http://192.168.0.105:8761/
eureka/
spring.cloud.stream.bindings.inventoryQ=inventoryQ
```

5. Change the RabbitMQ configuration file `rabbitmq.config` by uncommenting the following line to provide access to guest. By default, guest is restricted to be accessed from localhost only:

```
{loopback_users, []}
```

The location of `rabbitmq.config` will be different for different operating systems.

6. Create a Dockerfile under the root directory of the Search microservice, as follows:

```
FROM frolvlad/alpine-oraclejdk8
VOLUME /tmp
ADD  target/search-1.0.jar search.jar
EXPOSE 8090
ENTRYPOINT ["java","-jar","/search.jar"]
```

The following is a quick examination of the contents of the Dockerfile:

○ `FROM frolvlad/alpine-oraclejdk8`: This tells the Docker build to use a specific `alpine-oraclejdk8` version as the basic image for this build. The `frolvlad` indicates the repository to locate the `alpine-oraclejdk8` image. In this case, it is an image built with Alpine Linux and Oracle JDK 8. This will help layer our application on top of the base image without setting up Java libraries ourselves. In this case, as this image is not available on our local image store, the Docker build will go ahead and download this image from the remote Docker Hub registry.

- ◦ VOLUME /tmp: This enables access from the container to the directory specified in the host machine. In our case, this points to the tmp directory in which the Spring Boot application creates working directories for Tomcat. The tmp directory is a logical one for the container, which indirectly points to one of the local directories of the host.

- ◦ ADD target/search-1.0.jar search.jar: This adds the application binary file to the container with the destination filename specified. In this case, the Docker build copies target/search-1.0.jar to the container as search.jar.

- ◦ EXPOSE 8090: This is to tell the container how to do port mapping. This associates 8090 with external port binding for the internal Spring Boot service.

- ◦ ENTRYPOINT ["java","-jar", "/search.jar"]: This tells the container which default application to run when a container is started. In this case, we are pointing to the Java process and the Spring Boot fat JAR file to initiate the service.

7. The next step is to run docker build from the folder in which the Dockerfile is stored. This will download the base image and run the entries in the Dockerfile one after the other, as follows:

```
docker build -t search:1.0 .
```

The output of this command will be as follows:

```
rvslab:chapter8.search rajeshrv$ docker build -t search:1.0 .
Sending build context to Docker daemon 48.34 MB
Step 1 : FROM frolvlad/alpine-oraclejdk8
 ---> 5b8d90632c89
Step 2 : VOLUME /tmp
 ---> Using cache
 ---> c79a1b3275d4
Step 3 : ADD target/search-1.0.jar app.jar
 ---> 7766e630f139
Removing intermediate container f2ac976e781d
Step 4 : EXPOSE 8090
 ---> Running in 730300fa66a9
 ---> e058cc1615da
Removing intermediate container 730300fa66a9
Step 5 : ENTRYPOINT java -jar /app.jar
 ---> Running in b79116f3e54b
 ---> 5a8d0d6e0bf7
Removing intermediate container b79116f3e54b
Successfully built 5a8d0d6e0bf7
rvslab:chapter8.search rajeshrv$ ▌
```

8. Repeat the same steps for Search API Gateway and Website.

9. Once the images are created, they can be verified by typing the following command. This command will list out the images and their details, including the size of image files:

```
docker images
```

The output will be as follows:

```
rvslab:chapter8 rajeshrv$ docker images
REPOSITORY                    TAG           IMAGE ID
website                       1.0           263605f253f3
search-apigateway             1.0           322890ae3ec1
search                        1.0           f094b72d1b41
```

10. The next thing to do is run the Docker container. This can be done with the `docker run` command. This command will load and run the container. On starting, the container calls the Spring Boot executable JAR to start the microservice.

    Before starting the containers, ensure that the Config and the Eureka servers are running:

    ```
    docker run --net host -p 8090:8090 -t search:1.0

    docker run --net host -p 8095:8095 -t search-apigateway:1.0

    docker run --net host -p 8001:8001 -t website:1.0
    ```

    The preceding command starts the Search and Search API Gateway microservices and Website.

    In this example, we are using the host network (`--net host`) instead of the bridge network to avoid Eureka registering with the Docker container name. This can be corrected by overriding `EurekaInstanceConfigBean`. The host option is less isolated compared to the bridge option from the network perspective. The advantage and disadvantage of host versus bridge depends on the project.

11. Once all the services are fully started, verify with the `docker ps` command, as shown in the following screenshot:

```
rvslab:chapter8 rajeshrv$ docker ps
CONTAINER ID        IMAGE                      COMMAND
32af53b56945        website:1.0                "java -jar /website.j"
ce35355aea65        search-apigateway:1.0      "java -jar /search-ap"
5577c5107fc6        search:1.0                 "java -jar /search.ja"
4a423d0872b5        registry:2                 "/bin/registry /etc/d"
rvslab:chapter8 rajeshrv$
```

12. The next step is to point the browser to `http://192.168.99.100:8001`. This will open the BrownField PSS website.

    Note the IP address. This is the IP address of the Docker machine if you are running with Boot2Docker on Mac or Windows. In Mac or Windows, if the IP address is not known, then type the following command to find out the Docker machine's IP address for the default machine:

    ```
    docker-machine ip default
    ```

    If Docker is running on Linux, then this is the host IP address.

Apply the same changes to **Booking, Fares, Check-in**, and their respective gateway microservices.

Running RabbitMQ on Docker

As our example also uses RabbitMQ, let's explore how to set up RabbitMQ as a Docker container. The following command pulls the RabbitMQ image from Docker Hub and starts RabbitMQ:

```
docker run –net host rabbitmq3
```

Ensure that the URL in `*-service.properties` is changed to the Docker host's IP address. Apply the earlier rule to find out the IP address in the case of Mac or Windows.

Using the Docker registry

The Docker Hub provides a central location to store all the Docker images. The images can be stored as public as well as private. In many cases, organizations deploy their own private registries on premises due to security-related concerns.

Perform the following steps to set up and run a local registry:

1. The following command will start a registry, which will bind the registry on port `5000`:

   ```
   docker run -d -p 5000:5000 --restart=always --name registry
   registry:2
   ```

2. Tag `search:1.0` to the registry, as follows:

   ```
   docker tag search:1.0 localhost:5000/search:1.0
   ```

3. Then, push the image to the registry via the following command:

```
docker push localhost:5000/search:1.0
```

4. Pull the image back from the registry, as follows:

```
docker pull localhost:5000/search:1.0
```

Setting up the Docker Hub

In the previous chapter, we played with a local Docker registry. This section will show how to set up and use the Docker Hub to publish the Docker containers. This is a convenient mechanism to globally access Docker images. Later in this chapter, Docker images will be published to the Docker Hub from the local machine and downloaded from the EC2 instances.

In order to do this, create a public Docker Hub account and a repository. For Mac, follow the steps as per the following URL: https://docs.docker.com/mac/step_five/.

In this example, the Docker Hub account is created using the brownfield username.

The registry, in this case, acts as the microservices repository in which all the dockerized microservices will be stored and accessed. This is one of the capabilities explained in the microservices capability model.

Publishing microservices to the Docker Hub

In order to push dockerized services to the Docker Hub, follow these steps. The first command tags the Docker image, and the second one pushes the Docker image to the Docker Hub repository:

```
docker tag search:1.0brownfield/search:1.0
docker push brownfield/search:1.0
```

To verify whether the container images are published, go to the Docker Hub repository at https://hub.docker.com/u/brownfield.

Repeat this step for all the other BrownField microservices as well. At the end of this step, all the services will be published to the Docker Hub.

Microservices on the cloud

One of the capabilities mentioned in the microservices capability model is the use of the cloud infrastructure for microservices. Earlier in this chapter, we also explored the necessity of using the cloud for microservices deployments. So far, we have not deployed anything to the cloud. As we have eight microservices in total—Config-server, Eureka-server, Turbine, RabbitMQ, Elasticsearch, Kibana, and Logstash—in our overall BrownField PSS microservices ecosystem, it is hard to run all of them on the local machine.

In the rest of this book, we will operate using AWS as the cloud platform to deploy BrownField PSS microservices.

Installing Docker on AWS EC2

In this section, we will install Docker on the EC2 instance.

This example assumes that readers are familiar with AWS and an account is already created on AWS.

Perform the following steps to set up Docker on EC2:

1. Launch a new EC2 instance. In this case, if we have to run all the instances together, we may need a large instance. The example uses **t2.large**.

    In this example, the following Ubuntu AMI image is used: `ubuntu-trusty-14.04-amd64-server-20160114.5 (ami-fce3c696)`.

2. Connect to the EC2 instance and run the following commands:

    ```
    sudo apt-get update
    sudo apt-get install docker.io
    ```

3. The preceding command will install Docker on an EC2 instance. Verify the installation with the following command:

    ```
    docker version
    ```

Running BrownField services on EC2

In this section, we will set up BrownField microservices on the EC2 instances created. In this case, the build is set up in the local desktop machine, and the binaries will be deployed to AWS.

Perform the following steps to set up services on an EC2 instance:

1. Install Git via the following command:

   ```
   sudo apt-get install git
   ```

2. Create a Git repository on any folder of your choice.

3. Change the Config server's `bootstrap.properties` to point to the appropriate Git repository created for this example.

4. Change the `bootstrap.properties` of all the microservices to point to the config-server using the private IP address of the EC2 instance.

5. Copy all `*.properties` from the local Git repository to the EC2 Git repository and perform a commit.

6. Change the Eureka server URLs and RabbitMQ URLs in the `*.properties` file to match the EC2 private IP address. Commit the changes to Git once they have been completed.

7. On the local machine, recompile all the projects and create Docker images for the `search`, `search-apigateway`, and `website` microservices. Push all of them to the Docker Hub registry.

8. Copy the config-server and the Eureka-server binaries from the local machine to the EC2 instance.

9. Set up Java 8 on the EC2 instance.

10. Then, execute the following commands in sequence:

    ```
    java -jar config-server.jar
    java -jar eureka-server.jar
    docker run -net host rabbitmq:3
    docker run --net host -p 8090:8090 rajeshrv/search:1.0
    docker run --net host -p 8095:8095 rajeshrv/search-apigateway:1.0
    docker run --net host -p 8001:8001 rajeshrv/website:1.0
    ```

11. Check whether all the services are working by opening the URL of the website and executing a search. Note that we will use the public IP address in this case: http://54.165.128.23:8001.

Updating the life cycle manager

In *Chapter 6, Autoscaling Microservices*, we considered a life cycle manager to automatically start and stop instances. We used SSH and executed a Unix script to start the Spring Boot microservices on the target machine. With Docker, we no longer need SSH connections as the Docker daemon provides REST-based APIs to start and stop instances. This greatly simplifies the complexities of the deployment engine component of the life cycle manager.

In this section, we will not rewrite the life cycle manager. By and large, we will replace the life cycle manager in the next chapter.

The future of containerization – unikernels and hardened security

Containerization is still evolving, but the number of organizations adopting containerization techniques has gone up in recent times. While many organizations are aggressively adopting Docker and other container technologies, the downside of these techniques is still in the size of the containers and security concerns.

Currently, Docker images are generally heavy. In an elastic automated environment, where containers are created and destroyed quite frequently, size is still an issue. A larger size indicates more code, and more code means that it is more prone to security vulnerabilities.

The future is definitely in small footprint containers. Docker is working on unikernels, lightweight kernels that can run Docker even on low-powered IoT devices. Unikernels are not full-fledged operating systems, but they provide the basic necessary libraries to support the deployed applications.

The security issues of containers are much discussed and debated. The key security issues are around the user namespace segregation or user ID isolation. If the container is on root, then it can by default gain the root privilege of the host. Using container images from untrusted sources is another security concern. Docker is bridging these gaps as quickly as possible, but there are many organizations that use a combination of VMs and Docker to circumvent some of the security concerns.

Summary

In this chapter, you learned about the need to have a cloud environment when dealing with Internet-scale microservices.

We explored the concept of containers and compared them with traditional virtual machines. You also learned the basics of Docker, and we explained the concepts of Docker images, containers, and registries. The importance and benefits of containers were explained in the context of microservices.

This chapter then switched to a hands-on example by dockerizing the BrownField microservice. We demonstrated how to deploy the Spring Boot microservice developed earlier on Docker. You learned the concept of registries by exploring a local registry as well as the Docker Hub to push and pull dockerized microservices.

As the last step, we explored how to deploy a dockerized BrownField microservice in the AWS cloud environment.

9

Managing Dockerized Microservices with Mesos and Marathon

In an Internet-scale microservices deployment, it is not easy to manage thousands of dockerized microservices. It is essential to have an infrastructure abstraction layer and a strong cluster control platform to successfully manage Internet-scale microservice deployments.

This chapter will explain the need and use of Mesos and Marathon as an infrastructure abstraction layer and a cluster control system, respectively, to achieve optimized resource usage in a cloud-like environment when deploying microservices at scale. This chapter will also provide a step-by-step approach to setting up Mesos and Marathon in a cloud environment. Finally, this chapter will demonstrate how to manage dockerized microservices in the Mesos and Marathon environment.

By the end of this chapter, you will have learned about:

- The need to have an abstraction layer and cluster control software
- Mesos and Marathon from the context of microservices
- Managing dockerized BrownField Airline's PSS microservices with Mesos and Marathon

Reviewing the microservice capability model

In this chapter, we will explore the **Cluster Control & Provisioning** microservices capability from the microservices capability model discussed in *Chapter 3, Applying Microservices Concepts*:

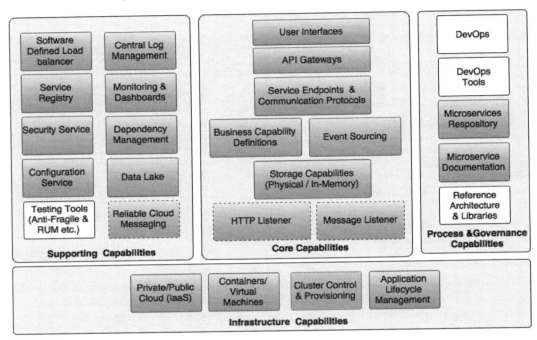

The missing pieces

In *Chapter 8, Containerizing Microservices with Docker*, we discussed how to dockerize BrownField Airline's PSS microservices. Docker helped package the JVM runtime and OS parameters along with the application so that there is no special consideration required when moving dockerized microservices from one environment to another. The REST APIs provided by Docker have simplified the life cycle manager's interaction with the target machine in starting and stopping artifacts.

In a large-scale deployment, with hundreds and thousands of Docker containers, we need to ensure that Docker containers run with their own resource constraints, such as memory, CPU, and so on. In addition to this, there may be rules set for Docker deployments, such as replicated copies of the container should not be run on the same machine. Also, a mechanism needs to be in place to optimally use the server infrastructure to avoid incurring extra cost.

There are organizations that deal with billions of containers. Managing them manually is next to impossible. In the context of large-scale Docker deployments, some of the key questions to be answered are:

- How do we manage thousands of containers?
- How do we monitor them?
- How do we apply rules and constraints when deploying artifacts?
- How do we ensure that we utilize containers properly to gain resource efficiency?
- How do we ensure that at least a certain number of minimal instances are running at any point in time?
- How do we ensure dependent services are up and running?
- How do we do rolling upgrades and graceful migrations?
- How do we roll back faulty deployments?

All these questions point to the need to have a solution to address two key capabilities, which are as follows:

- A cluster abstraction layer that provides a uniform abstraction over many physical or virtual machines
- A cluster control and init system to manage deployments intelligently on top of the cluster abstraction

The life cycle manager is ideally placed to deal with these situations. One can add enough intelligence to the life cycle manager to solve these issues. However, before attempting to modify the life cycle manager, it is important to understand the role of cluster management solutions a bit more.

Why cluster management is important

As microservices break applications into different micro-applications, many developers request more server nodes for deployment. In order to manage microservices properly, developers tend to deploy one microservice per VM, which further drives down the resource utilization. In many cases, this results in an overallocation of CPUs and memory.

In many deployments, the high-availability requirements of microservices force engineers to add more and more service instances for redundancy. In reality, though it provides the required high availability, this will result in underutilized server instances.

In general, microservice deployment requires more infrastructure compared to monolithic application deployments. Due to the increase in cost of the infrastructure, many organizations fail to see the value of microservices:

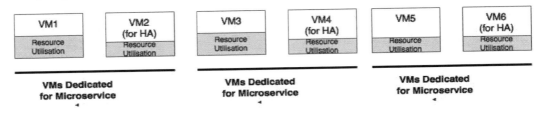

In order to address the issue stated before, we need a tool that is capable of the following:

- Automating a number of activities, such as the allocation of containers to the infrastructure efficiently and keeping it transparent to developers and administrators

- Providing a layer of abstraction for the developers so that they can deploy their application against a data center without knowing which machine is to be used to host their applications

- Setting rules or constraints against deployment artifacts

- Offering higher levels of agility with minimal management overheads for developers and administrators, perhaps with minimal human interaction

- Building, deploying, and managing the application's cost effectively by driving a maximum utilization of the available resources

Containers solve an important issue in this context. Any tool that we select with these capabilities can handle containers in a uniform way, irrespective of the underlying microservice technologies.

What does cluster management do?

Typical cluster management tools help virtualize a set of machines and manage them as a single cluster. Cluster management tools also help move the workload or containers across machines while being transparent to the consumer. Technology evangelists and practitioners use different terminologies, such as cluster orchestration, cluster management, data center virtualization, container schedulers, or container life cycle management, container orchestration, data center operating system, and so on.

Many of these tools currently support both Docker-based containers as well as noncontainerized binary artifact deployments, such as a standalone Spring Boot application. The fundamental function of these cluster management tools is to abstract the actual server instance from the application developers and administrators.

Cluster management tools help the self-service and provisioning of infrastructure rather than requesting the infrastructure teams to allocate the required machines with a predefined specification. In this automated cluster management approach, machines are no longer provisioned upfront and preallocated to the applications. Some of the cluster management tools also help virtualize data centers across many heterogeneous machines or even across data centers, and create an elastic, private cloud-like infrastructure. There is no standard reference model for cluster management tools. Therefore, the capabilities vary between vendors.

Some of the key capabilities of cluster management software are summarized as follows:

- **Cluster management**: It manages a cluster of VMs and physical machines as a single large machine. These machines could be heterogeneous in terms of resource capabilities, but they are, by and large, machines with Linux as the operating system. These virtual clusters can be formed on the cloud, on-premises, or a combination of both.

- **Deployments**: It handles the automatic deployment of applications and containers with a large set of machines. It supports multiple versions of the application containers and also rolling upgrades across a large number of cluster machines. These tools are also capable of handling the rollback of faulty promotes.

- **Scalability**: It handles the automatic and manual scalability of application instances as and when required, with optimized utilization as the primary goal.

- **Health**: It manages the health of the cluster, nodes, and applications. It removes faulty machines and application instances from the cluster.

- **Infrastructure abstraction**: It abstracts the developers from the actual machine on which the applications are deployed. The developers need not worry about the machine, its capacity, and so on. It is entirely the cluster management software's decision to decide how to schedule and run the applications. These tools also abstract machine details, their capacity, utilization, and location from the developers. For application owners, these are equivalent to a single large machine with almost unlimited capacity.

- **Resource optimization**: The inherent behavior of these tools is to allocate container workloads across a set of available machines in an efficient way, thereby reducing the cost of ownership. Simple to extremely complicated algorithms can be used effectively to improve utilization.

- **Resource allocation**: It allocates servers based on resource availability and the constraints set by application developers. Resource allocation is based on these constraints, affinity rules, port requirements, application dependencies, health, and so on.

- **Service availability**: It ensures that the services are up and running somewhere in the cluster. In case of a machine failure, cluster control tools automatically handle failures by restarting these services on some other machine in the cluster.

- **Agility**: These tools are capable of quickly allocating workloads to the available resources or moving the workload across machines if there is change in resource requirements. Also, constraints can be set to realign the resources based on business criticality, business priority, and so on.

- **Isolation**: Some of these tools provide resource isolation out of the box. Hence, even if the application is not containerized, resource isolation can be still achieved.

A variety of algorithms are used for resource allocation, ranging from simple algorithms to complex algorithms, with machine learning and artificial intelligence. The common algorithms used are random, bin packing, and spread. Constraints set against applications will override the default algorithms based on resource availability:

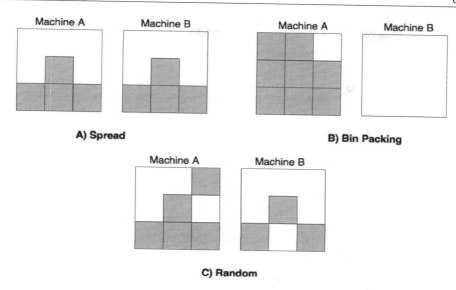

The preceding diagram shows how these algorithms fill the available machines with deployments. In this case, it is demonstrated with two machines:

- **Spread**: This algorithm performs the allocation of workload equally across the available machines. This is showed in diagram **A**.

- **Bin packing**: This algorithm tries to fill in data machine by machine and ensures the maximum utilization of machines. Bin packing is especially good when using cloud services in a pay-as-you-use style. This is shown in diagram **B**.

- **Random**: This algorithm randomly chooses machines and deploys containers on randomly selected machines. This is showed in diagram **C**.

There is a possibility of using cognitive computing algorithms such as machine learning and collaborative filtering to improve efficiency. Techniques such as **oversubscription** allow a better utilization of resources by allocating underutilized resources for high-priority tasks—for example, revenue-generating services for best-effort tasks such as analytics, video, image processing, and so on.

Relationship with microservices

The infrastructure of microservices, if not properly provisioned, can easily result in oversized infrastructures and, essentially, a higher cost of ownership. As discussed in the previous sections, a cloud-like environment with a cluster management tool is essential to realize cost benefits when dealing with large-scale microservices.

The Spring Boot microservices turbocharged with the Spring Cloud project is the ideal candidate workload to leverage cluster management tools. As Spring Cloud-based microservices are location unaware, these services can be deployed anywhere in the cluster. Whenever services come up, they automatically register to the service registry and advertise their availability. On the other hand, consumers always look for the registry to discover the available service instances. This way, the application supports a full fluid structure without preassuming a deployment topology. With Docker, we were able to abstract the runtime so that the services could run on any Linux-based environments.

Relationship with virtualization

Cluster management solutions are different from server virtualization solutions in many aspects. Cluster management solutions run on top of VMs or physical machines as an application component.

Cluster management solutions

There are many cluster management software tools available. It is unfair to do an apple-to-apple comparison between them. Even though there are no one-to-one components, there are many areas of overlap in capabilities between them. In many situations, organizations use a combination of one or more of these tools to fulfill their requirements.

The following diagram shows the position of cluster management tools from the microservices context:

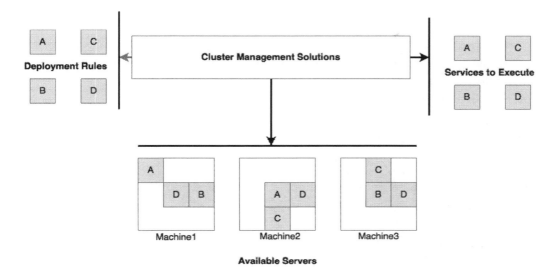

In this section, we will explore some of the popular cluster management solutions available on the market.

Docker Swarm

Docker Swarm is Docker's native cluster management solution. Swarm provides a native and deeper integration with Docker and exposes APIs that are compatible with Docker's remote APIs. Docker Swarm logically groups a pool of Docker hosts and manages them as a single large Docker virtual host. Instead of application administrators and developers deciding on which host the container is to be deployed in, this decision making will be delegated to Docker Swarm. Docker Swarm will decide which host to be used based on the bin packing and spread algorithms.

As Docker Swarm is based on Docker's remote APIs, its learning curve for those already using Docker is narrower compared to any other container orchestration tools. However, Docker Swarm is a relatively new product on the market, and it only supports Docker containers.

Docker Swarm works with the concepts of **manager** and **nodes**. A manager is the single point for administrations to interact and schedule the Docker containers for execution. Nodes are where Docker containers are deployed and run.

Kubernetes

Kubernetes (k8s) comes from Google's engineering, is written in the Go language, and is battle-tested for large-scale deployments at Google. Similar to Swarm, Kubernetes helps manage containerized applications across a cluster of nodes. Kubernetes helps automate container deployments, scheduling, and the scalability of containers. Kubernetes supports a number of useful features out of the box, such as automatic progressive rollouts, versioned deployments, and container resiliency if containers fail due to some reason.

The Kubernetes architecture has the concepts of **master**, **nodes**, and **pods**. The master and nodes together form a Kubernetes cluster. The master node is responsible for allocating and managing workload across a number of nodes. Nodes are nothing but a VM or a physical machine. Nodes are further subsegmented as pods. A node can host multiple pods. One or more containers are grouped and executed inside a pod. Pods are also helpful in managing and deploying co-located services for efficiency. Kubernetes also supports the concept of labels as key-value pairs to query and find containers. Labels are user-defined parameters to tag certain types of nodes that execute a common type of workloads, such as frontend web servers. The services deployed on a cluster get a single IP/DNS to access the service.

Kubernetes has out-of-the-box support for Docker; however, the Kubernetes learning curve is steeper compared to Docker Swarm. RedHat offers commercial support for Kubernetes as part of its OpenShift platform.

Apache Mesos

Mesos is an open source framework originally developed by the University of California at Berkeley and is used by Twitter at scale. Twitter uses Mesos primarily to manage the large Hadoop ecosystem.

Mesos is slightly different from the previous solutions. Mesos is more of a resource manager that relays on other frameworks to manage workload execution. Mesos sits between the operating system and the application, providing a logical cluster of machines.

Mesos is a distributed system kernel that logically groups and virtualizes many computers to a single large machine. Mesos is capable of grouping a number of heterogeneous resources to a uniform resource cluster on which applications can be deployed. For these reasons, Mesos is also known as a tool to build a private cloud in a data center.

Mesos has the concepts of the **master** and **slave** nodes. Similar to the earlier solutions, master nodes are responsible for managing the cluster, whereas slaves run the workload. Mesos internally uses ZooKeeper for cluster coordination and storage. Mesos supports the concept of frameworks. These frameworks are responsible for scheduling and running noncontainerized applications and containers. Marathon, Chronos, and Aurora are popular frameworks for the scheduling and execution of applications. Netflix Fenzo is another open source Mesos framework. Interestingly, Kubernetes also can be used as a Mesos framework.

Marathon supports the Docker container as well as noncontainerized applications. Spring Boot can be directly configured in Marathon. Marathon provides a number of capabilities out of the box, such as supporting application dependencies, grouping applications to scale and upgrade services, starting and shutting down healthy and unhealthy instances, rolling out promotes, rolling back failed promotes, and so on.

Mesosphere offers commercial support for Mesos and Marathon as part of its DCOS platform.

Nomad

Nomad from HashiCorp is another cluster management software. Nomad is a cluster management system that abstracts lower-level machine details and their locations. Nomad has a simpler architecture compared to the other solutions explored earlier. Nomad is also lightweight. Similar to other cluster management solutions, Nomad takes care of resource allocation and the execution of applications. Nomad also accepts user-specific constraints and allocates resources based on this.

Nomad has the concept of **servers**, in which all jobs are managed. One server acts as the **leader**, and others act as **followers**. Nomad has the concept of **tasks**, which is the smallest unit of work. Tasks are grouped into **task groups**. A task group has tasks that are to be executed in the same location. One or more task groups or tasks are managed as **jobs**.

Nomad supports many workloads, including Docker, out of the box. Nomad also supports deployments across data centers and is region and data center aware.

Fleet

Fleet is a cluster management system from CoreOS. It runs on a lower level and works on top of systemd. Fleet can manage application dependencies and make sure that all the required services are running somewhere in the cluster. If a service fails, it restarts the service on another host. Affinity and constraint rules are possible to supply when allocating resources.

Fleet has the concepts of **engine** and **agents**. There is only one engine at any point in the cluster with multiple agents. Tasks are submitted to the engine and agent run these tasks on a cluster machine.

Fleet also supports Docker out of the box.

Cluster management with Mesos and Marathon

As we discussed in the previous section, there are many cluster management solutions or container orchestration tools available. Different organizations choose different solutions to address problems based on their environment. Many organizations choose Kubernetes or Mesos with a framework such as Marathon. In most cases, Docker is used as a default containerization method to package and deploy workloads.

For the rest of this chapter, we will show how Mesos works with Marathon to provide the required cluster management capability. Mesos is used by many organizations, including Twitter, Airbnb, Apple, eBay, Netflix, PayPal, Uber, Yelp, and many others.

Diving deep into Mesos

Mesos can be treated as a data center kernel. DCOS is the commercial version of Mesos supported by Mesosphere. In order to run multiple tasks on one node, Mesos uses resource isolation concepts. Mesos relies on the Linux kernel's **cgroups** to achieve resource isolation similar to the container approach. It also supports containerized isolation using Docker. Mesos supports both batch workload as well as the OLTP kind of workloads:

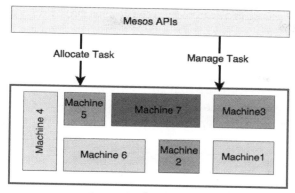

Cluster As A Single Machine

Mesos is an open source top-level Apache project under the Apache license. Mesos abstracts lower-level computing resources such as CPU, memory, and storage from lower-level physical or virtual machines.

Before we examine why we need both Mesos and Marathon, let's understand the Mesos architecture.

The Mesos architecture

The following diagram shows the simplest architectural representation of Mesos. The key components of Mesos includes a Mesos master node, a set of slave nodes, a ZooKeeper service, and a Mesos framework. The Mesos framework is further subdivided into two components: a scheduler and an executor:

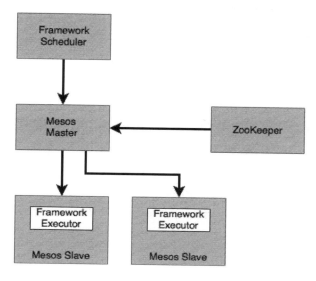

The boxes in the preceding diagram are explained as follows:

- **Master**: The Mesos master is responsible for managing all the Mesos slaves. The Mesos master gets information on the resource availability from all slave nodes and take the responsibility of filling the resources appropriately based on certain resource policies and constraints. The Mesos master preempts available resources from all slave machines and pools them as a single large machine. The master offers resources to frameworks running on slave machines based on this resource pool.

  For high availability, the Mesos master is supported by the Mesos master's standby components. Even if the master is not available, the existing tasks can still be executed. However, new tasks cannot be scheduled in the absence of a master node. The master standby nodes are nodes that wait for the failure of the active master and take over the master's role in the case of a failure. It uses ZooKeeper for the master leader election. A minimum quorum requirement must be met for leader election.

- **Slave**: Mesos slaves are responsible for hosting task execution frameworks. Tasks are executed on the slave nodes. Mesos slaves can be started with attributes as key-value pairs, such as *data center* = *X*. This is used for constraint evaluations when deploying workloads. Slave machines share resource availability with the Mesos master.

- **ZooKeeper**: ZooKeeper is a centralized coordination server used in Mesos to coordinate activities across the Mesos cluster. Mesos uses ZooKeeper for leader election in case of a Mesos master failure.

- **Framework**: The Mesos framework is responsible for understanding the application's constraints, accepting resource offers from the master, and finally running tasks on the slave resources offered by the master. The Mesos framework consists of two components: the framework scheduler and the framework executor:

  - The scheduler is responsible for registering to Mesos and handling resource offers

  - The executor runs the actual program on Mesos slave nodes

The framework is also responsible for enforcing certain policies and constraints. For example, a constraint can be, let's say, that a minimum of 500 MB of RAM is available for execution.

Frameworks are pluggable components and are replaceable with another framework. The framework workflow is depicted in the following diagram:

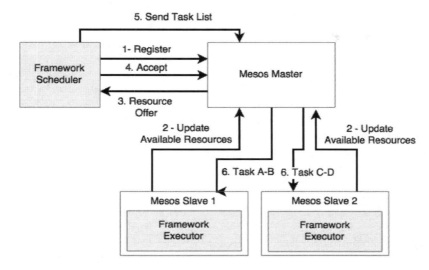

The steps denoted in the preceding workflow diagram are elaborated as follows:

1. The framework registers with the Mesos master and waits for resource offers. The scheduler may have many tasks in its queue to be executed with different resource constraints (tasks **A** to **D**, in this example). A task, in this case, is a unit of work that is scheduled—for example, a Spring Boot microservice.

2. The Mesos slave offers the available resources to the Mesos master. For example, the slave advertises the CPU and memory available with the slave machine.

3. The Mesos master then creates a resource offer based on the allocation policies set and offers it to the scheduler component of the framework. Allocation policies determine which framework the resources are to be offered to and how many resources are to be offered. The default policies can be customized by plugging additional allocation policies.

4. The scheduler framework component, based on the constraints, capabilities, and policies, may accept or reject the resource offering. For example, a framework rejects the resource offer if the resources are insufficient as per the constraints and policies set.

5. If the scheduler component accepts the resource offer, it submits the details of one more task to the Mesos master with resource constraints per task. Let's say, in this example, that it is ready to submit tasks **A** to **D**.

6. The Mesos master sends this list of tasks to the slave where the resources are available. The framework executor component installed on the slave machines picks up and runs these tasks.

Mesos supports a number of frameworks, such as:

- Marathon and Aurora for **long-running** processes, such as web applications
- Hadoop, Spark, and Storm for **big data** processing
- Chronos and Jenkins for **batch scheduling**
- Cassandra and Elasticsearch for **data management**

In this chapter, we will use Marathon to run dockerized microservices.

Marathon

Marathon is one of the Mesos framework implementations that can run both container as well as noncontainer execution. Marathon is particularly designed for long-running applications, such as a web server. Marathon ensures that the service started with Marathon continues to be available even if the Mesos slave it is hosted on fails. This will be done by starting another instance.

Marathon is written in Scala and is highly scalable. Marathon offers a UI as well as REST APIs to interact with Marathon, such as the start, stop, scale, and monitoring applications.

Similar to Mesos, Marathon's high availability is achieved by running multiple Marathon instances pointing to a ZooKeeper instance. One of the Marathon instances acts as a leader, and others are in standby mode. In case the leading master fails, a leader election will take place, and the next active master will be determined.

Some of the basic features of Marathon include:

- Setting resource constraints
- Scaling up, scaling down, and the instance management of applications
- Application version management
- Starting and killing applications

Some of the advanced features of Marathon include:

- Rolling upgrades, rolling restarts, and rollbacks
- Blue-green deployments

Implementing Mesos and Marathon for BrownField microservices

In this section, the dockerized Brownfield microservice developed in *Chapter 8, Containerizing Microservices with Docker,* will be deployed into the AWS cloud and managed with Mesos and Marathon.

For the purposes of demonstration, only three of the services (**Search, Search API Gateway,** and **Website**) are covered in the explanations:

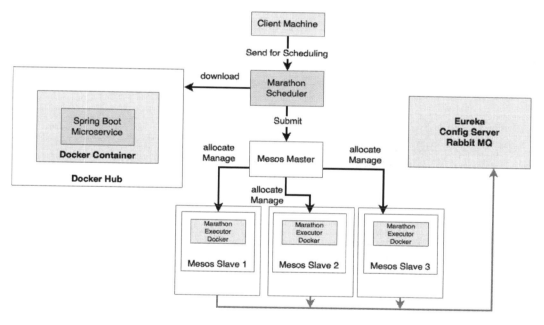

The logical architecture of the target state implementation is shown in the preceding diagram. The implementation uses multiple Mesos slaves to execute dockerized microservices with a single Mesos master. The Marathon scheduler component is used to schedule dockerized microservices. Dockerized microservices are hosted on the Docker Hub registry. Dockerized microservices are implemented using Spring Boot and Spring Cloud.

The following diagram shows the physical deployment architecture:

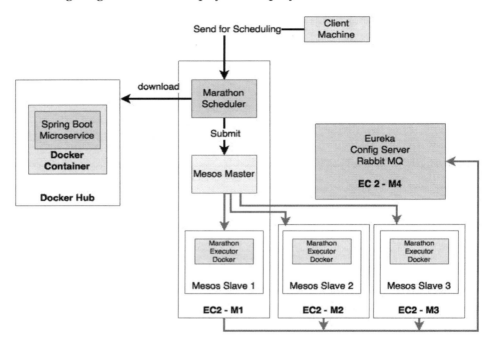

As shown in the preceding diagram, in this example, we will use four EC2 instances:

- **EC2-M1**: This hosts the Mesos master, ZooKeeper, the Marathon scheduler, and one Mesos slave instance
- **EC2-M2**: This hosts one Mesos slave instance
- **EC2-M3**: This hosts another Mesos slave instance
- **EC2-M4**: This hosts Eureka, Config server, and RabbitMQ

For a real production setup, multiple Mesos masters as well as multiple instances of Marathon are required for fault tolerance.

Setting up AWS

Launch the four **t2.micro** EC2 instances that will be used for this deployment. All four instances have to be on the same security group so that the instances can see each other using their local IP addresses.

The following tables show the machine details and IP addresses for indicative purposes and to link subsequent instructions:

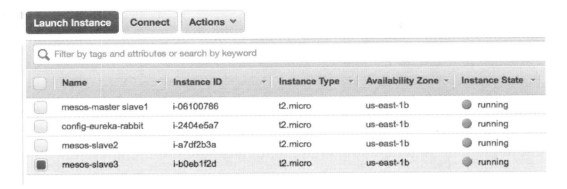

Instance ID	Private DNS/IP	Public DNS/IP
i-06100786	ip-172-31-54-69.ec2.internal 172.31.54.69	ec2-54-85-107-37.compute-1.amazonaws.com 54.85.107.37
i-2404e5a7	ip-172-31-62-44.ec2.internal 172.31.62.44	ec2-52-205-251-150.compute-1.amazonaws.com 52.205.251.150
i-a7df2b3a	ip-172-31-49-55.ec2.internal 172.31.49.55	ec2-54-172-213-51.compute-1.amazonaws.com 54.172.213.51
i-b0eb1f2d	ip-172-31-53-109.ec2.internal 172.31.53.109	ec2-54-86-31-240.compute-1.amazonaws.com 54.86.31.240

Replace the IP and DNS addresses based on your AWS EC2 configuration.

Installing ZooKeeper, Mesos, and Marathon

The following software versions will be used for the deployment. The deployment in this section follows the physical deployment architecture explained in the earlier section:

- Mesos version 0.27.1
- Docker version 1.6.2, build 7c8fca2
- Marathon version 0.15.3

The detailed instructions to set up ZooKeeper, Mesos, and Marathon are available at `https://open.mesosphere.com/getting-started/install/`.

Perform the following steps for a minimal installation of ZooKeeper, Mesos, and Marathon to deploy the BrownField microservice:

1. As a prerequisite, JRE 8 must be installed on all the machines. Execute the following command:

   ```
   sudo apt-get -y install oracle-java8-installer
   ```

2. Install Docker on all machines earmarked for the Mesos slave via the following command:

   ```
   sudo apt-get install docker
   ```

3. Open a terminal window and execute the following commands. These commands set up the repository for installation:

   ```
   sudo apt-key adv --keyserver hkp://keyserver.ubuntu.com:80 --recv
   E56151BF
   DISTRO=$(lsb_release -is | tr '[:upper:]' '[:lower:]')
   CODENAME=$(lsb_release -cs)
   # Add the repository
   echo "deb http://repos.mesosphere.com/${DISTRO} ${CODENAME} main"
   | \
      sudo tee /etc/apt/sources.list.d/mesosphere.list
   sudo apt-get -y update
   ```

4. Execute the following command to install Mesos and Marathon. This will also install Zookeeper as a dependency:

   ```
   sudo apt-get -y install mesos marathon
   ```

Repeat the preceding steps on all the three EC2 instances reserved for the Mesos slave execution. As the next step, ZooKeeper and Mesos have to be configured on the machine identified for the Mesos master.

Configuring ZooKeeper

Connect to the machine reserved for the Mesos master and Marathon scheduler. In this case, `172.31.54.69` will be used to set up ZooKeeper, the Mesos master, and Marathon.

There are two configuration changes required in ZooKeeper, as follows:

1. The first step is to set `/etc/zookeeper/conf/myid` to a unique integer between 1 and 255, as follows:

   Open vi /etc/zookeeper/conf/myid and set 1.

2. The next step is to edit `/etc/zookeeper/conf/zoo.cfg`. Update the file to reflect the following changes:

   ```
   # specify all zookeeper servers
   # The first port is used by followers to connect to the leader
   # The second one is used for leader election
   server.1= 172.31.54.69:2888:3888
   #server.2=zookeeper2:2888:3888
   #server.3=zookeeper3:2888:3888
   ```

   Replace the IP addresses with the relevant private IP address. In this case, we will use only one ZooKeeper server, but in a production scenario, multiple servers are required for high availability.

Configuring Mesos

Make changes to the Mesos configuration to point to ZooKeeper, set up a quorum, and enable Docker support via the following steps:

1. Edit `/etc/mesos/zk` to set the following value. This is to point Mesos to a ZooKeeper instance for quorum and leader election:

   ```
   zk:// 172.31.54.69:2181/mesos
   ```

2. Edit the `/etc/mesos-master/quorum` file and set the value as 1. In a production scenario, we may need a minimum quorum of three:

   vi /etc/mesos-master/quorum

3. The default Mesos installation does not support Docker on Mesos slaves. In order to enable Docker, update the following `mesos-slave` configuration:

   echo 'docker,mesos' > /etc/mesos-slave/containerizers

Running Mesos, Marathon, and ZooKeeper as services

All the required configuration changes are implemented. The easiest way to start Mesos, Marathon, and Zookeeper is to run them as services, as follows:

- The following commands start services. The services need to be started in the following order:

```
sudo service zookeeper start

sudo service mesos-master start

sudo service mesos-slave start

sudo service marathon start
```

- At any point, the following commands can be used to stop these services:

```
sudo service zookeeper stop

sudo service mesos-master stop

sudo service mesos-slave stop

sudo service marathon stop
```

- Once the services are up and running, use a terminal window to verify whether the services are running:

```
ubuntu@ip-172-31-54-69:~$
ubuntu@ip-172-31-54-69:~$ ps -ef | grep zookeeper
ubuntu    1240  1180  0 16:33 pts/0    00:00:00 grep --color=auto zookeeper
zookeep+ 17056     1  0 Apr10 ?        00:00:54 /usr/bin/java -cp /etc/zookeeper/conf:/usr/share/java/jline.jar:/usr/
share/java/log4j-1.2.jar:/usr/share/java/xercesImpl.jar:/usr/share/java/xmlParserAPIs.jar:/usr/share/java/netty.jar:/
usr/share/java/slf4j-api.jar:/usr/share/java/slf4j-log4j12.jar:/usr/share/java/zookeeper.jar -Dcom.sun.management.jmx
remote -Dcom.sun.management.jmxremote.local.only=false -Dzookeeper.log.dir=/var/log/zookeeper -Dzookeeper.root.logger
=INFO,ROLLINGFILE org.apache.zookeeper.server.quorum.QuorumPeerMain /etc/zookeeper/conf/zoo.cfg
ubuntu@ip-172-31-54-69:~$
ubuntu@ip-172-31-54-69:~$
ubuntu@ip-172-31-54-69:~$ ps -ef | grep sbin/mesos-master
ubuntu    1245  1180  0 16:33 pts/0    00:00:00 grep --color=auto sbin/mesos-master
root     17066     1  0 Apr10 ?        00:00:28 /usr/sbin/mesos-master --zk=zk://172.31.54.69:2181/mesos  --port=5050
  --log_dir=/var/log/mesos --quorum=1 --work_dir=/var/lib/mesos
ubuntu@ip-172-31-54-69:~$
ubuntu@ip-172-31-54-69:~$
ubuntu@ip-172-31-54-69:~$ ps -ef | grep marathon.Main
ubuntu    1252  1180  0 16:33 pts/0    00:00:00 grep --color=auto marathon.Main
root     17117     1  0 Apr10 ?        00:04:07 java -Djava.library.path=/usr/local/lib:/usr/lib:/usr/lib64 -Djava.ut
il.logging.SimpleFormatter.format=%2$s%5$s%6$s%n -Xmx512m -cp /usr/bin/marathon mesosphere.marathon.Main --zk zk://17
2.31.54.69:2181/marathon --master zk://172.31.54.69:2181/mesos
ubuntu@ip-172-31-54-69:~$
```

Running the Mesos slave in the command line

In this example, instead of using the Mesos slave service, we will use a command-line version to invoke the Mesos slave to showcase additional input parameters. Stop the Mesos slave and use the command line as mentioned here to start the slave again:

```
$sudo service mesos-slave stop
```

```
$sudo /usr/sbin/mesos-slave  --master=172.31.54.69:5050 --log_dir=/var/
log/mesos --work_dir=/var/lib/mesos --containerizers=mesos,docker --resou
rces="ports(*):[8000-9000, 31000-32000]"
```

The command-line parameters used are explained as follows:

- `--master=172.31.54.69:5050`: This parameter is to tell the Mesos slave to connect to the correct Mesos master. In this case, there is only one master running at `172.31.54.69:5050`. All the slaves connect to the same Mesos master.

- `--containerizers=mesos,docker`: This parameter is to enable support for Docker container execution as well as noncontainerized executions on the Mesos slave instances.

- `--resources="ports(*):[8000-9000, 31000-32000]`: This parameter indicates that the slave can offer both ranges of ports when binding resources. `31000` to `32000` is the default range. As we are using port numbers starting with `8000`, it is important to tell the Mesos slave to allow exposing ports starting from `8000` as well.

Perform the following steps to verify the installation of Mesos and Marathon:

1. Execute the command mentioned in the previous step to start the Mesos slave on all the three instances designated for the slave. The same command can be used across all three instances as all of them connect to the same master.

2. If the Mesos slave is successfully started, a message similar to the following will appear in the console:

   ```
   I0411 18:11:39.684809 16665 slave.cpp:1030] Forwarding total
   oversubscribed resources
   ```

   The preceding message indicates that the Mesos slave started sending the current state of resource availability periodically to the Mesos master.

3. Open `http://54.85.107.37:8080` to inspect the Marathon UI. Replace the IP address with the public IP address of the EC2 instance:

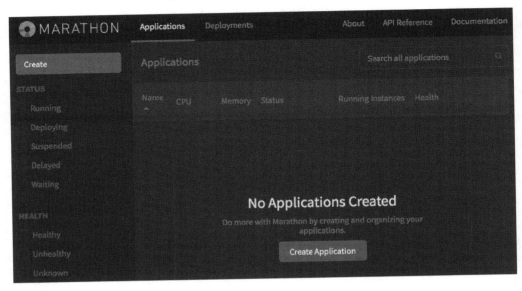

As there are no applications deployed so far, the **Applications** section of the UI is empty.

4. Open the Mesos UI, which runs on port `5050`, by going to `http://54.85.107.37:5050`:

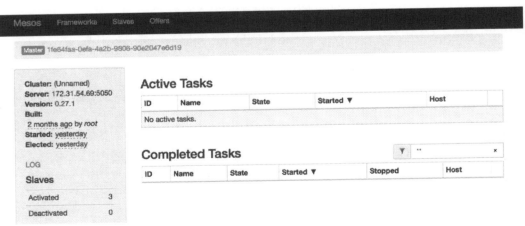

The **Slaves** section of the console shows that there are three activated Mesos slaves available for execution. It also indicates that there is no active task.

Preparing BrownField PSS services

In the previous section, we successfully set up Mesos and Marathon. In this section, we will take a look at how to deploy the BrownField PSS application previously developed using Mesos and Marathon.

> The full source code of this chapter is available under the Chapter 9 project in the code files. Copy `chapter8.configserver`, `chapter8.eurekaserver`, `chapter8.search`, `chapter8.search-apigateway`, and `chapter8.website` into a new STS workspace and rename them `chapter9.*`.

1. Before we deploy any application, we have to set up the Config server, Eureka server, and RabbitMQ in one of the servers. Follow the steps described in the *Running BrownField services on EC2* section in *Chapter 8, Containerizing Microservices with Docker*. Alternately, we can use the same instance as used in the previous chapter for this purpose.

2. Change all `bootstrap.properties` files to reflect the Config server IP address.

3. Before we deploy our services, there are a few specific changes required on the microservices. When running dockerized microservices with the BRIDGE mode on, we need to tell the Eureka client the hostname to be used to bind. By default, Eureka uses the **instance ID** to register. However, this is not helpful as Eureka clients won't be able to look up these services using the instance ID. In the previous chapter, the HOST mode was used instead of the BRIDGE mode.

   The hostname setup can be done using the `eureka.instance.hostname` property. However, when running on AWS specifically, an alternate approach is to define a bean in the microservices to pick up AWS-specific information, as follows:

```
@Configuration
class EurekaConfig {
@Bean
    public EurekaInstanceConfigBean eurekaInstanceConfigBean() {
    EurekaInstanceConfigBean config = new
EurekaInstanceConfigBean(new InetUtils(new
InetUtilsProperties()));
AmazonInfo info = AmazonInfo.Builder.newBuilder().
autoBuild("eureka");
        config.setDataCenterInfo(info);
```

```
        info.getMetadata().put(AmazonInfo.MetaDataKey.
publicHostname.getName(), info.get(AmazonInfo.MetaDataKey.
publicIpv4));
        config.setHostname(info.get(AmazonInfo.MetaDataKey.
localHostname));
config.setNonSecurePortEnabled(true);
config.setNonSecurePort(PORT);
config.getMetadataMap().put("instanceId", info.get(AmazonInfo.
MetaDataKey.localHostname));
return config;
}
```

The preceding code provides a custom Eureka server configuration using the Amazon host information using Netflix APIs. The code overrides the hostname and instance ID with the private DNS. The port is read from the Config server. This code also assumes one host per service so that the port number stays constant across multiple deployments. This can also be overridden by dynamically reading the port binding information at runtime.

The previous code has to be applied in all microservices.

4. Rebuild all the microservices using Maven. Build and push the Docker images to the Docker Hub. The steps for the three services are shown as follows. Repeat the same steps for all the other services. The working directory needs to be switched to the respective directories before executing these commands:

```
docker build -t search-service:1.0 .

docker tag search-service:1.0 rajeshrv/search-service:1.0

docker push rajeshrv/search-service:1.0


docker build -t search-apigateway:1.0 .

docker tag search-apigateway:1.0 rajeshrv/search-apigateway:1.0

docker push rajeshrv/search-apigateway:1.0


docker build -t website:1.0 .

docker tag website:1.0 rajeshrv/website:1.0

docker push rajeshrv/website:1.0
```

Deploying BrownField PSS services

The Docker images are now published to the Docker Hub registry. Perform the following steps to deploy and run BrownField PSS services:

1. Start the Config server, Eureka server, and RabbitMQ on its dedicated instance.

2. Make sure that the Mesos server and Marathon are running on the machine where the Mesos master is configured.

3. Run the Mesos slave on all the machines as described earlier using the command line.

4. At this point, the Mesos Marathon cluster is up and running and is ready to accept deployments. The deployment can be done by creating one JSON file per service, as shown here:

```
{
  "id": "search-service-1.0",
  "cpus": 0.5,
  "mem": 256.0,
  "instances": 1,
  "container": {
   "docker": {
    "type": "DOCKER",
     "image": "rajeshrv/search-service:1.0",
      "network": "BRIDGE",
      "portMappings": [
        {  "containerPort": 0, "hostPort": 8090 }
      ]
    }
  }
}
```

The preceding JSON code will be stored in the `search.json` file. Similarly, create a JSON file for other services as well.

The JSON structure is explained as follows:

- id: This is the unique ID of the application. This can be a logical name.

- cpus and mem: This sets the resource constraints for this application. If the resource offer does not satisfy this resource constraint, Marathon will reject this resource offer from the Mesos master.

- instances: This decides how many instances of this application to start with. In the preceding configuration, by default, it starts one instance as soon as it gets deployed. Marathon maintains the number of instances mentioned at any point.

- ○ `container`: This parameter tells the Marathon executor to use a Docker container for execution.

- ○ `image`: This tells the Marathon scheduler which Docker image has to be used for deployment. In this case, this will download the `search-service:1.0` image from the Docker Hub repository `rajeshrv`.

- ○ `network`: This value is used for Docker runtime to advise on the network mode to be used when starting the new docker container. This can be BRIDGE or HOST. In this case, the BRIDGE mode will be used.

- ○ `portMappings`: The port mapping provides information on how to map the internal and external ports. In the preceding configuration, the host port is set as `8090`, which tells the Marathon executor to use `8090` when starting the service. As the container port is set as `0`, the same host port will be assigned to the container. Marathon picks up random ports if the host port value is `0`.

5. Additional health checks are also possible with the JSON descriptor, as shown here:

```
"healthChecks": [
    {
        "protocol": "HTTP",
        "portIndex": 0,
        "path": "/admin/health",
        "gracePeriodSeconds": 100,
        "intervalSeconds": 30,
        "maxConsecutiveFailures": 5
    }
]
```

6. Once this JSON code is created and saved, deploy it to Marathon using the Marathon REST APIs as follows:

```
curl -X POST http://54.85.107.37:8080/v2/apps -d @search.json -H
"Content-type: application/json"
```

Repeat this step for all the other services as well.

The preceding step will automatically deploy the Docker container to the Mesos cluster and start one instance of the service.

Reviewing the deployment

The steps for this are as follows:

1. Open the Marathon UI. As shown in the following screenshot, the UI shows that all the three applications are deployed and are in the **Running** state. It also indicates that **1 of 1** instance is in the **Running** state:

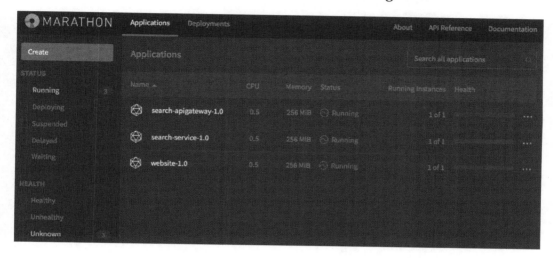

2. Visit the Mesos UI. As shown in the following screenshot, there are three **Active Tasks**, all of them in the **Running** state. It also shows the host in which these services run:

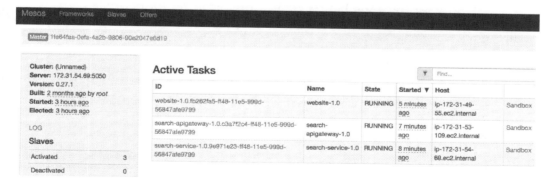

3. In the Marathon UI, click on a running application. The following screenshot shows the **search-apigateway-1.0** application. In the **Instances** tab, the IP address and port in which the service is bound is indicated:

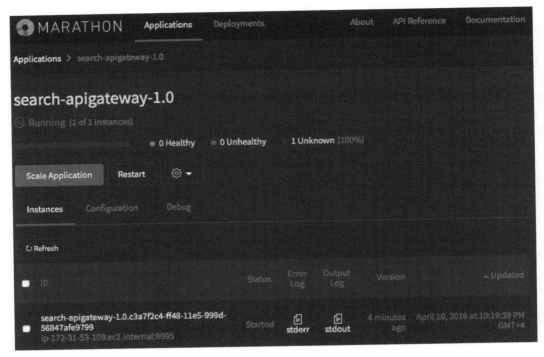

The **Scale Application** button allows administrators to specify how many instances of the service are required. This can be used to scale up as well as scale down instances.

4. Open the Eureka server console to take a look at how the services are bound. As shown in the screenshot, **AMIs** and **Availability Zones** are reflected when services are registered. Follow `http://52.205.251.150:8761`:

Instances currently registered with Eureka

Application	AMIs	Availability Zones	Status
SEARCH-APIGATEWAY	ami-fce3c696 (1)	us-east-1b (1)	UP (1) - ip-172-31-53-109.ec2.internal
SEARCH-SERVICE	ami-fce3c696 (1)	us-east-1b (1)	UP (1) - ip-172-31-54-69.ec2.internal
TEST-CLIENT	ami-fce3c696 (1)	us-east-1b (1)	UP (1) - ip-172-31-49-55.ec2.internal

5. Open `http://54.172.213.51:8001` in a browser to verify the
Website application.

A place for the life cycle manager

The life cycle manager introduced in *Chapter 6, Autoscaling Microservices*, has the
capability of autoscaling up or down instances based on demand. It also has the
ability to take decisions on where to deploy and how to deploy applications on
a cluster of machines based on polices and constraints. The life cycle manager's
capabilities are shown in the following figure:

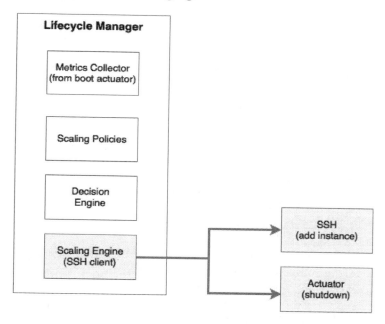

Marathon has the capability to manage clusters and deployments to clusters based
on policies and constraints. The number of instances can be altered using the
Marathon UI.

There are redundant capabilities between our life cycle manager and Marathon.
With Marathon in place, SSH work or machine-level scripting is no longer required.
Moreover, deployment policies and constraints can be delegated to Marathon. The
REST APIs exposed by Marathon can be used to initiate scaling functions.

Marathon autoscale is a proof-of-concept project from Mesosphere for autoscaling.
The Marathon autoscale provides basic autoscale features such as the CPU, memory,
and rate of request.

Rewriting the life cycle manager with Mesos and Marathon

We still need a custom life cycle manager to collect metrics from the Spring Boot actuator endpoints. A custom life cycle manager is also handy if the scaling rules are beyond the CPU, memory, and rate of scaling.

The following diagram shows the updated life cycle manager using the Marathon framework:

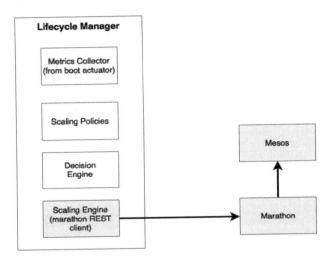

The life cycle manager, in this case, collects actuator metrics from different Spring Boot applications, combines them with other metrics, and checks for certain thresholds. Based on the scaling policies, the decision engine informs the scaling engine to either scale down or scale up. In this case, the scaling engine is nothing but a Marathon REST client. This approach is cleaner and neater than our earlier primitive life cycle manager implementation using SSH and Unix scripts.

The technology metamodel

We have covered a lot of ground on microservices with the BrownField PSS microservices. The following diagram sums it up by bringing together all the technologies used into a technology metamodel:

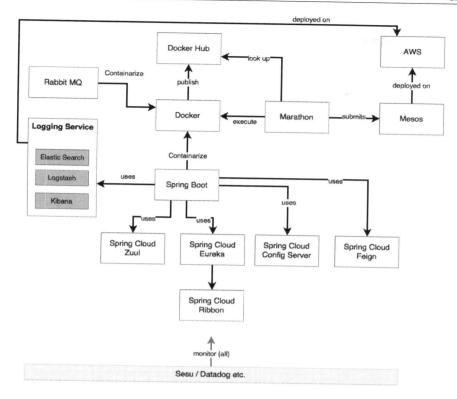

Summary

In this chapter, you learned the importance of a cluster management and init system to efficiently manage dockerized microservices at scale.

We explored the different cluster control or cluster orchestration tools before diving deep into Mesos and Marathon. We also implemented Mesos and Marathon in the AWS cloud environment to demonstrate how to manage dockerized microservices developed for BrownField PSS.

At the end of this chapter, we also explored the position of the life cycle manager in conjunction with Mesos and Marathon. Finally, we concluded this chapter with a technology metamodel based on the BrownField PSS microservices implementation.

So far, we have discussed all the core and supporting technology capabilities required for a successful microservices implementation. A successful microservice implementation also requires processes and practices beyond technology. The next chapter, the last in the book, will cover the process and practice perspectives of microservices.

10
The Microservices Development Life Cycle

Similar to the **software development life cycle (SDLC)**, it is important to understand the aspects of the microservice development life cycle processes for a successful implementation of the microservices architecture.

This final chapter will focus on the development process and practice of microservices with the help of BrownField Airline's PSS microservices example. Furthermore, this chapter will describe best practices in structuring development teams, development methodologies, automated testing, and continuous delivery of microservices in line with DevOps practices. Finally, this chapter will conclude by shedding light on the importance of the reference architecture in a decentralized governance approach to microservices.

By the end of this chapter, you will learn about the following topics:

- Reviewing DevOps in the context of microservices development
- Defining the microservices life cycle and related processes
- Best practices around the development, testing, and deployment of Internet-scale microservices

Reviewing the microservice capability model

This chapter will cover the following microservices capabilities from the microservices capability model discussed in *Chapter 3, Applying Microservices Concepts*:

- **DevOps**
- **DevOps Tools**
- **Reference Architecture & Libraries**
- **Testing Tools (Anti-Fragile, RUM etc)**

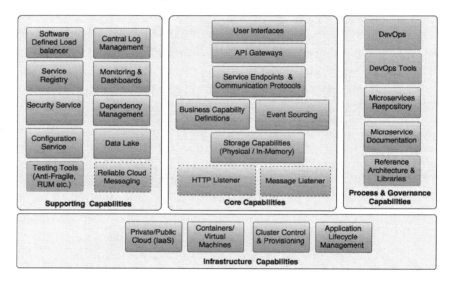

The new mantra of lean IT – DevOps

We discussed the definition of DevOps in *Chapter 2, Building Microservices with Spring Boot*. Here is a quick recap of the DevOps definition.

Gartner defines DevOps as follows:

> *"DevOps represents a change in IT culture, focusing on rapid IT service delivery through the adoption of agile, lean practices in the context of a system-oriented approach. DevOps emphasizes people (and culture), and seeks to improve collaboration between operations and development teams. DevOps implementations utilize technology — especially automation tools that can leverage an increasingly programmable and dynamic infrastructure from a life cycle perspective."*

DevOps and microservices evolved independently. *Chapter 1, Demystifying Microservices*, explored the evolution of microservices. In this section, we will review the evolution of DevOps and then take a look at how DevOps supports microservices adoption.

In the era of digital disruption and in order to support modern business, IT organizations have to master two key areas: speed of delivery and value-driven delivery. This is obviously apart from being expert in leading technologies.

Many IT organizations failed to master this change, causing frustration to business users. To overcome this situation, many business departments started their own shadow IT or stealth IT under their control. Some smart IT organizations then adopted a lean IT model to respond to these situations.

However, many organizations still struggle with this transformation due to the large baggage of legacy systems and processes. Gartner coined the concept of a **pace-layered application strategy**. Gartner's view is that high speed is required only for certain types of applications or certain business areas. Gartner termed this a **system of innovation**. A system of innovation requires rapid innovations compared to a **system of records**. As a system of innovations needs rapid innovation, a lean IT delivery model is essential for such applications. Practitioners evangelized the lean IT model as DevOps.

There are two key strategies used by organizations to adopt DevOps.

Some organizations positioned DevOps as a process to fill the gaps in their existing processes. Such organizations adopted an incremental strategy for their DevOps journey. The adoption path starts with Agile development, then incrementally adopts continuous integration, automated testing, and release to production and then all DevOps practices. The challenge in such organizations is the time to realize the full benefits as well as the mixed culture of people due to legacy processes.

Many organizations, therefore, take a disruptive approach to adopt DevOps. This will be achieved by partitioning IT into two layers or even as two different IT units. The high-speed layer of IT uses DevOps-style practices to dramatically change the culture of the organization with no connection to the legacy processes and practices. A selective application cluster will be identified and moved to the new IT based on the business value:

The Speed Carriage - New IT (DevOps)

The Legacy Carriage - Classic IT (Legacy Processes)

The intention of DevOps is not just to reduce cost. It also enables the business to disrupt competitors by quickly moving ideas to production. DevOps attacks traditional IT issues in multiple ways, as explained here.

Reducing wastage

DevOps processes and practices essentially speed up deliveries which improves quality. The speed of delivery is achieved by cutting IT wastage. This is achieved by avoiding work that adds no value to the business nor to desired business outcomes. IT wastage includes software defects, productivity issues, process overheads, time lag in decision making, time spent in reporting layers, internal governance, overestimation, and so on. By reducing these wastages, organizations can radically improve the speed of delivery. The wastage is reduced by primarily adopting Agile processes, tools, and techniques.

Automating every possible step

By automating the manually executed tasks, one can dramatically improve the speed of delivery as well as the quality of deliverables. The scope of automation goes from planning to customer feedback. Automation reduces the time to move business ideas to production. This also reduces a number of manual gate checks, bureaucratic decision making, and so on. Automated monitoring mechanisms and feedback go back to the development factory, which gets it fixed and quickly moved to production.

Value-driven delivery

DevOps reduces the gap between IT and business through value-driven delivery. Value-driven delivery closely aligns IT to business by understanding true business values and helps the business by quickly delivering these values, which can give a competitive advantage. This is similar to the shadow IT concept, in which IT is collocated with the business and delivers business needs quickly, rather than waiting for heavy project investment-delivery cycles.

Traditionally, IT is partially disconnected from the business and works with IT KPIs, such as the number of successful project deliveries, whereas in the new model, IT shares business KPIs. As an example, a new IT KPI could be that IT helped business to achieve a 10% increase in sales orders or led to 20% increase in customer acquisition. This will shift IT's organizational position from merely a support organization to a business partner.

Bridging development and operations

Traditionally, IT has different teams for development and operations. In many cases, they are differentiated with logical barriers. DevOps reduces the gap between the development and operations teams so that it can potentially reduce wastage and improve quality. Multidisciplinary teams work together to address problems at hand rather than throwing mud across the wall.

With DevOps, operations teams will have a fairly good understanding about the services and applications developed by development teams. Similarly, development teams will have a good handle on the infrastructure components and configurations used by the applications. As a result, operations teams can make decisions based exactly on service behaviors rather than enforcing standard organizational policies and rules when designing infrastructure components. This would eventually help the IT organization to improve the quality of the product as well as the time to resolve incidents and problem management.

In the DevOps world, speed of delivery is achieved through the automation of high-velocity changes, and quality is achieved through automation and people. Business values are achieved through efficiency, speed of delivery, quality, and the ability to innovate. Cost reduction is achieved through automation, productivity, and reducing wastage.

Meeting the trio – microservices, DevOps, and cloud

The trio — cloud, microservices, and DevOps — targets a set of common objectives: speed of delivery, business value, and cost benefit. All three can stay and evolve independently, but they complement each other to achieve the desired common goals. Organizations embarking on any of these naturally tend to consider the other two as they are closely linked together:

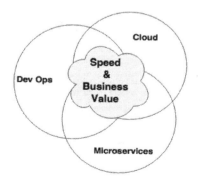

Many organizations start their journey with DevOps as an organizational practice to achieve high-velocity release cycles but eventually move to the microservices architecture and cloud. It is not mandatory to have microservices and cloud support DevOps. However, automating the release cycles of large monolithic applications does not make much sense, and in many cases, it would be impossible to achieve. In such scenarios, the microservices architecture and cloud will be handy when implementing DevOps.

If we flip a coin, cloud does not need a microservices architecture to achieve its benefits. However, to effectively implement microservices, both cloud and DevOps are essential.

In summary, if the objective of an organization is to achieve a high speed of delivery and quality in a cost-effective way, the trio together can bring tremendous success.

Cloud as the self-service infrastructure for Microservices

The main driver for cloud is to improve agility and reduce cost. By reducing the time to provision the infrastructure, the speed of delivery can be increased. By optimally utilizing the infrastructure, one can bring down the cost. Therefore, cloud directly helps achieve both speed of delivery and cost.

As discussed in *Chapter 9, Managing Dockerized Microservices with Mesos and Marathon*, without having a cloud infrastructure with cluster management software, it would be hard to control the infrastructure cost when deploying microservices. Hence, the cloud with self-service capabilities is essential for microservices to achieve their full potential benefits. In the microservices context, the cloud not only helps abstract the physical infrastructure but also provides software APIs for dynamic provisioning and automatic deployments. This is referred to as **infrastructure as code** or **software-defined infrastructure**.

DevOps as the practice and process for microservices

Microservice is an architecture style that enables quick delivery. However, microservices cannot provide the desired benefits by themselves. A microservices-based project with a delivery cycle of 6 months does not give the targeted speed of delivery or business agility. Microservices need a set of supporting delivery practices and processes to effectively achieve their goal.

DevOps is the ideal candidate for the underpinning process and practices for microservice delivery. DevOps processes and practices gel well with the microservices architecture's philosophies.

Practice points for microservices development

For a successful microservice delivery, a number of development-to-delivery practices need to be considered, including the DevOps philosophy. In the previous chapters, you learned the different architecture capabilities of microservices. In this section, we will explore the nonarchitectural aspects of microservice developments.

Understanding business motivation and value

Microservices should not be used for the sake of implementing a niche architecture style. It is extremely important to understand the business value and business KPIs before selecting microservices as an architectural solution for a given problem. A good understanding of business motivation and business value will help engineers focus on achieving these goals in a cost-effective way.

Business motivation and value should justify the selection of microservices. Also, using microservices, the business value should be realizable from a business point of view. This will avoid situations where IT invests in microservices but there is no appetite from the business to leverage any of the benefits that microservices can bring to the table. In such cases, a microservices-based development would be an overhead to the enterprise.

Changing the mindset from project to product development

As discussed in *Chapter 1, Demystifying Microservices*, microservices are more aligned to product development. Business capabilities that are delivered using microservices should be treated as products. This is in line with the DevOps philosophy as well.

The mindset for project development and product development is different. The product team will always have a sense of ownership and take responsibility for what they produce. As a result, product teams always try to improve the quality of the product. The product team is responsible not only for delivering the software but also for production support and maintenance of the product.

Product teams are generally linked directly to a business department for which they are developing the product. In general, product teams have both an IT and a business representative. As a result, product thinking is closely aligned with actual business goals. At every moment, product teams understand the value they are adding to the business to achieve business goals. The success of the product directly lies with the business value being gained out of the product.

Because of the high-velocity release cycles, product teams always get a sense of satisfaction in their delivery, and they always try to improve on it. This brings a lot more positive dynamics within the team.

In many cases, typical product teams are funded for the long term and remain intact. As a result, product teams become more cohesive in nature. As they are small in size, such teams focus on improving their process from their day-to-day learnings.

One common pitfall in product development is that IT people represent the business in the product team. These IT representatives may not fully understand the business vision. Also, they may not be empowered to take decisions on behalf of the business. Such cases can result in a misalignment with the business and lead to failure quite rapidly.

It is also important to consider a collocation of teams where business and IT representatives reside at the same place. Collocation adds more binding between IT and business teams and reduces communication overheads.

Choosing a development philosophy

Different organizations take different approaches to developing microservices, be it a migration or a new development. It is important to choose an approach that suits the organization. There is a wide verity of approaches available, out of which a few are explained in this section.

Design thinking

Design thinking is an approach primarily used for innovation-centric development. It is an approach that explores the system from an end user point of view: what the customers see and how they experience the solution. A story is then built based on observations, patterns, intuition, and interviews.

Design thinking then quickly devises solutions through solution-focused thinking by employing a number of theories, logical reasoning, and assumptions around the problem. The concepts are expanded through brainstorming before arriving at a converged solution.

Once the solution is identified, a quick prototype is built to consider how the customer responds to it, and then the solution is adjusted accordingly. When the team gets satisfactory results, the next step is taken to scale the product. Note that the prototype may or may not be in the form of code.

Design thinking uses human-centric thinking with feelings, empathy, intuition, and imagination at its core. In this approach, solutions will be up for rethinking even for known problems to find innovative and better solutions.

The start-up model

More and more organizations are following the start-up philosophy to deliver solutions. Organizations create internal start-up teams with the mission to deliver specific solutions. Such teams stay away from day-to-day organizational activities and focus on delivering their mission.

Many start-ups kick off with a small, focused team—a highly cohesive unit. The unit is not worried about how they achieve things; rather, the focus is on what they want to achieve. Once they have a product in place, the team thinks about the right way to build and scale it.

This approach addresses quick delivery through production-first thinking. The advantage with this approach is that teams are not disturbed by organizational governance and political challenges. The team is empowered to think out of the box, be innovative, and deliver things. Generally, a higher level of ownership is seen in such teams, which is one of the key catalysts for success. Such teams employ just enough processes and disciplines to take the solution forward. They also follow a fail fast approach and course correct sooner than later.

The Agile practice

The most commonly used approach is the Agile methodology for development. In this approach, software is delivered in an incremental, iterative way using the principles put forth in the Agile manifesto. This type of development uses an Agile method such as Scrum or XP. The Agile manifesto defines four key points that Agile software development teams should focus on:

- Individuals and interaction over processes and tools
- Working software over comprehensive documentation
- Customer collaboration over contract negotiation
- Responding to change over following a plan

The 12 principles of Agile software development can be found at http://www.agilemanifesto.org/principles.html.

Using the concept of Minimum Viable Product

Irrespective of the development philosophy explained earlier, it is essential to identify a **Minimum Viable Product (MVP)** when developing microservice systems for speed and agility.

Eric Ries, while pioneering the lean start-up movement, defined MVP as:

> *"A Minimum Viable Product is that version of a new product which allows a team to collect the maximum amount of validated learning about customers with the least effort."*

The objective of the MVP approach is to quickly build a piece of software that showcases the most important aspects of the software. The MVP approach realizes the core concept of an idea and perhaps chooses those features that add maximum value to the business. It helps get early feedback and then course corrects as necessary before building a heavy product.

The MVP may be a full-fledged service addressing limited user groups or partial services addressing wider user groups. Feedback from customers is extremely important in the MVP approach. Therefore, it is important to release the MVP to the real users.

Overcoming the legacy hotspot

It is important to understand the environmental and political challenges in an organization before embarking on microservices development.

It is common in microservices to have dependencies on other legacy applications, directly or indirectly. A common issue with direct legacy integration is the slow development cycle of the legacy application. An example would be an innovative railway reservation system relaying on an age-old **transaction processing facility (TPF)** for some of the core backend features, such as reservation. This is especially common when migrating legacy monolithic applications to microservices. In many cases, legacy systems continue to undergo development in a non-Agile way with larger release cycles. In such cases, microservices development teams may not be able to move so quickly because of the coupling with legacy systems. Integration points might drag the microservices developments heavily. Organizational political challenges make things even worse.

There is no silver bullet to solve this issue. The cultural and process differences could be an ongoing issue. Many enterprises ring-fence such legacy systems with focused attention and investments to support fast-moving microservices. Targeted C-level interventions on these legacy platforms could reduce the overheads.

Addressing challenges around databases

Automation is key in microservices development. Automating databases is one of the key challenges in many microservice developments.

In many organizations, DBAs play a critical role in database management, and they like to treat the databases under their control differently. Confidentiality and access control on data is also cited as a reason for DBAs to centrally manage all data.

Many automation tools focus on the application logic. As a result, many development teams completely ignore database automation. Ignoring database automation can severely impact the overall benefits and can derail microservices development.

In order to avoid such situations, the database has to be treated in the same way as applications with appropriate source controls and change management. When selecting a database, it is also important to consider automation as one of the key aspects.

Database automation is much easier in the case of NoSQL databases but is hard to manage with traditional RDBMs. **Database Lifecycle Management (DLM)** as a concept is popular in the DevOps world, particularly to handle database automation. Tools such as DBmaestro, Redgate DLM, Datical DB, and Delphix support database automation.

Establishing self-organizing teams

One of the most important activities in microservices development is to establish the right teams for development. As recommended in many DevOps processes, a small, focused team always delivers the best results.

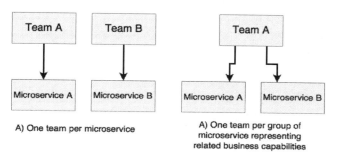

A) One team per microservice

A) One team per group of microservice representing related business capabilities

As microservices are aligned with business capabilities and are fairly loosely coupled products, it is ideal to have a dedicated team per microservice. There could be cases where the same team owns multiple microservices from the same business area representing related capabilities. These are generally decided by the coupling and size of the microservices.

Team size is an important aspect in setting up effective teams for microservices development. The general notion is that the team size should not exceed 10 people. The recommended size for optimal delivery is between 4 and 7. The founder of Amazon.com, Jeff Bezos, coined the theory of two-pizza teams. Jeff's theory says the team will face communication issues if the size gets bigger. Larger teams work with consensus, which results in increased wastage. Large teams also lose ownership and accountability. A yardstick is that the product owner should get enough time to speak to individuals in the team to make them understand the value of what they are delivering.

Teams are expected to take full ownership in ideating for, analyzing, developing, and supporting services. Werner Vogels from Amazon.com calls this *you build it and you run it*. As per Werner's theory, developers pay more attention to develop quality code to avoid unexpected support calls. The members in the team consist of fullstack developers and operational engineers. Such a team is fully aware of all the areas. Developers understand operations as well as operations teams understand applications. This not only reduces the changes of throwing mud across teams but also improves quality.

Teams should have multidisciplinary skills to satisfy all the capabilities required to deliver a service. Ideally, the team should not rely on external teams to deliver the components of the service. Instead, the team should be self-sufficient. However, in most organizations, the challenge is on specialized skills that are rare. For example, there may not be many experts on a graph database in the organization. One common solution to this problem is to use the concept of consultants. Consultants are SMEs and are engaged to gain expertise on specific problems faced by the team. Some organizations also use shared or platform teams to deliver some common capabilities.

Team members should have a complete understanding of the products, not only from the technical standpoint but also from the business case and the business KPIs. The team should have collective ownership in delivering the product as well as in achieving business goals together.

Agile software development also encourages having self-organizing teams. Self-organizing teams act as a cohesive unit and find ways to achieve their goals as a team. The team automatically align themselves and distribute the responsibilities. The members in the team are self-managed and empowered to make decisions in their day-to-day work. The team's communication and transparency are extremely important in such teams. This emphasizes the need for collocation and collaboration, with a high bandwidth for communication:

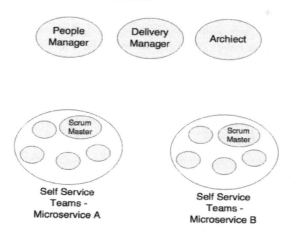

In the preceding diagram, both **Microservice A** and **Microservice B** represent related business capabilities. Self-organizing teams treat everyone in the team equally, without too many hierarchies and management overheads within the team. The management would be thin in such cases. There won't be many designated vertical skills in the team, such as team lead, UX manager, development manager, testing manager, and so on. In a typical microservice development, a shared product manager, shared architect, and a shared people manager are good enough to manage the different microservice teams. In some organizations, architects also take up responsibility for delivery.

Self-organizing teams have some level of autonomy and are empowered to take decisions in a quick and Agile mode rather than having to wait for long-running bureaucratic decision-making processes that exist in many enterprises. In many of these cases, enterprise architecture and security are seen as an afterthought. However, it is important to have them on board from the beginning. While empowering the teams with maximum freedom for developers in decision-making capabilities, it is equally important to have fully automated QA and compliance so as to ensure that deviations are captured at the earliest.

Communication between teams is important. However, in an ideal world, it should be limited to interfaces between microservices. Integrations between teams ideally has to be handled through consumer-driven contracts in the form of test scripts rather than having large interface documents describing various scenarios. Teams should use mock service implementations when the services are not available.

Building a self-service cloud

One of the key aspects that one should consider before embarking on microservices is to build a cloud environment. When there are only a few services, it is easy to manage them by manually assigning them to a certain predesignated set of virtual machines.

However, what microservice developers need is more than just an IaaS cloud platform. Neither the developers nor the operations engineers in the team should worry about where the application is deployed and how optimally it is deployed. They also should not worry about how the capacity is managed.

This level of sophistication requires a cloud platform with self-service capabilities, such as what we discussed in *Chapter 9, Managing Dockerized Microservices with Mesos and Marathon*, with the Mesos and Marathon cluster management solutions. Containerized deployment discussed in *Chapter 8, Containerizing Microservices with Docker*, is also important in managing and end to-end-automation. Building this self-service cloud ecosystem is a prerequisite for microservice development.

Building a microservices ecosystem

As we discussed in the capability model in *Chapter 3, Applying Microservices Concepts*, microservices require a number of other capabilities. All these capabilities should be in place before implementing microservices at scale.

These capabilities include service registration, discovery, API gateways, and an externalized configuration service. All are provided by the Spring Cloud project. Capabilities such as centralized logging, monitoring, and so on are also required as a prerequisite for microservices development.

Defining a DevOps-style microservice life cycle process

DevOps is the best-suited practice for microservices development. Organizations already practicing DevOps do not need another practice for microservices development.

In this section, we will explore the life cycle of microservices development. Rather than reinventing a process for microservices, we will explore DevOps processes and practices from the microservice perspective.

Before we explore DevOps processes, let's iron out some of the common terminologies used in the DevOps world:

- **Continuous integration (CI)**: This automates the application build and quality checks continuously in a designated environment, either in a time-triggered manner or on developer commits. CI also publishes code metrics to a central dashboard as well as binary artifacts to a central repository. CI is popular in Agile development practices.

- **Continuous delivery (CD)**: This automates the end-to-end software delivery practice from idea to production. In a non-DevOps model, this used to be known as **Application Lifecycle Management (ALM)**. One of the common interpretations of CD is that it is the next evolution of CI, which adds QA cycles into the integration pipeline and makes the software ready to release to production. A manual action is required to move it to production.

- **Continuous deployment**: This is an approach to automating the deployment of application binaries to one or more environments by managing binary movement and associated configuration parameters. Continuous deployment is also considered as the next evolution of CD by integrating automatic release processes into the CD pipeline.

- **Application Release Automation (ARA)**: ARA tools help monitor and manage end-to-end delivery pipelines. ARA tools use CI and CD tools and manage the additional steps of release management approvals. ARA tools are also capable of rolling out releases to different environments and rolling them back in case of a failed deployment. ARA provides a fully orchestrated workflow pipeline, implementing delivery life cycles by integrating many specialized tools for repository management, quality assurance, deployment, and so on. XL Deploy and Automic are some of the ARA tools.

The following diagram shows the DevOps process for microservices development:

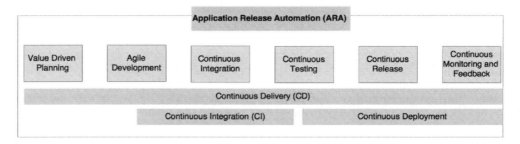

Let's now further explore these life cycle stages of microservices development.

Value-driven planning

Value-driven planning is a term used in Agile development practices. Value-driven planning is extremely important in microservices development. In value-driven planning, we will identify which microservices to develop. The most important aspect is to identify those requirements that have the highest value to business and those that have the lowest risks. The MVP philosophy is used when developing microservices from the ground up. In the case of monolithic to microservices migration, we will use the guidelines provided in *Chapter 3, Applying Microservices Concepts*, to identify which services have to be taken first. The selected microservices are expected to precisely deliver the expected value to the business. Business KPIs to measure this value have to be identified as part of value-driven planning.

Agile development

Once the microservices are identified, development must be carried out in an Agile approach following the Agile manifesto principles. The scrum methodology is used by most of the organizations for microservices development.

Continuous integration

The continuous integration steps should be in place to automatically build the source code produced by various team members and generate binaries. It is important to build only once and then move the binary across the subsequent phases. Continuous integration also executes various QAs as part of the build pipeline, such as code coverage, security checks, design guidelines, and unit test cases. CI typically delivers binary artefacts to a binary artefact repository and also deploys the binary artefacts into one or more environments. Part of the functional testing also happens as part of CI.

Continuous testing

Once continuous integration generates the binaries, they are moved to the testing phase. A fully automated testing cycle is kicked off in this phase. It is also important to automate security testing as part of the testing phase. Automated testing helps improve the quality of deliverables. The testing may happen in multiple environments based on the type of testing. This could range from the integration test environment to the production environment to test in production.

Continuous release

Continuous release to production takes care of actual deployment, infrastructure provisioning, and rollout. The binaries are automatically shipped and deployed to production by applying certain rules. Many organizations stop automation with the staging environment and make use of manual approval steps to move to production.

Continuous monitoring and feedback

The continuous monitoring and feedback phase is the most important phase in Agile microservices development. In an MVP scenario, this phase gives feedback on the initial acceptance of the MVP and also evaluates the value of the service developed. In a feature addition scenario, this further gives insight into how this new feature is accepted by users. Based on the feedback, the services are adjusted and the same cycle is then repeated.

Automating the continuous delivery pipeline

In the previous section, we discussed the life cycle of microservices development. The life cycle stages can be altered by organizations based on their organizational needs but also based on the nature of the application. In this section, we will take a look at a sample continuous delivery pipeline as well as toolsets to implement a sample pipeline.

There are many tools available to build end-to-end pipelines, both in the open source and commercial space. Organizations can select the products of their choice to connect pipeline tasks.

 Refer to the XebiaLabs periodic table for a tool reference to build continuous delivery pipelines. It is available at `https://xebialabs.com/periodic-table-of-devops-tools/`.

The pipelines may initially be expensive to set up as they require many toolsets and environments. Organizations may not realize an immediate cost benefit in implementing the delivery pipeline. Also, building a pipeline needs high-power resources. Large build pipelines may involve hundreds of machines. It also takes hours to move changes through the pipeline from one end to the other. Hence, it is important to have different pipelines for different microservices. This will also help decoupling between the releases of different microservices.

Within a pipeline, parallelism should be employed to execute tests on different environments. It is also important to parallelize the execution of test cases as much as possible. Hence, designing the pipeline based on the nature of the application is important. There is no one size fits all scenario.

The key focus in the pipeline is on end-to-end automation, from development to production, and on failing fast if something goes wrong.

The following pipeline is an indicative one for microservices and explores the different capabilities that one should consider when developing a microservices pipeline:

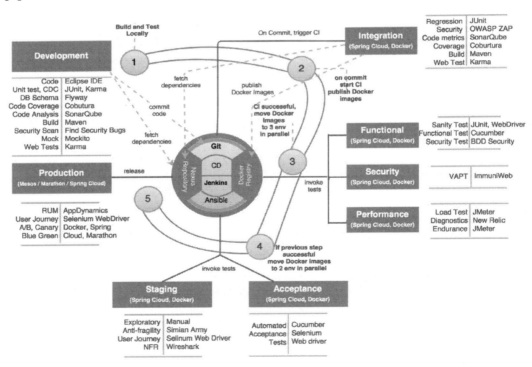

The continuous delivery pipeline stages are explained in the following sections.

Development

The development stage has the following activities from a development perspective. This section also indicates some of the tools that can be used in the development stage. These tools are in addition to the planning, tracking, and communication tools such as Agile JIRA, Slack, and others used by Agile development teams. Take a look at the following:

- **Source code**: The development team requires an IDE or a development environment to cut source code. In most organizations, developers get the freedom to choose the IDEs they want. Having said this, the IDEs can be integrated with a number of tools to detect violations against guidelines. Generally, Eclipse IDEs have plugins for static code analysis and code matrices. SonarQube is one example that integrates other plugins such as Checkstyle for code conventions, PMD to detect bad practices, FindBugs to detect potential bugs, and Cobertura for code coverage. It is also recommended to use Eclipse plugins such as ESVD, Find Security Bugs, SonarQube Security Rules, and so on to detect security vulnerabilities.

- **Unit test cases**: The development team also produces unit test cases using JUnit, NUnit, TestNG, and so on. Unit test cases are written against components, repositories, services, and so on. These unit test cases are integrated with the local Maven builds. The unit test cases targeting the microservice endpoints (service tests) serve as the regression test pack. Web UI, if written in AngularJS, can be tested using Karma.

- **Consumer-driven contracts**: Developers also write CDCs to test integration points with other microservices. Contract test cases are generally written as JUnit, NUnit, TestNG, and so on and are added to the service tests pack mentioned in the earlier steps.

- **Mock testing**: Developers also write mocks to simulate the integration endpoints to execute unit test cases. Mockito, PowerMock, and others are generally used for mock testing. It is good practice to deploy a mock service based on the contract as soon as the service contract is identified. This acts as a simple mechanism for service virtualization for the subsequent phases.

- **Behavior driven design (BDD)**: The Agile team also writes BDD scenarios using a BDD tool, such as Cucumber. Typically, these scenarios are targeted against the microservices contract or the user interface that is exposed by a microservice-based web application. Cucumber with JUnit and Cucumber with Selenium WebDriver, respectively, are used in these scenarios. Different scenarios are used for functional testing, user journey testing, as well as acceptance testing.

- **Source code repository**: A source control repository is a part and parcel of development. Developers check-in their code to a central repository, mostly with the help of IDE plugins. One microservice per repository is a common pattern used by many organizations. This disallows other microservice developers from modifying other microservices or writing code based on the internal representations of other microservices. Git and Subversion are the popular choices to be used as source code repositories.

- **Build tools**: A build tool such as Maven or Gradle is used to manage dependencies and build target artifacts—in this case, Spring Boot services. There are many cases, such as basic quality checks, security checks and unit test cases, code coverage, and so on, that are integrated as part of the build itself. These are similar to the IDE, especially when IDEs are not used by developers. The tools that we examined as part of the IDEs are also available as Maven plugins. The development team does not use containers such as Docker until the CI phase of the project. All the artifacts have to be versioned properly for every change.

- **Artifact repository**: The artifact repository plays a pivotal role in the development process. The artifact repository is where all build artifacts are stored. The artifact repository could be Artifactory, Nexus, or any similar product.

- **Database schemas**: Liquibase and Flyway are commonly used to manage, track, and apply database changes. Maven plugins allow interaction with the Liquibase or Flyway libraries. The schema changes are versioned and maintained, just like source code.

Continuous integration

Once the code is committed to the repository, the next phase, continuous integration, automatically starts. This is done by configuring a CI pipeline. This phase builds the source code with a repository snapshot and generates deployable artifacts. Different organizations use different events to kickstart the build. A CI start event may be on every developer commit or may be based on a time window, such as daily, weekly, and so on.

The CI workflow is the key aspect of this phase. Continuous integration tools such as Jenkins, Bamboo, and others play the central role of orchestrating the build pipeline. The tool is configured with a workflow of activities to be invoked. The workflow automatically executes configured steps such as build, deploy, and QA. On the developer commit or on a set frequency, the CI kickstarts the workflow.

The following activities take place in a continuous integration workflow:

1. **Build and QA**: The workflow listens to Git webhooks for commits. Once it detects a change, the first activity is to download the source code from the repository. A build is executed on the downloaded snapshot source code. As part of the build, a number of QA checks are automatically performed, similarly to QA executed in the development environment. These include code quality checks, security checks, and code coverage. Many of the QAs are done with tools such as SonarQube, with the plugins mentioned earlier. It also collects code metrics such as code coverage and more and publishes it to a central database for analysis. Additional security checks are executed using OWASP ZAP Jenkins' plugins. As part of the build, it also executes JUnit or similar tools used to write test cases. If the web application supports Karma for UI testing, Jenkins is also capable of running web tests written in Karma. If the build or QA fails, it sends out alarms as configured in the system.

2. **Packaging**: Once build and QA are passed, the CI creates a deployable package. In our microservices case, it generates the Spring Boot standalone JAR. It is recommended to build Docker images as part of the integration build. This is the one and only place where we build binary artifacts. Once the build is complete, it pushes the immutable Docker images to a Docker registry. This could be on Docker Hub or a private Docker registry. It is important to properly version control the containers at this stage itself.

3. **Integration tests**: The Docker image is moved to the integration environment where regression tests (service tests) and the like are executed. This environment has other dependent microservices capabilities, such as Spring Cloud, logging, and so on, in place. All dependent microservices are also present in this environment. If an actual dependent service is not yet deployed, service virtualization tools such as MockServer are used. Alternately, a base version of the service is pushed to Git by the respective development teams. Once successfully deployed, Jenkins triggers service tests (JUnits against services), a set of end-to-end sanity tests written in Selenium WebDriver (in the case of web) and security tests with OWASP ZAP.

Automated testing

There are many types of testing to be executed as part of the automated delivery process before declaring the build ready for production. The testing may happen by moving the application across multiple environments. Each environment is designated for a particular kind of testing, such as acceptance testing, performance testing, and so on. These environments are adequately monitored to gather the respective metrics.

In a complex microservices environment, testing should not be seen as a last-minute gate check; rather, testing should be considered as a way to improve software quality as well as to avoid last-minute failures. Shift left testing is an approach of shifting tests as early as possible in the release cycle. Automated testing turns software development to every-day development and every-day testing mode. By automating test cases, we will avoid manual errors as well as the effort required to complete testing.

CI or ARA tools are used to move Docker images across multiple test environments. Once deployed in an environment, test cases are executed based on the purpose of the environment. By default, a set of sanity tests are executed to verify the test environment.

In this section, we will cover all the types of tests that are required in the automated delivery pipeline, irrespective of the environment. We have already considered some types of tests as part of the development and integration environment. Later in this section, we will also map test cases against the environments in which they are executed.

Different candidate tests for automation

In this section, we will explore different types of tests that are candidates for automation when designing an end-to-end delivery pipeline. The key testing types are described as follows.

Automated sanity tests

When moving from one environment to another, it is advisable to run a few sanity tests to make sure that all the basic things are working. This is created as a test pack using JUnit service tests, Selenium WebDriver, or a similar tool. It is important to carefully identify and script all the critical service calls. Especially if the microservices are integrated using synchronous dependencies, it is better to consider these scenarios to ensure that all dependent services are also up and running.

Regression testing

Regression tests ensure that changes in software don't break the system. In a microservices context, the regression tests could be at the service level (Rest API or message endpoints) and written using JUnit or a similar framework, as explained earlier. Service virtualizations are used when dependent services are not available. Karma and Jasmine can be used for web UI testing.

In cases where microservices are used behind web applications, Selenium WebDriver or a similar tool is used to prepare regression test packs, and tests are conducted at the UI level rather than focusing on the service endpoints. Alternatively, BDD tools, such as Cucumber with JUnit or Cucumber with Selenium WebDriver, can also be used to prepare regression test packs. CI tools such as Jenkins or ARA are used to automatically trigger regression test packs. There are other commercial tools, such as TestComplete, that can also be used to build regression test packs.

Automated functional testing

Functional test cases are generally targeted at the UIs that consume the microservices. These are business scenarios based on user stories or features. These functional tests are executed on every build to ensure that the microservice is performing as expected.

BDD is generally used in developing functional test cases. Typically in BDD, business analysts write test cases in a domain-specific language but in plain English. Developers then add scripts to execute these scenarios. Automated web testing tools such as Selenium WebDriver are useful in such scenarios, together with BDD tools such as Cucumber, JBehave, SpecFlow, and so on. JUnit test cases are used in the case of headless microservices. There are pipelines that combine both regression testing and functional testing as one step with the same set of test cases.

Automated acceptance testing

This is much similar to the preceding functional test cases. In many cases, automated acceptance tests generally use the screenplay or journey pattern and are applied at the web application level. The customer perspective is used in building the test cases rather than features or functions. These tests mimic user flows.

BDD tools such as Cucumber, JBehave, and SpecFlow are generally used in these scenarios together with JUnit or Selenium WebDriver, as discussed in the previous scenario. The nature of the test cases is different in functional testing and acceptance testing. Automation of acceptance test packs is achieved by integrating them with Jenkins. There are many other specialized automatic acceptance testing tools available on the market. FitNesse is one such tool.

Performance testing

It is important to automate performance testing as part of the delivery pipeline. This positions performance testing from a gate check model to an integral part of the delivery pipeline. By doing so, bottlenecks can be identified at very early stages of build cycles. In some organizations, performance tests are conducted only for major releases, but in others, performance tests are part of the pipeline. There are multiple options for performance testing. Tools such as JMeter, Gatling, Grinder, and so on can be used for load testing. These tools can be integrated into the Jenkins workflow for automation. Tools such as BlazeMeter can then be used for test reporting.

Application Performance Management tools such as AppDynamics, New Relic, Dynatrace, and so on provide quality metrics as part of the delivery pipeline. This can be done using these tools as part of the performance testing environment. In some pipelines, these are integrated into the functional testing environment to get better coverage. Jenkins has plugins in to fetch measurements.

Real user flow simulation or journey testing

This is another form of test typically used in staging and production environments. These tests continuously run in staging and production environments to ensure that all the critical transactions perform as expected. This is much more useful than a typical URL ping monitoring mechanism. Generally, similar to automated acceptance testing, these test cases simulate user journeys as they happen in the real world. These are also useful to check whether the dependent microservices are up and running. These test cases could be a carved-out subset of acceptance test cases or test packs created using Selenium WebDriver.

Automated security testing

It is extremely important to make sure that the automation does not violate the security policies of the organization. Security is the most important thing, and compromising security for speed is not desirable. Hence, it is important to integrate security testing as part of the delivery pipeline. Some security evaluations are already integrated in the local build environment as well as in the integration environment, such as SonarQube, Find Security Bugs, and so on. Some security aspects are covered as part of the functional test cases. Tools such as BDD-Security, Mittn, and Gauntlt are other security test automation tools following the BDD approach. VAPT can be done using tools such as ImmuniWeb. OWASP ZAP and Burp Suite are other useful tools in security testing.

Exploratory testing

Exploratory testing is a manual testing approach taken by testers or business users to validate the specific scenarios that they think automated tools may not capture. Testers interact with the system in any manner they want without prejudgment. They use their intellect to identify the scenarios that they think some special users may explore. They also do exploratory testing by simulating certain user behavior.

A/B testing, canary testing, and blue-green deployments

When moving applications to production, A/B testing, blue-green deployments, and canary testing are generally applied. A/B testing is primarily used to review the effectiveness of a change and how the market reacts to the change. New features are rolled out to a certain set of users. Canary release is moving a new product or feature to a certain community before fully rolling out to all customers. Blue-green is a deployment strategy from an IT point of view to test the new version of a service. In this model, both blue and green versions are up and running at some point of time and then gracefully migrate from one to the other.

Other nonfunctional tests

High availability and antifragility testing (failure injection tests) are also important to execute before production. This helps developers unearth unknown errors that may occur in a real production scenario. This is generally done by breaking the components of the system to understand their failover behavior. This is also helpful to test circuit breakers and fallback services in the system. Tools such as Simian Army are useful in these scenarios.

Testing in production

Testing in Production (TiP) is as important as all the other environments as we can only simulate to a certain extend. There are two types of tests generally executed against production. The first approach is running real user flows or journey tests in a continuous manner, simulating various user actions. This is automated using one of the **Real User Monitoring (RUM)** tools, such as AppDynamics. The second approach is to wiretap messages from production, execute them in a staging environment, and then compare the results in production with those in the staging environment.

Antifragility testing

Antifragility testing is generally conducted in a preproduction environment identical to production or even in the production environment by creating chaos in the environment to take a look at how the application responds and recovers from these situations. Over a period of time, the application gains the ability to automatically recover from most of these failures. Simian Army is one such tool from Netflix. Simian Army is a suite of products built for the AWS environment. Simian Army is for disruptive testing using a set of autonomous monkeys that can create chaos in the preproduction or production environments. Chaos Monkey, Janitor Monkey, and Conformity Monkey are some of the components of Simian Army.

Target test environments

The different test environments and the types of tests targeted on these environments for execution are as follows:

- **Development environment**: The development environment is used to test the coding style checks, bad practices, potential bugs, unit tests, and basic security scanning.

- **Integration test environment**: Integration environment is used for unit testing and regression tests that span across multiple microservices. Some basic security-related tests are also executed in the integration test environment.

- **Performance and diagnostics**: Performance tests are executed in the performance test environment. Application performance testing tools are deployed in these environments to collect performance metrics and identify bottlenecks.

- **Functional test environment**: The functional test environment is used to execute a sanity test and functional test packs.

- **UAT environment**: The UAT environment has sanity tests, automated acceptance test packs, and user journey simulations.

- **Staging**: The preproduction environment is used primarily for sanity tests, security, antifragility, network tests, and so on. It is also used for user journey simulations and exploratory testing.

- **Production**: User journey simulations and RUM tests are continuously executed in the production environment.

Making proper data available across multiple environments to support test cases is the biggest challenge. Delphix is a useful tool to consider when dealing with test data across multiple environments in an effective way.

Continuous deployment

Continuous deployment is the process of deploying applications to one or more environments and configuring and provisioning these environments accordingly. As discussed in *Chapter 9, Managing Dockerized Microservices with Mesos and Marathon*, infrastructure provisioning and automation tools facilitate deployment automation.

From the deployment perspective, the released Docker images are moved to production automatically once all the quality checks are successfully completed. The production environment, in this case, has to be cloud based with a cluster management tool such as Mesos or Marathon. A self-service cloud environment with monitoring capabilities is mandatory.

Cluster management and application deployment tools ensure that application dependencies are properly deployed. This automatically deploys all the dependencies that are required in case any are missing. It also ensures that a minimum number of instances are running at any point in time. In case of failure, it automatically rolls back the deployments. It also takes care of rolling back upgrades in a graceful manner.

Ansible, Chef, or Puppet are tools useful in moving configurations and binaries to production. The Ansible playbook concepts can be used to launch a Mesos cluster with Marathon and Docker support.

Monitoring and feedback

Once an application is deployed in production, monitoring tools continuously monitor its services. Monitoring and log management tools collect and analyze information. Based on the feedback and corrective actions needed, information is fed to the development teams to take corrective actions, and the changes are pushed back to production through the pipeline. Tools such as APM, Open Web Analytics, Google Analytics, Webalizer, and so on are useful tools to monitor web applications. Real user monitoring should provide end-to-end monitoring. QuBit, Boxever, Channel Site, MaxTraffic, and so on are also useful in analyzing customer behavior.

Automated configuration management

Configuration management also has to be rethought from a microservices and DevOps perspective. Use new methods for configuration management rather than using a traditional statically configured CMDB. The manual maintenance of CMDB is no longer an option. Statically managed CMDB requires a lot of mundane tasks to maintain entries. At the same time, due to the dynamic nature of the deployment topology, it is extremely hard to maintain data in a consistent way.

The new styles of CMDB automatically create CI configurations based on an operational topology. These should be discovery based to get up-to-date information. The new CMDB should be capable of managing bare metals, virtual machines, and containers.

Microservices development governance, reference architectures, and libraries

It is important to have an overall enterprise reference architecture and a standard set of tools for microservices development to ensure that development is done in a consistent manner. This helps individual microservices teams to adhere to certain best practices. Each team may identify specialized technologies and tools that are suitable for their development. In a polyglot microservices development, there are obviously multiple technologies used by different teams. However, they have to adhere to the arching principles and practices.

For quick wins and to take advantage of timelines, microservices development teams may deviate from these practices in some cases. This is acceptable as long as the teams add refactoring tasks in their backlogs. In many organizations, although the teams make attempts to reuse something from the enterprise, reuse and standardization generally come as an afterthought.

It is important to make sure that the services are catalogued and visible in the enterprise. This improves the reuse opportunities of microservices.

Summary

In this chapter, you learned about the relationship between microservices and DevOps. We also examined a number of practice points when developing microservices. Most importantly, you learned the microservices development life cycle.

Later in this chapter, we also examined how to automate the microservices delivery pipeline from development to production. As part of this, we examined a number of tools and technologies that are helpful when automating the microservices delivery pipeline. Finally, we touched base with the importance of reference architectures in microservices governance.

Putting together the concepts of microservices, challenges, best practices, and various capabilities covered in this book makes a perfect recipe for developing successful microservices at scale.

Index

Made in the USA
San Bernardino, CA
23 February 2017